"A wonderfully engaging and heartfelt account of prison life by one of Burma's most distinguished literary voices, a story of fortitude and political commitment, but also of the uplifting powers of Vipassana meditation. A very special memoir."

—Thant Myint-U, author of
The River of Lost Footsteps: A Personal History of Burma

"In calm, vivid, and clear prose reflecting her unwavering faith and practice of Vipassana meditation, Ma Thida tells her inspiring story without bitterness as we learn of her steadfast commitment to human rights and of how she turns adversity into strength. Her integrity offers hope to a nation emerging from dictatorship, and her compassion is vital in a land that seeks to heal its wounds."

—Salil Tripathi, Chair, Writers in Prison Committee,
PEN International

"Life in prison corrodes the soul, but Ma Thida's memoir shows that it doesn't have to kill the human spirit. It may seem strange to say, but her account of the depravity wrought by Burma's generals on people who simply spoke out for democracy is captivating. This is hardly surprising from a doctor, activist, and writer who represents the best and brightest in Burma and belatedly has a leading role in the development of a country that, through its collective will, has now defeated a brutal dictatorship."

—Brad Adams, Asia Director, Human Rights Watch

"Like Ma Thida herself, this book is a powerful blend of literary, medical, political, and spiritual forces. Part personal memoir, prison diary, meditation manual, and human rights manifesto, Ma Thida's indomitable spirit shines through on every page. Essential reading for anyone who wants to understand Burma today."

—Emma Larkin, author of *Finding George Orwell in Burma*

T0375143

PRISONER OF CONSCIENCE

My Steps through Insein

MA THIDA

Silkworm Books

ISBN: 978-616-215-123-1

First published in 2016 by
Silkworm Books
430/58 M. 7, T. Mae Hia, Chiang Mai 50100, Thailand
info@silkwormbooks.com
www.silkwormbooks.com

The e-book is available on Kindle and iBooks.

Cover photo by Mette Karlsvik
Typeset in Minion Pro 11 pt. by Silk Type

Printed and bound in the United States by Lightning Source

CONTENTS

FOREWORD

After I was released from Insein Prison where I was incarcerated from 1989 to 2008, I wrote a book about my experiences, titled *Hell on Earth*. Here is Ma Thida's own "hell on earth," and I must say the story of her hell and mine are different in one significant aspect: her story is better than mine.

I wrote as a journalist. I wrote a record of my days behind bars; I was informing readers that prison is both hell and a school of life. She wrote as a talented writer, laying bare her *vedana* (pains) and her *cedana* (goodwill). She was saying to readers, "Prison is a state of mind, you know!" and, "Prison is just another state of existence."

When I read in her book how in prison she stopped using a male form of the first-person pronoun, I recalled that when we were working together at the information department of the National League for Democracy (NLD) she was even using an old-fashioned male version of "I"; I had felt as if I were talking to Shwe Udaung, the late and very famous writer from the colonial days, who always spoke his mind. At the time, Ma Thida was already an established writer and a doctor. Young as she was then, she was smart; she was tough and had no problem speaking her mind to anyone.

In her book are accounts of the great times, full of hope, during the early months of the NLD, and of Daw Suu's campaign trips, of which records no longer exist. The sounds and scenes of the water festival come alive in her description of the celebration and competition held at the NLD office. At the same time, she has included international news along with the timeline of important events in our country, so it is a joy for readers like me to be able to see the bigger picture. The Military Intelligence had tried their best to harass her, both in prison and after her release, and it seems to me that she had roundly "tortured" them, in addition to giving them a few life lessons.

Being involved in political activities in Myanmar is something like the sport of pole vaulting: you run as hard as you can with an unwieldy, long pole in hand, hoping to go over the bar without a hitch and to land gracefully on the other side. As luck would have it, you could take a hard tumble; landing in prison would mean years of a disrupted life, from which some would not be able to recover.

In my years in Insein, I was kept in solitary confinement and often threatened or urged to give in to their demands for one promise or another, all of which I firmly refused. On the evening of my release, I told the media that the whole of Myanmar was like a prison, and Ma Thida says the same thing.

Her book is a sharp reminder of the injustice and cruelties that happen under dictatorships; let none of us forget, and may all of us continue to voice reminders of our own.

U Win Tin
(1930–2014)

Chapter 1

Young Dreams

The huge cast-iron gate stood open, as if heartily welcoming me into Adipati[1] Road. My father held my hand; I was five years old and still in primary school. Along the sides of this road were the colonial-era buildings of the Rangoon Arts and Science University, with the Convocation Hall at the far end. On either side of the entrance to the Convocation Hall sit two statues of *chinthé*, the stylized Burmese lion. Not far from the hall is the tall *thitpoat*[2] tree, believed to be as old as the university, and the symbol of the campus. To the right of the gate there is an empty plot, overrun with weeds.

My father bent down and said in his quiet voice, "See that empty plot? The Students' Union building used to be there, but the army blew it up in July 1972[3] during the students' demonstrations. Many of them were shot down, and many were jailed. The previous day, I was in town and had to stay overnight for some family business. When I returned the next morning I was not allowed to enter the grounds. When I could in the evening, the Students' Union building was no longer there. That was the very place where student activists like Aung San and Nu[4] used to hold their meetings or relaxed in the teashop on the ground floor."

At that age the only places I had been to were the Shwe Hpone Pwint Pagoda near our house, and this campus. My father loved his university so much so that he often took my younger brother and me there on

---

1. Chancellor.
2. Large tree with a pale-colored bark (*Dalbergia kurzii*).
3. Under the regime of General Ne Win.
4. Student leaders fighting for independence from the British.

weekends. We found out about what had happened to the students over the decades, the names of all the dormitories, and how the campus was poetically referred to as Myakyuntha—the "emerald island"—with its thick-leafed flowering trees and position next to Inya Lake.

The history of this university could not be ignored if we were to learn anything about the colonial period and our independence. The story of the university had happy moments of romance and fun but also its share of loss, bloodshed, struggles, and challenges. That history—set among old colonial buildings, lush green trees, beautiful Inya Lake, and images of past students—filled me with fascination.

Those weekends were the reason for my dream of graduating with pride from this Convocation Hall, and that dream was the reason I studied hard starting in primary school. My mother, who was once a schoolteacher, wanted me to be a doctor. As for me, I was too young to know what I wanted to be and was only interested in graduating in such a beautiful hall.

However, I have had problems with my health since I was little. My father had wanted to be a doctor but had needed to graduate as quickly as possible because, being an orphan since World War II, his older siblings were contributing toward his education and he did not want to prolong their burden. He got a degree in economics yet kept a deep interest in medicine. My two younger brothers and I were used to the smell of Western medicine in our house—which I actually did not mind.

However, I have allergies, and various things like strong smells, pets, seafood, and very cold or hot weather cause rashes to break out all over my body. During primary school, I was even admitted to the Rangoon (later Yangon) Children's Hospital after unknowingly taking fake antibiotic capsules,[5] which completely incapacitated me with a fever of 107 degrees Fahrenheit (41.7°C). I am still suffering from the impact of that encounter. After that, my allergic reactions became much more intense and also lasted longer. Despite being in

---

5. In the 1960s–1980s, under a socialist regime of economic isolation, medicines were smuggled in from India and China, and many were fake.

and out of consciousness during my time in the hospital, I can still remember the strong smell of the place and the huge red gates of the Chinese embassy across the road. Having to frequent clinics and hospitals as a child, I became very fond of doctors and nurses. Young as I was, I appreciated their help in easing my sufferings. It was thus not only my mother's wish—I myself wanted to be a doctor, and this soon became a vivid dream.

Among the many stories told to me when I was young, it was the lives of Mother Teresa and Daw[6] Oo Zunn whose empathy, goodwill, and sacrifices not only entered my ears but also went right through to my heart. From my schoolbooks I learned a little about the Rakhine lady living in Mandalay called Daw Oo Zunn and how she helped elderly people by setting up free Homes for the Aged Poor. I was more familiar with the Albanian-born Mother Teresa—who helped anyone and everyone, even people who suffered from leprosy—because my father bought foreign magazines for us and we also listened to the British Broadcasting Corporation's Burmese Service. The inspiration of Mother Teresa was about not only helping others but also, for a child still in primary school, the praising of others.

One experience made it forever abhorrent for me to take undue advantage or claim special privileges. When I was eleven years old, my out-of-town cousins were visiting us, and my father allowed me to take them around Yangon. We were overjoyed, as we were on our own and had been given some money to spend. At the luxurious Karawaik Hotel, which was under the Ministry of Hotels and Tourism, where my father worked, we used his name to get ice cream for free and without even having to queue like the others; I was even thinking that the others in the queue must surely be impressed with us. However, when we got home and told my father, he scolded us soundly for taking advantage of his position. Under his anger, the taste of ice cream, as well as my happiness, evaporated. From then on, even in dreams I found myself queuing up and paying for my ice cream.

---

6. Formal female name prefix for older or respected women.

Regular family trips during summer holidays were the happiest times of my childhood, as my mother loved to travel and to visit our grandparents in Mawlamyaing.[7] We were very happy as well as in awe of the beautiful scenery, architecture, local food, different weather, ethnic cultures, and their languages and accents on the side trips to places near Mawlamyaing, such as Belu Island and Hpa An, or to places in Upper Myanmar such as Bagan, Mandalay, and the whole of Shan State. My father would then say to us, "See how beautiful our country is! We could earn a lot of foreign money if we had cable cars and big parks like in some of those countries. Foreigners would also see how beautiful our country is and how rich with natural resources." That was my father's dream, and he talked about this often. Every time I heard it I got goose bumps and felt very proud to be born in Myanmar.

Although too young to fully appreciate all these places and new things, while walking among the endless temples of eleventh-century Bagan I was very proud of the high architectural standards of our ancient civilizations. Still unable to fully understand the loss of sovereignty to the British, I would feel sad as I gazed at the Mandalay Palace and paid homage to the Maha Muni Buddha image. I loved my father's Shan relatives when we visited them in Thibaw and some parts of the Shan State. I would tell my friends and neighbors about our trips when we got home and I felt more confident in myself after finding out I had traveled more than my friends. Though still very young, my dreams were big because my ideas and general knowledge were not confined to my classroom or to our twelve-by-fifty-foot apartment.

I went to bed late every night—perhaps I matured very early because I stayed up with my father and mother who were often discussing social and economic matters. I was quite familiar with and understood how grownups thought by listening to my parents talk on different issues. Every night before I went to bed, I would pray to the Buddha for the sake of those who faced hardship and who were not fortunate. I do not remember if I wished to be like those who were more fortunate than

---

7. Moulmein, a town on the southern seacoast.

us, but I remember very well that I was worried for and wanted to help those who are poor, and it would take me that much longer to pray than my brothers.

My family and I relied on public transport since we could not afford a car. The roofless bus stop near our home could be known as such only because of the sign tacked to the lamppost, though the people clustered around it like ants meant no one needed to look up at the sign. Although they were not lined up in a queue it looked as if they were line dancing as all of their faces were turned in the same direction, as full of hope for the arrival of a bus as Stone Age humans who might have longed for the sun or moon to rise. I stood at many crowded bus stops like that one. The experience of bus rides—or rather, waiting for one—was a part of our lives. Even as a teenager, I never dreamt of one day having my own car but would wonder about how to solve our public transport problem; that is one of my yet-to-be-fulfilled dreams.

When I was about eleven, my grandparents from Mawlamyaing moved to Yangon, so our family moved into a bigger place in Sanchaung, a district of Yangon not far from the Shwedagon Pagoda. It turned out to be a significant move for me: I got to know my grandfather intimately. He had been expelled from his high school in Mawlamyaing for participating in the very first students' boycott against the British in 1920 and became self-taught. I was very much influenced by him, particularly in my manner of speaking and thinking, which was nothing like my peers'. He was almost eighty at that time and the life experiences he shared with me left a strong impression—so much so that I took them as models for my own life. I learned of how he had dealt with colonials— neither obedience nor resistance—and it somewhat influenced my own way of dealing with life.

My teenage dreams also shifted because my grandfather encouraged me to read more. Although I had not let go of my dream to become a doctor, I began to get passionate about literature; it became yet another dream. Grandfather read all kinds of books in both English and Burmese, ranging from astronomy, medicine, and other sciences to ancient history and literature. He always had a notebook handy while he read to mark down anything he liked. As a kid I used to play so wildly with my two younger brothers as to almost tear the roof down, but when I reached adolescence I became caught up in the magic of literature and was more interested in reading quietly by myself.

The power of the written word overtook my other dreams during my early teen years after being introduced to Grandfather's cupboard of books. I was not satisfied with reading only the books we had at home but would also borrow magazines and novels from book-lending shops.[8] Besides, I often visited any relatives and family friends who owned books so I could read at their place or borrow if they allowed me to. From childhood onward, books fascinated me and I was reading so much that I often missed out on other experiences that I "should" have had. I often read all night long, which was not good for my health. If my parents saw a light from my room they would tell me to stop reading and to go to sleep. It got so serious that once my hair caught fire because I was reading under the blankets with a lamp. I would become a bit panicky just from not having a book in my hands—as if I were committing a crime.

As I grew up with brothers, I was a bit boyish and could not see myself as a girl. I was also not very interested in pretty clothes or being girly either. I loved playing football and took part in street matches, up to the time I graduated from high school. During my teen years, Russian literature and leftist novels were popular, but in fact it was books on Buddhism that drew my attention. Those books brought ideas that were like new colors to my dreams. I would skip passages on how women should behave, or even anything at all to do with women, and read only how a good man should live, and try to be like that. Although I was boyish in manner, I was tamed and softened at heart by religious literature.

The first articles on Buddhism that I took to heart were on the *Metta Sutta*[9] and were written by U[10] Thukha, a famous writer.

---

8. To this day, they can be found in many neighborhoods and villages.

9. *Metta Sutta* is a Buddhist discourse in Pali on the development of *metta*, meaning "loving-kindness" through virtuous behavior and meditation.

10. Formal male prefix for names of older or respected men.

They were serialized in a monthly magazine and I would wait eagerly to read it. U Thukha wrote that the *Metta Sutta* is not just for chanting but that it is the word of the Buddha that we should follow and practice. He wrote with conviction and with many explanations; it touched my heart so deeply that I, still only in my teens, made up my mind to practice the teachings of the Buddha for the rest of my life.

Excerpts from religious books by U Thuka and other writers I liked were:

> When a person cannot show any respect to herself or himself, she or he will have to change as it is not a manner in which the Buddha wanted anyone to behave and act. And only when they can respect themselves can they expect others to respect them. We must be righteous; we must not lie to others or to ourselves.

> It is not the nature of *mudu,* or gentleness, that we stand firm on our own idea but that we be gentle in striving for justice and fairness.

> If we are not first of all sincerely gentle in our intentions (*manawkan*), our word (*wazikan*) or deed (*karyakan*) will only be meaningless and pretentious.

> No matter who censures you, it is more important not to be censured by the Buddha.

Unlike others, I did not have pretty or fashionable clothes, and I understood that my father's integrity meant we had just enough to eat. I tried to live in accordance with the *Metta Sutta*, which teaches one to be satisfied and contented with what one has, but nevertheless it was in conflict with the normal wants of a young person.

I wanted to respect myself and I did not wish to be censured by the Buddha. Because of our family's economic situation, I had to create a way to be contented with what I had and to ignore my wishes as a teenager—I had to try very hard to be truly contented with what I had instead of just pretending. For a teenager, it was quite a challenge to abide by my own rules and not to lie to myself as well as abiding by what the Buddha taught. In the end, it was the story of Padasari Theri, in one of the Buddha's sermons, that gave me the answer.

Pasada Theri was a young woman who lived during the lifetime of the Buddha. Her husband, children, and parents died from various causes, and she went completely insane, to the point that she discarded her clothes and remained unaware that she was naked. She attained *sawtapan*, which is the first stage of *ariya* (sainthood), after accepting the truth of the Buddha's dharma,[11] and finally attained the state of *ariya*. However, some who did not know the full story of this transformation thought that it was inappropriate for her to approach the Buddha in a state of nakedness.

The truth was that once she attained the state of *ariya*, though she was naked in physical terms, she was in fact regarded as fully clothed for knowing the Three Gems—the Buddha, the dharma, and the sangha;[12] the Five Precepts—namely, not to kill, steal, commit adultery, lie, or drink intoxicants; and the Seven Good Deeds of a virtuous person—namely, *thadha, sila, suta, saga, pannya, hiri,* and *ottapa*.[13]

From this I began to understand the way of living a contented life.

I tried to take refuge in the Three Gems instead of wearing flowers in my hair and to abide by the Five Precepts of daily life instead of wearing fashionable clothes. It was something I could do with my own will, and I was relieved of the burden of wanting things I could not afford. Although I was not able to live completely in accordance with all Seven Good Deeds of a virtuous person, I was able to ignore a teenage girl's desire for worldly things, from the fragrance of good Thanakha bark paste[14] to gold and diamonds.

---

11. Teachings.

12. The Sangha is the order of monks established by the Buddha.

13. *Thadha* means faith; *sila* means morality; *suta* means knowledge or learning; *saga* means merit practice; *paññya* means wisdom; *hiri* means shame; and *ottapa* means fear of sinning.

14. Bark from the Thanakha tree *(Limonia acidissima Linn)* ground to a paste.

As a young teen sometimes I would become a temporary nun or enter a meditation retreat for nine days[15] at a time, which helped me in many ways. I was able to experience how one can abide by the rules of a religious life, and I also had the chance to practice the basics of Vipassana[16] meditation, which would help significantly when I took it up seriously in prison. Once I became a nun, I did not even want to leave but knew I was not yet strong enough to remain in the religious life. Then I realized I could create a life that would contribute to the secular as well as religious worlds if I abided by the Eight Precepts.[17] Only then could I go back to being a layperson again.

---

15. A number significant in Buddhism.

16. Vipassana means insight or mindfulness meditation in the practice of conscious awareness.

17. Not to kill, steal, indulge in sex, lie, take intoxicants, eat after noon, take pleasure in music or dance or use cosmetics and perfumes, or live in luxury.

Chapter 2

Dreams of a Young Adult

As I enjoyed reading, I was soon wishing I could write. Besides, although I did not know much about the outside world during the socialist era's[1] dearth of information, I read about and was inspired by state leaders, nation builders, revolutionists, and peacemakers. I thought that one day I would have my own biography, just like them. When my mother opened a private tuition school in Pazundaung Township, I also taught there, and even though I was in high school I had to read primary- and middle-school textbooks to teach over sixty students. This kept me in touch with people, and I become very familiar with public transport, which also gave me a chance to know the city better.

As a teenager during the socialist era, I did not have much time to observe my own country,[2] yet I was able to grasp and understand the hardship and poverty that my society was facing. I did not know how people were doing in other parts of the world, but I knew very well that those around me were facing extreme hardship. I myself came from one of those families, but we had enough—just enough—to sustain ourselves. People around me were not that different from us or were worse off. I started writing some short stories based on the people I saw who were earning meager incomes. In my late teenage years I started to send my short stories to magazines; when I went to submit my work,

---

1. 1962–88.

2. Travel to remote regions was limited due to armed insurgencies and a lack of proper transportation and roads.

often the editors thought I had been sent on behalf of a writer parent since they supposed I was only of high-school age.

In the first term of my final year in medical school, my classmates and I had to go on trips to rural areas to volunteer in providing health care, and I began writing short stories based on the people of Bagan after I went there in 1986 and on a couple of trips after that. Contrary to the majestic temples and beautiful landscape of their surroundings, the people of Bagan suffered when fewer tourists came. I visited Bagan again in late 1987 after the government had demonetized some currency notes without compensation. In Bagan, people were desperate. Some men abandoned their craft businesses to mine gold when rumors told of a mother lode. Land around Bagan was dug up by hordes of people whose hands once made beautiful traditional crafts. I, who love Bagan, saw all of it and had pen and paper ready, but I could hardly write as my heart was breaking. I was then just twenty-one years old and was shocked by the question of how and to what extent our people were suffering.

The years 1985–87 were the busiest as well as the most important for me as I needed to do well in medical school. I had to study very hard and could not allow myself to fail just because I was writing and reading a lot outside of my schoolwork. My hard work paid off as my short stories were printed in two or three magazines in a single month. Senior and veteran writers started to notice and read my writings, which were of ordinary lives but in a different style, as I wanted readers to continue thinking after they reached the end. I was barely out of my teens at the time, and my writings did not reflect my age.

Some readers could not even believe that I wrote them myself; their assumptions irritated me. I was angry that they measured my work not by a literary standard but by age. Instead of being supportive, some older writers hinted at wanting me to be their "disciple,"[3] so I began to use quotes from literature in retaliation against their

---

3. In conservative literati society, younger members are expected to hang around older and seemingly wiser ones so that while the latter look good as "leaders" the former earn privileges through connections.

arrogance. I used the best quotes of condemnation I could muster, because at that time I was unaware that I had yet to encounter people with more malice. However, I said that as I had no respect for their writings I would not want to know them in person. I refused to give my work to magazines that asked me to unless they could clearly state their objectives. Thus I was soon regarded as being a prickly porcupine of a writer. With earnings from my writing, I was able to pay my school fees, go on short trips, and even contribute toward family expenses, but I did not realize at the time that my gentleness *(mudu)* was decreasing. Nonetheless, I was fulfilling some of my childhood dreams, so I was able to ignore both praise and criticism.

After our final med-school trips we had to submit reports as part of the exams. Unfortunately, I had witnessed some unseemly behavior: I heard a township medical chief ask his driver to make up statistics in his report, and another time, I got into a heated argument with a medic in one village who had pocketed all the villagers' donations for a new clinic. As a result, the papers I wrote on these trips were more like complaints than reports. I became openly resistant to the normal practice of pretending not to know what was going on in order to pass exams, and I was ostracized because of it. With this experience, my previous dream of becoming a specialist turned into wishing to be someone who could create a reliable system in the public health sector. My biggest dream at that point was to open a free hospital.

At that point in history, we had fewer media restrictions, so some magazines were able to publish more international news, such as stories on notable women like Benazir Bhutto from Pakistan or Corazon Aquino of the Philippines, as well as welcome news of perestroika and glasnost in the USSR. Though Myanmar at this point was still untouched by the fledgling Internet access that was starting to make headway in other parts of the world, I was aware of the world around us.

Literary talks where established writers opened people's minds to new ideas were allowed in many parts of Myanmar, and audiences turned up in the thousands to stay and listen until the early hours of dawn. There were also round-table discussions on different topics by different literary groups, and so I kept updated regarding world affairs even if I missed reading some books or magazines. I learned even more about the world through research for my writing, and at the same time I was saddened to learn that my country was one of the world's least-developed nations.

Criticism of U Ne Win,[4] who was at that time the chairman of the Burma Socialist Program Party (BSPP) and the president of the country, began in whispers but soon became loud, although never in the media. He too said a few words regarding the need for some economic changes during the party conference on August 10, 1987. Amidst all this, the country started to show signs of unrest when 75-, 35-, and 25-kyat banknotes were demonetized without compensation. Almost everyone lost money from the move and could not survive on what little was left. As a result, students tried to protest and so universities around the country were closed. Strangely enough, my mother had never liked these notes so she had saved up others. I lost out on some of my writing fees, though, and my grandmother lost quite a bit.

However, most households did not keep money in the bank—they still don't—and they suffered enormously. Some even died of cardiac arrest after the announcement. I decided to travel to Bagan while the universities were closed, and throughout that trip I learned more about the situation outside of the city. Although I was miserable about the situation, I was not politically active, and day by day I became increasingly aware of the mood of unrest. Sensing the possibility of change was very exciting, but still I thought that I would be able to attend my graduation ceremony the following year, 1988, at the Convocation Hall on the campus of Rangoon Arts and Science University—my unforgotten childhood dream.

---

4. Chief of Staff General Ne Win had taken over the country on March 2, 1962, in a coup d'état.

Chapter 3

Reality of Revolution

We all had to line up to wash our hands at the few taps that worked before we entered the operating theater—a normal start of day at Rangoon General Hospital in early 1988. That particular day, March 14, I was feeling drowsy as it was rainy and cold.

All I wanted to do was to get some sleep, but excited words I overheard suddenly woke me up: "The body of the boy who was shot dead last night was brought to the mortuary but they took it away early this morning! There's another one in ward 9/10, he was shot too but is still alive. Poor guy! The bullet went through his intestines."

"The medical chief got into trouble for writing death by gunshot wound on the death certificate."

"I heard that they first cut off the power in the whole township before they started shooting."

"What's with them, shooting into a brawl between young men? Everyone is already on the brink of exploding!"

I could not fully understand what was going on as I had gone to bed without listening to the news from the state TV station or the BBC. I found out later that the *lone htain* (riot police) had used full force to stop a brawl the previous night between students from the Rangoon Institute of Technology and some blue-collar workers living in the neighborhood, at a teashop called Sandar Win.

Everyone in the hospital was talking about it, and my friends and I planned to check on the wounded student. The famous movie star Win Oo was also hospitalized for colon cancer in the same ward, so we thought that if anyone asked we could say we were going to see him. The student's name was Soe Naing, and when we peeped in, he was

14

alone in a small room and looked almost lifeless. He was barely conscious, still in his blood-stained clothes and wired to medical equipment, with tubes in him. Despite his condition, his ankles were chained to the bed. The room was murky and filled with the unpleasant smell of medicine, blood, and sweat. There were uniformed and armed men standing around him. We were deeply disheartened as from experience we knew he could not survive; he passed away that night.

We also heard that the body of Hpone Maw, a civil engineering student, was taken to the mortuary at the new Japanese Hospital.[1] We hurried over, but both the new hospital and our medical school next to it were under tight security, so no one could go in. Then we heard that his body had been secretly cremated at Tamwe Cemetery and that his family was not allowed to hold the requisite seven-day vigil at his home. We were students and they had been students as well; knowing this stirred our consciences.

As a result of this brutality and insensitivity toward the family, students of the Rangoon Institute of Technology began to demonstrate on the streets the same day and were joined by students from Rangoon Arts and Science University on March 15; that day, many were brutally beaten up and arrested by the riot police. At a spot known as White Bridge, on Pyay Road right on the western shores of Inya Lake, badly beaten students who were unable to run were crammed into two trucks and sent to Insein Prison. Forty-one of them died from suffocation on the way, and the prison officials refused to accept the bodies, so they were taken to Kyandaw Cemetery and secretly cremated. When the news became widely known, even the government-run newspaper had to admit it. About six hundred students were arrested on that day, and in remembrance of the bloody crackdown on the White Bridge this incident was dubbed the "Red Bridge uprising."

At the time, my classmates and I were final-year students and did not have to attend classes as we were being sent to various hospitals

---

1. An extension of Rangoon General Hospital across Bogyoke Aung San St., donated by the Japanese government through the Japanese International Cooperation Agency and known either as JICA or the Japanese Hospital.

for hands-on training, so we did not actively experience the student uprising. In fact, we learned only by word of mouth what was going on, and it made us even sadder. We were frustrated with our inability to join in and became angrier since we could only imagine what it was like out there. However, we still had to sit for tests every other day. People who previously had no idea of the existence of the BBC tuned in at 8:15 every night now to listen to the news from the Burmese Service. While preparing to do my best in the final exams, these unfolding events shook me to the core.

Then, copies of an open letter to U Ne Win by his former aide Brigadier General Aung Gyi were widely distributed. Many people were unhappy about the failure of the socialist economy, and we heard more stories about the time when the Revolutionary Council first came into power in 1962. The report of the enquiry commission set up to investigate the unrest in March came out on May 15, but no one believed it. We were all uneasy in this tense political situation. Meanwhile, we heard that some astrologers had suggested people should offer limes to the Buddha images[2] in order to bring peace, so I too did that, prayed, and counted my prayer beads. No matter how well versed in religious reading or how well I knew the Buddha's teachings, I knew that the only way we could escape from this samsara was to rely on dharma only. I relied heavily on religion as an escape from or answer to the political and social problems we were facing. I needed my country to be peaceful, but I did not know how I could participate to ensure peace. What I knew was to keep my morality pure, to pray, and to write about things as they were.

It was June 21. The test that would decide where we were to be posted was coming up, so my friends and I were studying hard. We heard there could be student demonstrations but kept preparing for the test at the children's hospital, where we were being trained. When we got tired of studying, we talked about the events of last few months and about whatever news we had heard from the BBC. That afternoon

---

2. In a ritual called Yadaya Chay, to prevent bad events from happening or to bring good ones.

we heard that speeches were being made by activists at the Rangoon Arts and Science University campus and our medical school in Lanmadaw Township, and that there was a huge demonstration in Myaynegone Township not far from my home, all of which were being surrounded by the riot police. We were in a state of turmoil and were wondering what to do when a lecturer announced there would be no exam that afternoon. We also heard that there were no more buses and that roads had been closed. Although we were relieved to hear the exam had been canceled, many of us began to worry about how to get home.

On that day, a friend and I were lucky to get a ride back to Sanchaung from Myo Myint Nyein, an editor of the successful literary magazine *Pay Hpoo Lwar* (Message), which had published several of my short stories. On the way we stopped at the Lanmadaw Medical University campus to listen to some speeches. When I got home, I heard that the situation at Myaynegone was getting very tense, so my siblings and I walked to the Padonmar football field close to where it was happening. When we were almost at the field we heard rapid gunfire and came face-to-face with the crowd running for their lives away from Myaynegone. We walked home as fast as we could. That night, it was announced on state media that all universities, including Rangoon Arts and Science University, would be closed down indefinitely, and I suspected that my dream of graduating was fast vanishing. The next day the same was announced for the medical universities; curfew was imposed from 6:00 p.m. to 6:00 a.m.

In early July, some students were released from jail, but there were some uprisings by young monks in Taunggyi and Pyay. Martial law was imposed in Pyay, and everyone around the country was in the state of alarm. On July 23, an emergency meeting of the Central Executive Committee of the BSPP was held, and people were hoping U Ne Win would say something about the demonetized notes and whether the government might offer some sort of reimbursement. Instead, he issued an open threat: "I want everyone to know that if you gather and cause unrest, the army will shoot to hit; it won't be shooting in the air." He then resigned from the party's chairmanship.

However the people still believed he was wielding power from behind the scenes. He also gave a brief explanation about the dynamiting of the Students' Union building in 1962 and asked the people whether they wanted to continue with a one-party system or preferred a multiparty system. On July 27, U Sein Lwin became president of the country, and U Aung Gyi[3] and ten veteran politicians were arrested on August 1.

A sizable crowd of students gathered on August 2 at the Shwedagon Pagoda, and the next day martial law was announced. Students who were sent home to the provinces were organizing for the largest-yet nationwide demonstrations on August 8—a day that would become known as 8.8.88—by handing out pamphlets to those who might not have heard the target date announced on the BBC. Since all the schools and universities were shut down there was no excuse for me to go out. My family would not want me to go to the magazines' offices which for various reasons had very few people around during those days. I only talked to my friends over the phone, and no one had asked me to join the demonstration either. I was wondering if I should keep studying for my exams in case all schools and universities reopened or if I should just write down my feelings. At the end, I did not do anything except keep an ear out for news of what was happening and became more frustrated and angry about the situation.

August 8 arrived and nationwide demonstrations started, but I was unable to go out. My grandfather had passed away in 1986 and my grandmother was too gentle, so there was no one to help me persuade my parents to allow me to go. They were very concerned that something would happen to their children, so they banned all three of us from going out. I got phone calls from friends who were about to hold a

---

3. U Aung Gyi was an ex-military general and once worked closely with U Ne Win. After the bombing of the Students' Union building in 1962, it was never clear exactly who was responsible—Aung Gyi or Ne Win. Then he was dismissed. In May 1988, he wrote a forty-two-page open letter to U Ne Win and was recognized as one of the earliest critics of Ne Win. But people did not believe him much since his relationship with Ne Win was never very clear. His release from prison just before Daw Aung San Suu Kyi's speech at the Shwedagon pagoda in late August also made people wonder what the true situation was, but still no one knew.

hunger strike in front of the Rangoon General Hospital. They said there had been fatalities when the riot police opened fire directly into the crowd—wounding or killing not only students but also some patients, doctors, and nurses. My friends told me that bullet holes could still be seen on the wall of the hospital and that the riot police had knowingly shot into the crowd of doctors and nurses.

I could not tolerate this any longer; it was unacceptable to be at home and doing nothing in this situation. Although my love for my parents had stopped me from getting involved from the beginning, I could no longer stand by and watch while the ruling party's troops were firing into the crowd of medical staff without justification. I decided to try and persuade my parents to allow me to go do something, as I realized that abiding by the *Metta Sutta* also meant strongly opposing brutality. For the very first time in my life, I lied to my parents, saying there were many wounded patients at the hospital and that I had to go help. My parents then easily allowed me to go. In fact, they already knew where all of us should stand in this unfolding event; they were just being parents and trying to keep us safe. Nonetheless, their compassion for others won over their worry for their children and allowed me to do what I really wanted to do. From that day, I immersed myself completely in the movement—our revolution.

After the massacre of early August, the curfew was relaxed, now lasting from 8:00 p.m. to 4:00 a.m. U Sein Lwin resigned from his position as president of the country on August 12. During those days, there were nonstop demonstrations in all areas of the country, and even civil servants had begun to join in. Meanwhile, government-owned buildings, factories, and storerooms were looted and destroyed at the instigation of the army; they wanted to downplay the intent of the demonstrators by portraying their actions as mere looting. Meanwhile the whole government apparatus began to collapse as personnel abandoned their posts and took to the streets among rows upon rows of peaceful demonstrators. On August 19, Dr. Maung Maung of the BSPP State Council became the president.

Young people from all parts of Yangon were preparing to reestablish the students' union. The space in front of the Rangoon General

Hospital's wards 19 and 20 became the central gathering spot. Although I told my parents that I wanted to volunteer by caring for the wounded demonstrators, I was in the wards for only a week; after that I was mostly marching with the demonstrators and following mobile speechmakers, like famous author Maung Thaw Ka, as they moved from one stage to the next. Ma[4] Hmwe, an artist and a neighbor of mine, had similar interests to me, so the two of us would go around all day looking for opportunities to heighten momentum for the movement.

On the morning of August 24, Daw Aung San Suu Kyi, daughter of our national hero Bogyoke[5] Aung San, appeared in public for the first time at the Rangoon General Hospital and announced that she would be giving a speech at the western stairway of the Shwedagon Pagoda

Aung San Suu Kyi gives her first public speech on August 24, 1988, in front of the cardiac ward of Rangoon General Hospital. Writer and satirist Maung Thaw Ka is standing at her side. On the other side is actress Khin Thida Tun.

---

4. Feminine name prefix meaning "Sister."
5. Major General.

on August 26. We then heard that the martial law would be removed starting at midday. President Dr. Maung Maung promised to hold a national referendum on September 12, but it was already too late as the public, extremely bitter at the actions of the authorities, had lost all faith in their promises. On the same day, the government released detained students and politicians in the evening. Freshly released from jail, U Aung Gyi gave a speech at Padonmar Field on September 25. However, the public was outraged when he said, "Don't even think ill of the army."

On August 26, Daw Aung San Suu Kyi gave a speech at the Shwedagon Pagoda's western entrance as planned. The large fields on either side of the pagoda's western stairway were normally covered only with tall, tangled weeds, but on that day there was a sea of people. With roads blocked by crowd after crowd of demonstrators wanting to greet her, Daw Aung San Suu Kyi could not arrive on time for her speech. Previously, many suspected Daw Aung San Suu Kyi would not understand Myanmar's politics as she was married to a foreigner and had lived abroad most of her life. However, her speech unequivocally reassured them that these things could not prohibit her from helping the country change for the better.

Afterward we decided that it was not enough for us just to join in demonstrations, so we discussed what else we could do to be more effective. Many governmental departments, including the Press Scrutiny Board, had stopped operating, and the staff from the state-owned newspapers Working People's Daily and the Mirror were already participating in the demonstrations. Even state-run papers started to feature news of the demonstrations, and we also saw cheaply printed magazines and journals being published privately; we thought we should do the same with a handwritten bulletin. While we were planning it we heard that there was a riot at Insein Prison. Before 1980 there had been a general amnesty in which political prisoners as well as criminals were freed; now we heard that the criminal prisoners were rioting and that there had been some shooting, in which thirty-six prisoners died. After that, hundreds of inmates (apart from those on death row) were freed into the general population, and these criminal elements with nowhere to go soon became a burden to the general strike forces and demonstrators.

The situation became increasingly chaotic as more and more people took to the streets. There were endless numbers of unions and protest committees. Our group was named *Ayaung Thit* (New Color) by artist Min Wai Aung. I was the resident writer and editor, with Swe Nyo as photographer. Our newsletter was published by a group of painters and cartoonists, so we prioritized cartoons and illustrations while I was the main writer for the headlines and articles. Others contributed articles as well and we published our paper every other day. In addition, as a student I could attend meetings held in the universities and the Rangoon General Hospital, so I was writing news and articles for our paper, *Ayaung Thit; Doh Ayay* (Our Cause), a paper published by a group of editors; and *Tha Megga* (The Union), published by the students' union. Although I often missed meals I was happy and excited with the new experiences.

By the first week of September, vandalism and lootings were happening everywhere in Yangon and also in the provinces. Hysteria took hold of the mobs, and a few people began decapitating those they suspected of being government spies. There were almost no buses, so everyone had to walk to and from our impromptu workplaces. Mistrust among the demonstrators heightened as rumors flew. On September 9 soldiers from the air force joined the demonstrations, and on September 10 incumbent president Dr. Maung Maung announced at his party's conference that general elections would be held "soon."

The protest committees and the public had no faith in this and only wanted to form an interim government. On September 16, the student unions and strike committees banded together to hold a meeting at the Institute of Medicine 1, attended at their request by the former Prime Minister U Nu,[6] former Defense Minister U Tin Oo, ex–Brigadier General U Aung Gyi, Bo Yan Naing—who was another

---

6. Who on September 9 had declared himself the legitimate prime minister.

hero of independence—and Daw Aung San Suu Kyi, to form an interim government. Nonetheless, all of them responded that they would like to take time to think this through. On September 17, tempers were on the brink of erupting at the Ministry of Trade when armed soldiers were spotted on the rooftop and angry crowds surrounded the building; then monks intervened and managed to ease the situation. We heard that the next day, September 18, there was to be a mass rally in the Convocation Hall for all the student organizations and unions.

On that morning, although I had a cold and a fever and was exhausted, I took some medicine, pulled on a jumper, and left for downtown. This mass meeting was only for students and the media was not allowed, so my colleagues from the *Doh Ayay* journal wanted me, a student, to attend and write something for them. I was running around all morning and it was already 2:30 p.m. when I reached the Convocation Hall. I had not eaten since waking up that morning; I took a handout meal box from the organizers and climbed the steps of the hall. Once inside, I saw students and unionists systematically lining up to take their places. The large, high-ceilinged hall with a wide stage at the far end looked just like many other colonial buildings, yet my heart was thumping in excitement; I got goose bumps all over. This place had been part of my dreams since childhood. But my dream of how I would walk into the hall was definitely nothing like this; I was supposed to be wearing my graduation gown, cap on my head, with my parents by my side. Yet there I was in the Convocation Hall—hungry, sweaty, feverish, and with a runny nose.

I was holding a recorder and camera in my hand, and I was soon surrounded by thousands of students and demonstrators. Our journal, *Ayaung Thit*, would be out in two days, but I had to be quick since the *Doh Ayay* journal was published daily. I had taken some photos and had witnessed the opening part of the proceedings, so I knew the agenda of the meeting. With an article to finish, I calculated the time needed to finish my work and then get home before dark; I gave my tape recorder to my friend Soe Win Oo, thinking I would come back for it later. I caught a bus outside the campus and when it reached the Myaynegon stop, passengers who got on told everyone that the military had taken over the country. It was announced at four in the afternoon on the state radio and TV stations, which since morning had been broadcasting military marches over and over.

I saw people running around and screaming before I reached our office. Everyone sighed with relief when they saw me. We decided that we should go home straight away since the curfew was at six o'clock. We would come back tomorrow to discuss how we could continue to produce *Ayaung Thit*. Colleagues from *Doh Ayay* decided that they would be publishing the next day, and all of them were already gathered in their office. They asked me to read the news to them over the phone when I got home. I promised that I would write a short article for them, reasoning that although I would not be able to retrieve the recorder from my friend, he could at least tell me what happened over the phone. After a few packed bus rides and long walks, Ma Hmwe and I reached home, both of us perspiring profusely. My parents, grandmother, and brothers were waiting anxiously for me. We listened to the radio the whole evening and could hear the repeated announcements of Statements 1/88 and 2/88 from the "State Law and Order Restoration Council."

With my mind in turmoil I tried to write an article but found it difficult. Soe Win Oo called and said it did not look good. The military had surrounded the campus. He told me what was going on and said that he and the others would try to get to the University of Medicine, spend the night there, and continue demonstrating the next morning. I finished writing one short news article. While I was eating dinner, the *Doh Ayay* journal called. I read out the three-page article I had finally written to them over the phone. My voice was garbled with the sound of the official announcement as we both had our radios on. The rice grains on my hand dried out as I'd had no time to wash my hands, and my throat was dry from nervousness. Extremely concerned, my parents got angry with me. Although I was not sure whether *Doh Ayay* could be published tomorrow, I was certain I would not be allowed to go out of the house again.

But then, the phone began to ring nonstop. I learned of how demonstrators had been shot down and killed. Colleagues from *Doh*

Ayay could not do anything despite being ready to produce the journal. Soe Win Oo also called and asked me to get help as he was trapped in the University of Dentistry. I heard gunshots in the background—and then the phone went dead. My family did not want me to even talk on the phone anymore. I was, however, plotting how to get out of the house. I was not thinking about the danger I might face; all I thought about was how to increase the pace of the revolution toward its end as, at the time, I could not foresee that it was going to be a long fight.

The military was firmly in power after killing nearly 4,000 demonstrators and innocent bystanders throughout the country. But then, we thought the government could not operate without civil servants. I used the usual white lie to my parents of there being many wounded patients at the hospital that needed my help, but I instead went to a place where U Win Tin[7] and some other editors were meeting. U Win Tin tried everything he could to continue the civil servants' strike, but in vain—almost all civil servants went back to work.[8] After that we gathered at a teashop, where we normally would not have gone, to discuss what to do next since we did not want to flee across the border as many were doing. By that time, I had no income and was mostly walking to get from one place to another. With all our money combined, our group of friends did not even have the two kyats needed to buy the recently published book *La Sandar Hnint Chuu Paiksan*,[9] which we all wanted to read.

The military government announced that it would allow political parties to be formed[10] with the aim of holding elections "soon." The National League for Democracy (NLD) was formed on September 24 with former brigadier general Aung Gyi as chairman, former defense

---

7. Late editor and internationally known political leader.

8. Those who did not go back to work were fired and many from Myanmar embassies abroad sought political asylum.

9. The Burmese translation of *The Moon and Sixpence* by Somerset Maugham.

10. About two hundred political parties were registered in return for a phone line and other privileges; most were made up of a few family members. SLORC had thought more parties would mean fewer votes for the NLD.

minister U Tin Oo as the deputy chairman, Daw Aung San Suu Kyi as general secretary, and U Win Tin as assistant general secretary.[11]

Our *Ayaung Thit* group was asked to help out at the NLD office. We had nothing else to do since all schools and universities were closed and no more magazines were allowed to be published. The problem was that we did not want to be members of any party; we decided to help out until we could return to our careers in art or literature, so we went to the NLD's headquarters, just one house away from Daw Aung San Suu Kyi's home. A committee for registering new members was set up in an empty plot next to the main road, within the compound of her residence at 54 University Avenue, and Myo Myint Nyein was put in charge. We not only issued application forms but were also in charge of the party flags and signboards to be used for the party's branch offices, which would soon be in operation.

Our newly established committee office had no furniture and no money to buy any, so we had to ask for donations from friends and well-wishers. We put up the NLD headquarters signboard on September 27 at 56 University Avenue on the day of its registration. Initially, we were only selling membership application forms, but with U Win Tin's advice we issued membership cards with numbered codes according to the township of the member. I also had to take care of keeping a record of the members. Although I was good at math and could calculate large sums in my head, I was not very happy with the task at hand since it was not what I wanted to do.

We all missed a lot of meals as the people came in droves to buy the forms, and we could not spare any time because no one wanted to wait even a few minutes for us to eat since they had lived under the BSPP for too long—26 years—and wanted out. Once the applications

---

11. Each of the founders brought in three members for the central executive committee:
   1. Daw Aung San Suu Kyi brought editor U Win Tin, attorney Daw Myint Myint Khin, and actor U Aung Lwin.
   2. U Tin Oo brought U Chit Khaing, U Aung Shwe and U Lwin, all ex-military.
   3. U Aung Gyi brought U Kyi Han, U Ba Shwe and U Kyi Maung, all ex-military.

came back we had to issue the cards. U Win Tin arranged for us to assign membership numbers according to the township and its population; by the number it could be instantly known which township a member came from. Accordingly, I came up with the codes for every card.

I was also given the task of maintaining the list of all members and keeping it confidential. It was of utmost importance to keep it secret, since even having an application form could very well mean detention or jail (despite political parties supposedly having been made "legal"). Those who worked for the registration of members at the township level did not need to memorize much, but as for me, having to remember nearly five hundred different codes was leaving me feeling befuddled. Besides, we had to speed up the process of issuing cards since some Central Executive Committee members were about to leave for campaign trips. Having lived under the BSPP with its high-ranking officials always having "VIP" status, I felt furious just hearing that word, so if someone asked me to prioritize membership for a VIP I snapped at them that I could not accept anyone asking me to do favors for "important" people and that I would only do so if the situation was urgent.

My head was still filled with the codes even when I returned home each day. I could not stop myself from calling out the relevant area code whenever I heard the name of a township or district over the radio; I was under enormous stress. We even worked late into the night and slept at the office to prepare the cards. Even my colleagues were surprised to see me being such a workaholic, pushing them to go back to work right after a meal during those late nights; I was only twenty-two then and expected others to work just like me. I would give a stern look to anyone asking for a break. However diligent I was, it was far from what I wanted to do. I was even dubbed the "human computer," but it was this good memory that was causing mental torture. By this time I had confessed to my family what I was doing; I was never comfortable with lying.

As usual when I was stressed, I thought I should go on a trip. Wanting to revive my *mudu*, I thought it would be good to go alone to the place I love most—Bagan. Previously, I had been requested by artist Ma Thanegi, who was volunteering as Ma Suu's secretary,[12] to volunteer by compiling records of campaign trips, but I had not been interested in that sort of work. Now, I was wrestling with numbers and codes. I explained everything about my participation in the NLD to my parents and they understood my feelings. I told them that I wanted to go to Bagan alone, and I informed people at the office so that they could find a replacement. At the same time, U Win Tin advised Ma Suu to go on campaign trips before the rainy season, and she decided to go to four divisions[13] leaving on October 30, 1988. Knowing of my desire to travel, writer U Moe Thu and Myo Myint Nyein arranged for me to go along as a representative of the information section; Ma Suu's student supporters in the Tri-Color youth group, who were already acting as guards in her compound, took care of the security, headed by two brothers who were sons of her late father's bodyguard.[14]

---

12. All we young adults called her Ma Suu or *Ahma,* meaning elder sister, while the students called her Aunty Suu.

13. Magwé, Bago, Sagaing, and Mandalay.

14. The Tri-Color group was made up of young men and women students volunteering for Daw Aung San Suu Kyi, the boys serving as bodyguards and living in an incomplete building in her compound while the girls would come during the day. The group's name (Thone Yaung Chal in Burmese) refers to the three colors of our flag in former times (and used again in the flag since 2011): yellow, green, and red.

Chapter 4

Campaign Trips

We representatives of the registration and information committee had a separate covered pickup truck. Photographer Tekkatho Aye Myint was in charge of taking stills, and we also hired a professional video team. Myo Myint Nyein was assigned to issue membership cards during the trip and I, being a final-year medical student, was put in charge of the health care for about thirty people in addition to helping with issuing cards and selling flags, seals, and NLD constitution booklets. I was also writing down everything Ma Suu discussed at the NLD district offices. Initially, Myo Myint Nyein was to do it but he had too many things to oversee, and the video camera could not record everything.

On the very first day of the trip our pickup broke down near the small town of Zeegone, so photographer Aye Myint, the video team, and I went on by rented car to meet up with the others at Pyay while Myo Myint Nyein was left behind with the pickup truck. During those days, anyone found with the NLD's membership application form, especially in the provinces, could be arrested so all of us were worried sick for one another. With important materials, including the moneybox, we arrived in Pyay.

By day, I was a documenter, vendor of membership applications, and filler of miscellaneous other roles, and by night I was a medic. Everyone running around during the day in the crowds invariably suffered bruises or at least exhaustion. So my mobile "clinic" was full in the evenings wherever we stopped for the night. I will never forget this trip and seeing how the public welcomed Ma Suu and all of us so warmly, despite knowing there were Military Intelligence personnel following us. Deep into the night, I wrote down everything in my diary after I finished my work as a medic; I wanted to hand over all the records to the Central Executive Committee as soon as we got back to Yangon. Despite being busy, I never forgot to pray, recite sutras, and count my prayer beads before going to bed, because those were the fundamental tasks of my life.

When we reached Pakokku, known for its many monasteries, the support we saw was unbelievable; we struggled to stay upright in the sea of people. Our feet barely touched the ground, and at times we were lifted up bodily by the press of people and turned completely around. It was both joyous and touching to see the massive crowds of people following Ma Suu with such great expectations. On one dusty road, a young woman on a bicycle pedaled furiously to keep up with our car.

Aye Myint, the photographer, called out to her, "Aren't you tired?"

She answered, "Nope! This is like reuniting with my own mother. I'm so happy!"

We were speechless at her sheer love for Ma Suu.

When we stopped for the night, writer U Moe Thu said, "I just found out that the government refused to extend Michael Aris's visa and they've asked him to leave. So he has to go back soon, and if Daw Suu decides to go back to Yangon we will have to cancel the whole trip." We wondered what she would do.

Her response was, "It doesn't matter. Why don't we extend our trip by three more days? Then we can go to northern Shan State."

It did not really surprise me to hear it, but still, I found myself staring at her face in amazement for quite some time.

The next day, we arrived in Bagan. While we were at the Ananda Temple, I could not even pray properly as I was trying to find out what had become of little Mi Mi Kan, who was a main character in one of my short stories. It seemed that the situation in Bagan after the '88 uprising had deteriorated. (Soon after coming back from this trip, I received a letter from friends in Bagan saying they could no longer afford to eat rice but were eating maize. I immediately wrote a short story about this, but no magazine dared publish it, so my readers have yet to see it.)

We then traveled to Magwe, Mandalay, and Sagaing Divisions—including a small town called Nat Mauk, which was the birthplace of

Ma Suu's father. In some townships, the local State Law and Order Restoration Council (SLORC) contingent tried to harass us, but we were able to successfully and peacefully hold our rallies. The trip to northern Shan State was quite short since we only went to Kyaukme and Thibaw, where I was delighted to see relatives from my father's side; in fact, we all stayed the night at their house.

I was able to hand in our report to the Central Executive Committee on November 15, the day after we arrived back from the trip. Although we were feeling happy at our accomplishment, we were soon upset to hear that U Aung Gyi was planning to publicly announce his concerns that the NLD was being influenced by communists, which he could have discussed with his fellow committee members in private.

We were also just about to publish the first newsletter of the campaign trip. I had to rewrite my diary to be an article for the newsletter, transcribe the speeches, and select photos. We began to work more on the documentation of NLD affairs than on providing

Party meeting in early November 1988 at the Yenangchaung Township NLD office. Front row (from left): U Khin Maung Swe (NLD central committee member, now National Democratic Front party head), Daw Aung San Suu Kyi, U Moe Thu (NLD central committee member), Maung Sein Win (NLD member from Pegu Division). Back row (from left): Win Thein (Tri-Color student group), Ma New (poet), Ma Thida.

membership cards. Whatever duty we performed, those of us who worked in the information committee were almost all the same people from its start, and we worked well together. We also came to form a close bond with the students from the Tri-Color group because we went on campaign trips together. I had no time to write anymore as I was very busy assisting with documentation, arranging debates and speaking competitions, covering Ma Suu's press conferences, and publishing newsletters and bulletins.

On November 24, Ma Suu gave a speech to the NLD youth who were about to go on their own campaign trip, and she recited and explained the poem "If—" by Rudyard Kipling. I liked it so much that I translated it into Burmese. Ma Suu liked what I had done and we agreed that it should be published. At the bottom I inserted a footnote that it was "rewritten as explained by Daw Aung San Suu Kyi" since I was not confident enough to call myself a translator, but everyone ended up thinking this poem was translated by her.

On November 25, U Aung Gyi publicly accused some NLD Central Executive Committee and Central Committee members—U Win Tin, Daw Myint Myint Khin, U Aung Lwin, U Moe Thu, U Ko Yu, U Chan Aye (writer Maung Suu Sann), U Tun Tin, Monywa U Tin Shwe, and U Ba Thaw (writer Maung Thaw Ka)—of being communists and demanded that they be removed. The NLD responded by issuing a statement that the matter would be decided with a secret vote of the committee on December 3. U Aung Gyi was defeated; he had thirteen votes and the other side had twenty-eight. He was expelled from the NLD along with all those who voted with him. U Kyi Maung, who did not vote in favor of U Aung Gyi, also remained in the party. A new Central Executive Committee was formed with U Tin Oo as chairman, U Win Tin as deputy chairman, and Daw Aung San Suu Kyi as general secretary. Members were U Kyi Maung, U Lwin, U Chit Khaing, U Aung Lwin, and Daw Myint Myint Khin.

We worked hard to be able to inform the eagerly awaiting public of the meeting's outcome. I had to transcribe the recordings of that meeting so that we could publish as quickly as possible. With this, my wish to contribute to the movement with my skills was at last fulfilled. I was also fortunate enough to learn how to do newspaper layout and design from U Win Tin and Myo Myint Nyein. From being purely a writer, I now became a journalist. It also happened around this time that one of the short stories I had sent to *Shumawa* magazine was removed by order of the Press Scrutiny Board. I started to suspect I might be blacklisted, although, as usual, no reason was given for why the story was banned.

~

At the time, people in Myanmar were also aware that South Korean President Chun Doo-hwan had admitted to corruption and had resigned following a students' protest. The news of Benazir Bhutto becoming prime minister of Pakistan was greeted with joy in Myanmar. On November 30, the military government changed the country's economic policy from the socialist state-run system to a free-market model.

~

At the NLD, we were preparing for a campaign trip to Mon State and its capital, Mawlamyine. As travel plans were being finalized, the illness of Ma Suu's mother, Daw Khin Kyi, grew worse. Since it was a short trip we did not cancel and went ahead with the plan of leaving on November 14. Chairman U Tin Oo and his group also left Yangon at the same time for their campaign trip to Bago Division and Rakhine State. The public wholeheartedly welcomed and supported them as well.

On our trip to Mawlamyine with Ma Suu, the car in which the MIs were following us broke down, and Ma Suu offered to give a lift to two of them in our committee's small covered pickup truck. There was not enough space so I sat on the roof or clung upright to the back frame. I was so busy selling our materials and booklets that I asked the two MIs to help me. I thought that since they were getting a free ride they should make themselves useful.

On her campaign trips, Ma Suu sometimes brought along two members from the student party, the Democratic Party for a New Society, and on this trip these were Moe Hein and Moe Thee Zun. There were no obstacles and problems on this trip and we were even able to travel to small villages in Belu Island, where on our way one old man stopped us to ask for a lift. He said, "I, a farmer, want to have a quick glance at her!" He did not say anything but looked deeply at her face and nodded his head approvingly several times—it was a moment that left a deep impression.

We arrived back in Yangon on December 18, and as usual I had to prepare the publication of a newsletter and edit the documentary video of the trip. Apart from editing, I also had to write the narration for the video. One advantage for this trip was that I was able to tape Ma Suu's speeches as well as write them down as I had finally gotten a tape recorder. Besides, Mawlamyaing was our base, so I had the time and conditions to write all necessary notes as well as pray to the Buddha every night.

While we were planning for another campaign trip, this time to the Ayeyarwaddy Division, Daw Khin Kyi passed away, on December 27. Saying they would like to help out with the funeral arrangements, the military government sent some officers to Ma Suu's residence. Our group from the information committee got very busy with designing the coffin and having an architect draw plans for the tomb. On top of it all, we had to prepare the documentation and program of the funeral, which was held on January 2, 1989. In the midst of all that work, we were able to publish a book of poetry, *Victory from Father to Daughter*, by the famous poet Tin Moe, written in honor of Ma Suu and her father. Later, we published more collections of his poems but "only for NLD members" as he had insisted.

We started preparing to campaign in Ayeyarwaddy Division after the funeral. At that time, I was shuttling between the hospital, where my grandmother was recovering from a bleeding gastric ulcer, and the NLD information office. This particular trip turned out to be very stressful but exciting—we faced danger and countless hardships as the divisional commander, Brigadier General Myint Aung, was determined to sabotage our efforts. The more dangerous and difficult it got, the better our committee members worked together. Unlike on previous trips, we traveled on a double-decker boat, and we faced some harassment even before we left Yangon. We also heard that the military had beaten up some villagers who were planning to welcome us and to arrange our meals. At the town of Laputta, all microphones and amplifiers were confiscated and kept at the police station for the whole time we were there, so for Ma Suu's speeches we used FM microphones, a shortwave radio, and the amps we had on our boat. In Kyon Ma Ngay, soldiers were placed in positions where they could shoot us if ordered to do so.

Finally, we arrived at Pathein, the capital of Ayeyarwaddy Division, but the military had already imposed a daytime curfew so that no one could come out to listen to Ma Suu's speeches; the roads were completely empty. Even that was not enough; the military stationed a checkpoint at each end of the street in front of our hotel. They made every effort to inconvenience us, so we had difficulty in even finding food.

The next morning, trouble was already waiting for us when we came out of the hotel. As we tried to walk through the checkpoint, the soldiers aimed their guns and bayonets directly at us and stood in the alert position. However, Ma Suu calmly walked through those soldiers without a glance at them, and then we all followed her through the guns and bayonets. After that, the officer on duty came and pleaded with her, "Please, Elder Sister, don't go. Don't go, please." People who were watching this saga were first stunned to silence, and then they started to shout, "Daw Aung San Suu Kyi! Good health to you!" Finally, our whole group was allowed to go to the pagoda by car. The public dared not approach us since the military trucks were following closely.

Meanwhile, no boats or canoes were allowed to leave the nearby villages, in case anyone was thinking of coming to support Ma Suu. As soon as this ban was imposed, NLD members and supporters swam across rivers to reach Pathein. They told us how they had placed their clothes in earthenware pots and pushed them along as they swam across in the night with their heads under water, breathing through lengths of reeds. They were very proud of their strategy, and we were deeply touched. Their steadfast love and brave hearts gave us, including Ma Suu, so much strength. She remarked that if everyone in Myanmar were like the people of Ayeyarwaddy Division, victory would soon be ours.

The divisional commander was so furious for some reason that we had gone to a pagoda that he did everything he could to prevent us reaching Hinegyi Island by forbidding any boat to take us there. Ma Suu then announced that if that was the case we would all stay in Pathein for a longer period so that we would have the time to walk to villages and towns in the vicinity; right after that we were allowed to hire transportation to go to Hinegyi Island. Once there, Ma Suu was only allowed to give speeches in the offices of the NLD, and it took a long time to get a chance to talk to more people. Many local NLD organizers of Pathein had been arrested when we got back. Then, Ma Suu fell ill with indigestion and I too was suffering from my usual monthly cramps; I had also passed out in Hinegyi Island, much to the alarm of my colleagues. We all felt we could not spend another day in that place so that very night started to make plans for our trip back to Yangon.

The day after our return to Pathein from Hinegyi, Ma Suu thought we should all ride around town on bicycles that we had earlier borrowed from supporters. Troops surrounding the hotel that day had no idea what we were up to until she rode out with the rest of us following on our bikes. They tried to follow in a car, but it was too late as crowds of supporters, even children, came out on their bikes, and no cars could penetrate the dense procession. That evening, the whole town was packed with people on bikes as word had spread. The next evening, as she always did, Ma Suu stood on the uncovered back of a Hilux pickup truck and talked and greeted the public as we rode around the city. We realized that the situation in Pathein could get really rough for our supporters, and since we had been there quite a while we decided to leave the next morning.

Following close on our heels as we drove to the jetty to board our boat was a fire engine washing down the street as we passed: the powers that be were implying, according to traditional superstitions, that they were washing away our "evilness." We thought it was funny, and I am sure they must have been more furious than ever to see our laughing faces.

Meanwhile all of us, including supporters, were still being harassed in one way or another. The public was becoming aware of the situation so it became more important than ever that we spread the news. The Burmese Service of the BBC arranged to interview Ma Suu, while we made plans to publish a daily bulletin from the NLD headquarters in Yangon. At every stop we made on the way back, a staff member from our Yangon office would come to meet us; I would hand over the articles and news that I had ready, and he would go back to Yangon the next day. In this manner our colleagues in Yangon could publish the most recent news. Of course there were no mobile phones—let alone email or Internet—during those days, and the authorities had already cut almost all landline phones—so we had to resort to the medieval method of communication, using runners. Thus, staff from our committee were being trained on the job and getting quite good at it, for we had to improvise often.

Our communication system of messengers was so effective that not only Yangon but also the whole country was made aware of the harassment we were facing. People were following the developments of our trip as if it were a thriller movie. As for me, I gained many new experiences as a media person. This trip had also left me with many different feelings—confusion, anger, excitement, and satisfaction, as well as elation. We usually had not used all the footage we shot of previous trips, but this time we thought we should produce it without any edits and as quickly as we could. We spent many nights without sleep and I still feel very proud of the narration I wrote for it.

January had ended and the trip to Tanintharyi was waiting. There was unfinished work from the Ayeyarwaddy trip and a need to rotate our staff, so our committee sent out a different group for this trip. Besides, we had to plan for trips to Shan and Kayah States, which would begin right after the Tanintharyi campaign.

Since it had been decided that we must be in Panglong[1] on Union Day, which is February 12, we did not have much time to organize. Compared to the Ayeyarwaddy Division, this trip to the southern Shan State and Kayah State was peaceful; most of us had never been to Kayah State before, and the different culture I saw cast a spell on me. The weather was very cold and my health was not so kind to me; as I am allergic to cold, I suffered from severe rashes during the whole trip. I was ill the whole way, so instead of me tending to the health issues of others, they were taking care of me.

While we were on our trip, a paper titled "Analysis of the Political Movement and Daw Aung San Suu Kyi" came out in which the author, Moe Thee Zun of the Democratic Party for a New Society, strongly criticized her as someone with overconfidence in her own abilities.

〜

At that time, there was unrest and tension in the Middle East; Iran's religious leader Ayatollah Khomeini accused author Salman Rushdie of being anti-Islamic for writing *The Satanic Verses.*

〜

The memorial service for the one-year death anniversary of the student Hpone Maw was held at the Rangoon Institute of Technology on March 13, and Ma Suu, U Tin Oo, and the NLD headquarters staff attended the event. Among the long speeches by several student leaders, Ma Suu's speech was short and to the point: "Courage is not doing whatever you want by wielding arms. Courage is doing what we desire to do without taking to arms." The audience applauded her fervently.

We were preparing a trip to Kachin State, and our committee staff and the NLD security would be leaving by train ahead of Ma Suu and a few others, who would fly out to join us later. I was on the train,

---

1. Panglong is the town where General Aung San and ethnic leaders signed an agreement in 1947 to be of one country, one union.

and the day after we reached Myitkyina, March 27, we heard that there was a huge problem at the NLD headquarters. March 27 was Revolutionary Day,[2] and security was so tight that we thought Ma Suu would not be able to leave Yangon. As we expected, there was no one when we went to pick them up at the airport the next day. We could not even make phone calls to Yangon or Mandalay.

We then decided to go back to Yangon; we would take the train to Mandalay the next morning and from there take the evening train to Yangon. That evening I was coughing unbearably, so without knowing I was allergic to penicillin, I took ampicillin and began to suffer from a bad bout of diarrhea and then fainted as a result. After regaining consciousness I took some pills and gave myself some injections of medicine that a local doctor had helped me to get. I tried but could not sleep through the heavy rain and lashing hailstorm. We went to the train station around three in the morning but we could not get any seats to Mandalay. Finally, after begging the ticket office we managed to get only two seats, so most of us had to ride in the goods car.

That was not all. The train derailed between Naba and Hser Mhaw. We had to spend the night there, in such a remote place and with nothing to eat. My condition was pretty bad and my colleagues wanted to give me all the food we had. My blood pressure was so low that I was out of breath with the slightest movement. They tried to fetch a nurse from a nearby village but she was also stuck on her way back from town, where she had gone for her salary. The heat of March was so intense that I could not stay in the carriage. I lay down by the tracks in the shade of the train. My colleagues could not find anything to eat in this deserted place and were worried that I might die. In the end, they were able to find the NLD branch office in Naba and managed to get me a plate of rice and an omelet. That one dish saved my life on that trip; we were stuck for forty-eight hours.

---

2. In 1990 it was renamed Armed Forces Day

Finally we reached Mandalay around five in the morning and then had to line up for tickets to Yangon that evening. We only got seats up to Pyinmana and were to continue our trip without seats from there. As I was too sick to stand, my colleagues insisted that I sit on a wooden chest we had brought with us. My weight was down to eighty pounds (about thirty-six kg.) by the time we got back to Yangon. My parents gave me the ultimatum that I must not go on any more trips, so I was not able to go along when Ma Suu took a short trip to Nyaung Don in early April. Another reason I did not go was the *thangyat*[3] competition.

After the ill-fated Myitkyina trip, while we were just chatting informally Ma Suu thought it would be a good idea to hold a competition for the best *thangyat*. So I sent a memo to all NLD branch offices and asked them to send groups to compete at the NLD headquarters in Yangon. Everyone was enthusiastic. We at the information and registration committee again got busy as we all thought there should also be a group competing from the headquarters, too. We applied for a permit at the local township administrator's office to build a stage in the compound of the NLD headquarters, and we were asked to get seven guarantors. All of us were happy to sign, and we began writing verses and rehearsing.

We were all set by the time Ma Suu came back from Nyaung Don, but on her arrival a car from Ma Suu's convoy was stopped just before it entered her gate because one man in it had unfurled the NLD flag.[4] Ma Suu's car was already in her compound when those in the offending car were arrested and taken away in a truck. Immediately she walked out to the street and sat on a concrete block on the pavement and refused to budge until her followers were released. Only when they were sent back did she go back into the house.

---

3. *Thangyat* is satirical and mostly political verses chanted by groups during the Water Festival that precedes the Myanmar New Year. *Thangyat* chanting by groups of people is one of our own unique old cultural traditions for the lunar New Year celebration.

4. One of the many new laws imposed during those days was that no other flag apart from the state flag could be flown.

At last, we were able to celebrate the Water Festival and hold the *thangyat* competition, which would be the most significant activity the IRC had organized so far. We asked several writers and performing artistes to be the judges. We decided to give an audience choice award as well to the group that received the loudest and longest applause. At the competition, the audience packed the street and grew bigger by the hour. People also awarded cash to *thangyat* groups they liked, as is the tradition. I was stressed out with doing so many things at once, such as announcing the awards, tallying the scores, and managing the health care of the competitors. We knew an opportunity like this would not readily come again. All the competitors were funny and hard-hitting, and soon the whole length of University Avenue was packed with people.

We were not allowed to build the stage on the road, so it was rather small. Those who were further down the street could not see much, but nonetheless people sat on the ground and listened to the performances. At the time, the mayor of Yangon was on a campaign to clean up the city and had put up signposts all over town with a slogan that said, "This is your city!" One group twisted this slogan around as they chanted while using their fingers like they were shooting guns: "This is your city, and *this* is what is happening in your city!"

Funds were tight so contestants lacked nice costumes, but their dancing, chanting, and satire were outstanding; it was both a celebration and an act of defiance. The next day, our competition was criticized in the state-owned newspaper the *Mirror*—which in fact showed that we had hit the mark. Later, about thirty people from different groups of *thangyat* competitors were arrested, but the seven of us who were guarantors were spared. Ma Suu left for Kachin State on April 24 to make up for the canceled trip. Having to work on *thangyat* tapes as well as do the accounting for the show and trips, I could not go along.

~

Right after the Water Festival, we learned that students in China had initiated their democracy movement, and on April 21 the Tiananmen Square uprising took shape. Then the iron curtain crashed in Europe—

41

the 150-mile wall between Hungary and Austria came down. General Secretary Zhao Ziyang went to see the Chinese protestors on May 19 but the next day the Chinese authorities declared martial law. On May 30, Chinese students erected the Goddess of Democracy statue at Tiananmen Square and on the same day in Myanmar, the election law was announced by the government. On June 4, Tiananmen Square was stained with blood as many students were killed or arrested. On the same day, Poland's opposition party won the elections in Europe. The politics of the world was like oil boiling in a wok.

～

The only personal routine I was able to keep during that period was praying to the Buddha while completely ignoring both schoolwork and writing. In June, my short story titled "May Young Leaves Unscarred by Thorns Flourish," written during the Shan State trip in February, was printed in *Yokeshin Amyutay* magazine[5] where Myo Myint Nyein was editor. In this story, Ma Suu was the disguised main character and June was the month she was born, so I gave a copy of the magazine to Ma Suu as a birthday present. Painter Myo Myint did the illustrations for the story and he drew her wearing glasses to further mislead the censors. In the same month, the Information Ministry issued guidelines for publishers while trying to suppress our publications, although we had made them "for NLD members only." That month, primary schools reopened.

On June 21, Ma Suu attended the first anniversary of the Myaynegone massacre and laid a wreath in honor of the fallen. It was alleged that the gathering turned into a riot and the army shot to disperse the crowd. As a result, one member of the National Unity Party, which was a new name for the BSPP, was killed. An announcement was issued promising the students who had fled across the border that they would not be punished if they returned; a list of those who had already returned was broadcast as well.

---

5. The title means "Essence of Movies" but the magazine had a strong bent for literature.

Chapter 5

The Beginning of the End

As tension rose, U Win Tin was arrested on trumped-up charges. Soe Thein, one of the NLD youth leaders, and his pregnant girlfriend had been arrested while trying to get an abortion. Soe Thein's father was worried when his son did not come home for some days, so he called the NLD headquarters to ask if he was there. The phone was on U Win Tin's desk so he answered it and said no, Soe Thein was not there. For this, U Win Tin was charged with harboring "the accused." U Win Tin's trial was open to the public, so many of us went to give him food during breaks, check his health, and attend the court sessions. Obviously it was a false charge meant to undermine his role in politics. He was sentenced to three years[1] and we were all furious although we could not even fathom then that later on sixteen more years would be added to it. Without his advice and guidance, our work in the information and registration committee was considerably weakened. Yet we could not concentrate only on this disaster, as the NLD plan for Martyrs' Day[2] was already underway. In early July, there had been explosions in Thanlyin (a port city across the river from Yangon) and at Yangon City Hall, so everyone was on edge.

One hundred forty-four legally registered political parties gathered to discuss how they were going to observe Martyrs' Day on July 19.

---

1. In Insein Prison he was kept in a cell in a walled compound that prisoners called the VIP (very important prisoners) section. In the same section were offices of the Military Intelligence.
2. Martyrs' Day commemorates the day in 1947 when Bogyoke Aung San and seven other leaders were assassinated.

I was busy assisting with drawing up a plan to form a sister party in case the NLD was abolished by the regime; we also needed to select a candidate through an election within the NLD, for which necessary rules and procedures had already been set up by U Win Tin. Other in-party elections were to take place to reform the NLD youth and the office staff of the NLD headquarters.

On July 16, the military regime announced that on Martyrs' Day anyone attending a gathering of more than five people, regardless of the circumstances, would be arrested. As news of the announcement spread, different opinions emerged on the meeting of the 144 parties. Some of them wanted to stay home while others wanted to go ahead and march. On July 17, the authorities imposed martial law, but Ma Suu expressed her wish to lay her wreath at the Martyrs' Mausoleum together with the public, after the official ceremony, to which she had been invited but had sent a refusal. Usually we slept at the office after working late and attended whatever morning event there was the following day, but on the night of July 18 we all decided to go home instead since we did not have time to obtain the necessary equipment for recording the event. We planned to meet up at the Evergreen Café the next morning, since that evening there were hundreds of soldiers, police, and riot police stationed around Shwedagon Pagoda with many even patrolling residential areas. However, as I went to bed my understanding was that the next day Ma Suu would lead the public in a march to the Martyrs' Mausoleum.

Ma Thanegi rang me from Ma Suu's home office before seven the next morning and said the march had been canceled and for me to stay away, as there were a lot of soldiers around Ma Suu's house and the NLD headquarters. She asked me not only to alert the other members of the information committee but also to watch the developments of the day. I was frightened and tried to phone whomever I could. Ma Hmwe thought she should go check out the situation, so she left. Meanwhile, members of our committee met in Myaynegone and then tried to go to our office, but streets leading to that area were already blocked, so they had to turn back, as did Ma Hmwe. People from some townships who thought the planned march was still on came out marching with flags flying and were beaten up, shot at, and arrested. Later, I was able to go near the NLD headquarters but could not enter the compound. That night the state television station broadcast the news that Ma Suu had been put under house arrest, and all those found in the NLD headquarters and in Ma Suu's compound had been sent to Insein Prison.

We had worked in the committee shed for nearly ten months, with many late nights, and often had to stay overnight. Our reports, documents, books, photos, video footage, and journals were irreplaceable; it was very upsetting to think of all our documents—including my personal belongings—in the office being taken away by Military Intelligence. I was now parted from my colleagues, including Ma Suu. Although I was fortunate enough to escape arrest this time, I was worried that my colleagues might be tortured and that I might be implicated. It was unbearable; I could do nothing except turn to my usual routine of counting my beads and chanting sutras for protection from evil. Those of us who weren't detained recorded the names of our colleagues who had been arrested and sent food and other necessities to them through their families.

The NLD headquarters and our office within Ma Suu's compound were both shut down,[3] so as usual, we discussed the future by meeting in teashops. Some magazines resumed publication. In August, middle schools were reopened and we heard that all the schools and universities would be reopened soon. I reminded myself that I should go back to medical school. I had been a final-year student with only nine months left until graduation when all colleges were closed, and news that the University of Medicine might reopen was spreading among my classmates. Final-year students are not taught in classrooms but given hands-on training at hospitals, so I had no idea where to start and how we would be chosen for the hospital assignments. Nor did I know what I should be studying in preparation. My desire to be a doctor was by this time quite strong. I wanted to learn a lot more than what I had picked up helping at the NLD and also wanted to learn

---

3. Later the NLD headquarters was moved to new premises on Shwegondine Rd.

more about publication and journalism. By then Myo Myint Nyein had resumed his part-time job at *Yokeshin Amyutae* magazine, and I decided to train with him. Meanwhile, painters Ma Hmwe and Myo Myint reopened their studio.

At the magazine office and the printing press, I learned how to do layout for the magazine and it was not easy like today since everything had to be done manually. The workplace atmosphere was nothing like our old committee office. Not being a very feminine person, I often said things in a very straightforward manner and I had always spoken my mind when discussing anything with my colleagues at the NLD office. I did not like to be regarded as a girl either. I had a short haircut and most of the time wore the small-patterned men's *pasoe*[4] and a men's Shan jacket so that even Ma Suu sometimes confused me with young men from the Tri-Color group, who also teased and laughed at me if they saw me wearing a woman's *htamein*.[5] However people who did not know me did not appreciate my manner of speaking frankly. Once I told an older journalist who said he would like to take an afternoon nap, "Don't come to the office if you want to sleep. You have to work sixty seconds in a minute, period."

I even talked this way to the elderly writer U Moe Thu: "Bagyi[6] Moe, I am coming to argue with you, I'm not happy with you." I have to admit I behaved badly. Once, for example, I had banged the tabletop with my fist while talking to U Win Tin about youth affairs. I usually wore my shoulder bag slung not on my shoulder but across my chest like a boy, and if I was feeling upset with anyone I had my fists up as if to sock him. I always wore a sullen look or a frown, and I was never quick to smile; I did not care much about others and was not interested in listening to them, either.

When I was twenty-two, I was still neither masculine nor feminine in my manner, but I was about to become a doctor and was trying hard to become a serious writer. But I thought I was right all the time and

---

4. Men's waist garment, sewn in a tube.
5. Women's waist garment, sewn in a tube.
6. Elder Uncle.

was not a pleasant person; those who knew me well, young and old, took no offense and were very understanding of me, as they knew I had already done a lot at my age. Because of this type of behavior, Myo Myint Nyein asked me to promise him one thing when I asked to be an intern at *Yokeshin Amyutae* magazine: "Some people who come here may be eccentric, but you have to be able to relate to them since they are all writers or trying to be writers. You must address everyone respectfully as *Saya* or *Sayama*."[7] I promised him readily, since at the time I really wanted to learn the workings of a publication.

The magazine was being managed from a small front room of a private residence and there was not much space to work, but it was convenient as the printing press was on the same street. The monsoon of 1989 went by quickly while I memorized the symbols of proofreading and such things as how to do layout. There was no computer so we had to mark by hand the size of every font along with typesetting instructions for the printer. Proofreading was done first and printed out if approved, and then we pasted the illustrations and cartoons on to the master plate, which was essentially a piece of thick cardboard. I also had to draw some fonts and headings with a stencil. Although formatting and layout were the jobs of a designer, I was assisting with all the tasks, from proofreading, printing film, and sending the master copy to press to the final stage of binding. In other words, I was an unofficial editor. In the office, I remained quiet because of my promise, but when we were at the teashops or outside of the office I was my usual self and went on behaving as I wished. I was unable to see that many people were reluctant to talk to me because I had been arrogant to them before. More than sixty of my short stories had been published in various magazines during the four years of my writing career, and I was also getting hands-on experience in publishing, so I was happily caught up in my own life. My only frustration was not being politically active.

While the USSR was disintegrating in front of the rest of the world, I was a med-school student who was at the same time proudly

---

7. Meaning "teacher" but also functioning as a polite form of address. *Saya* is the male version and *Sayama* is for females.

juggling different career choices; my social circle was also expanding. In September 1989, vocational schools were reopened. In November, the SLORC began their plan of building roads and bridges in an operation named "All-Myanmar Nation Building and Restoration" and at the same time declared ethnic organizations like the Karen National Union, Kachin Independence Organization, and the New Mon State Party illegal. Meanwhile, classes for part II of the final year of medical school ("Final Part II" in university parlance) resumed and we were assigned to various hospitals. I continued to work at the magazine while doing my medical training.

∼

About the same time, Europe was undergoing several changes: the Berlin wall between East and West Germany came down. The Communist Party of Czechoslovakia lost its power after a massive students' uprising in Prague, and Vaclav Havel was elected president. Gorbachev and George H. W. Bush began taking steps toward ending the Cold War. Many changes took place in other countries as well: For the first time, free and fair elections were held in Brazil and Chile. President Fredrik Willem de Klerk abolished apartheid in South Africa. The Armed Forces of the Philippines staged a coup d'état against President Corazon Aquino's government. Leaving communism behind, Mongolia transformed itself into a democratic society. In Myanmar, however, NLD chairman U Tin Oo was sentenced to three years in prison. Ma Suu, still under house arrest, announced she would compete in the forthcoming election.[8]

∼

Although universities had reopened there were not many students around, and I noticed that some students from my year were missing;

---

8. Held on May 27, 1990.

some of them had fled to the jungle to take up arms against the regime and some had emigrated to other countries. Relationships between friends who had been as close as siblings became strained due to opposing political views. I did not want my med-school friends to get into trouble, so I kept all my political activities and views to myself when I was with them. I concentrated only on the work I was assigned, but whenever I was at the magazine I would look frantically for news of friends in prison.

Ma Suu's wish to stand as a candidate in the elections was opposed by one member of the state-backed National Unity Party and was refused permission. Having no backing—and not even recognition from Western countries—the SLORC solved some of its financial problems by selling part of the land owned by the Myanmar embassy in Tokyo. The Karen National Union's Thae Baw Boe Camp was attacked and taken over by the military. The military stepped up it dominance of the economy by setting up Myanmar Economic Holdings, Ltd. in February 1990.

∼

During the same period, thousands of people lined up to view the intelligence records of the Stasi of East Germany, made public for the first time. On February 11, 1989, South Africa's popular leader Nelson Mandela, who had been imprisoned for twenty-seven years, was freed. Gorbachev became the president of the USSR, and separatist Lithuania announced their independence from the union.

∼

In early March, competing political parties were allowed to campaign on television for fifteen minutes each. The public wholeheartedly supported U Kyi Maung when he represented the NLD. However, some people were not happy at how NLD candidates were chosen in some townships, as these local NLD offices had not followed the rules established by U Win Tin and published in the NLD's election byaws. Others were so keen to vote for the NLD that they did not care who the candidate was. Also, as expected, the military government was unfairly backing the National Unity Party by allowing it to lure members in exchange for them being able to get a national registration card immediately;[9] the government was also unjustly restricting the NLD and its members.

The NLD had chosen the farmer's hat as its symbol. As a result, these hats were worn throughout the country, whereas before they would not have worn in towns or cities. Most members of the NLD, male or female, wore the white-on-black patterned cotton waist garments produced in Yaw, a central Myanmar region, and the reddish homespun cotton called *pinni* for jackets. Both became the height of fashion as everyone wore them to show their support of the NLD. I happily voted for U Khin Maung Swe, the NLD's candidate for my township, Sanchaung. We had been on many trips together, and I shared his views and aspirations.

We never believed that the elections would be free and fair. In the weeks leading up to them, oppression and intimidation pf the NLD grew worse. It was obvious that the majority of the people regarded this election as a chance to finally escape military rule. General Saw Maung, chairman of SLORC, had repeatedly given his promise that they would go back to the barracks after the elections; we thought it would be one year at most to wait before we would have a civilian government. Voters queued up at the ballot stations long before they were opened, and the public stood around the voting stations late into the evening while the votes were being counted. Very soon, it was apparent that the NLD had won most of the townships in Yangon and surrounding areas. We also heard from the BBC and VOA that the NLD had won most of its constituencies in the provinces. Finally, an official vote count was announced on July 1: a total of 2,380 candidates from ninety-three political parties had contested 485 seats, and the NLD had won 392 of them. The public had shown their enormous support by voting for the NLD despite

---

9. To this day, this usually takes a long time.

being hindered, harassed, and intimidated by the authorities. Most of us cried in joy.[10]

U Win Nyein, Myo Myint Nyein's journalist older brother, started his own magazine, *Shwe Amyutae*,[11] which covered both pop culture and literature, so we were both working for it as well as for the revived literary magazine *Message*,[12] for which I was soon interviewing famous writers under the pen name Lay Net (meaning "serious"). I was still in medical training at the same time, but I did my best to meet the deadline for every issue of each magazine. Min Lu assisted us for the Aspiring Young Writers section, "Kalaung Nge,"[13] and for this my classmate and designer Soe Kyaw and I came up with a logo of a pen that looked like a fighting peacock.

Soon, the SLORC started to hint at their real intention by saying the military's duty was not completed just with the holding of elections. Sensing what was going to happen, the NLD's elected members of parliament wrote an open letter to the SLORC on July 9 calling for the convening of the parliament. The SLORC responded that parliament would be convened only after a new constitution was drawn. All political parties and the public were beginning to be aware that the opportunity for a democratic government would be lost. Everyone felt confused and alarmed at the uncertainty after holding such high expectations.

On July 28 and 29, the elected MPs from the NLD convened in a meeting at Gandhi Hall on Bo Aung Kyaw Road. The public waited

---

10. It became apparent later that the military had been certain the National Unity Party would win. In many townships they had made preparations to celebrate by ordering food and drink, which ended up all being thrown away; in some cases, they refused to pay the caterers.

11. For nine years running, *Shwe Amyutae* (meaning "Essence of Gold"), has been giving literary awards for short stories, poetry, and articles published in any magazine in the country, the first award of its kind. The State Literary Awards are 300,000 kyat (about US$300) each for books only. However, no private award was allowed to be higher than the government's, so for the *Shwe* Literary Awards, readers' personal gifts at the ceremony were often several times more than the basic 300,000 kyat. The panel of judges (of which I am one) has to read about five thousand short stories a year.

12. *Pay Hpu Lywar.*

13. Kalaung Nge means young or new writer.

to see whether the elected MPs were going to form a parallel government and whether it would gain international recognition. Most of us were certain that the NLD would get international support since even the Chinese ambassador had gone to the NLD headquarters to congratulate them after their election victory. Nonetheless, it did not happen as we expected: the MPs only called for the convening of the parliament by a certain date.[14]

~

While our country was in political turmoil the Gulf War against Iraq began in retaliation for their invasion of Kuwait.

~

While this political situation was causing tension in Yangon, monks in Mandalay started their boycott in line with the Buddha's dharma by refusing to attend ceremonies or give religious services to the families of the military who had oppressed the will of the public. This movement was led by respected monks and was a remarkable and unprecedented move. Famous and revered abbots and monks were sentenced to twenty years' imprisonment each. The absurdity and lawlessness of the raids on monasteries and arrests of monks were revealed in the SLORC statement describing the crime of one monk: "He was at the monastery to attend the dharma class." Worse still, the arrested monks were sent to prisons in remote parts of the country and were forcibly disrobed. While I was preparing for my Final Part II exams, I felt battered by this bad news.

I was eager to publish pamphlets of protest that our writer-artist group had planned. Writer and poet Min Lu showed us his poem titled "What is going on?" which was written in his usual satirical style, and

---

14. Apparently to discourage any plans for a parallel government, the day before the Ghandi Hall meeting a notification was issued by the government that only SLORC had the right to exercise executive, legislative, and judiciary power and would not accept the formation of any interim government.

both Myo Myint Nyein and I wanted to publish it. We entrusted the job to Sein Hlaing from the Tri-Color group, and later this poem got so popular that people made photocopies to pass around.

On September 9, 10, and 12, Sein Hlaing, Myo Myint Nyein, and Min Lu were arrested for their parts in the writing and publication of the hard-hitting poem. Myo Myint Nyein knew I had helped from the beginning in publishing the poem, and the others also knew I had played a role. If one of the three confessed to my involvement during interrogation, it was very possible that I would not be sitting the exam for my final year. Not only could I not take a break from my studies, I also had to take over most of Myo Myint Nyein's work at *Shwe Amyutae,* so I was at the magazine from early morning until late. The magazine would fold if I did not help, because the chief editor U Win Nyein was still working as a civil servant and so did not have time to do the final layouts and various other necessary tasks. I also had to take up Min Lu's Aspiring Young Writers section. Unfortunately, my exam was scheduled for the same day as the deadline for an issue of the magazine. Despite the fact that I was worried about the exam and my colleagues as well as for my own safety, I was in a frenzy working to publish two magazines while preparing for my finals.

Everyone in medical school feared the Final Part II exam most because it was the last, the most important, and above all the most difficult. Written exams were held on September 24. During the written exams, which were from 9:00 a.m. to noon, every time someone walked past the room I got goose bumps. After each test I ran to 33rd Street to go through submitted articles, choose ones to publish, do the dummy, proofread, arrange for illustrations, and so on. Photographer Sein Myo Myint came from another magazine to help out and we would travel home together since he too lived in Sanchaung. When I got home I would study for the next day's test. I was working and living like a robot. On the other hand, to ease my worries, I stuck to my daily routine of praying to the Buddha, counting prayer beads, and chanting sutras. In this way I tried everything I could to endure the situation while doing my best to fulfill my commitments at work. I was well prepared beforehand, so I was not too concerned about the exams.

I would also be able to take them again in six months if I should fail—assuming I would not be in prison. After the exams were over, I had still not been arrested, so I realized none of my three colleagues in jail had given me up. Yet I could not be certain till they were released or were put on trial and sentenced. When the results of the oral exams were announced, I found I had passed with high marks in surgery, obstetrics, and gynecology.

When U Win Nyein suffered a stroke I had to fill in for him while commuting between the office and hospital where I would visit him. At the magazine, writers Mya Hnaung Nyo and Lin Naing Oo and artist Myint Maung Kyaw were helping out. It was getting more difficult for me as my rotating internship at various hospitals did not allow me much time for the magazine. When Myo Myint Nyein and the other two were sentenced to seven years in prison, all I could do was volunteer to fill in for them at the literary magazine while doing what I could for their families.

Most of the responsibilities I took on there did not give me much trouble; I could easily do interviews and write analytical articles, as my work focused on interviews of popular short story writers and essayists. However, the Aspiring Young Writers pages required a lot of effort. There were many submissions because the section had produced a number of famous writers and editors. I had a sentimental attachment to it and read all the stories to choose the best, sometimes allotting more pages as necessary. It was this section that most often drew questions from the Press Scrutiny Board; we thus needed more time to negotiate with them so that the stories could be published. Then, for various reasons we had to ask the publisher to work with another editorial team and so I only had to deal with the pop magazine, which could be maintained at its own pace easily enough. This enabled me to devote more time to my internship and to resume my career as a freelance writer.

~

The world was transforming: the two Germanys reunited in early October of that year, and Gorbachev was awarded the Nobel Peace

Prize. But in the Middle East, Israel and Palestine continued to fight. In December 1990, eight elected MPs who had fled to the border formed the National Coalition Government of the Union of Burma with Dr. Sein Win, Ma Suu's cousin, as prime minister. Many MPs who had helped them were arrested and sentenced to twenty-five years' imprisonment. In the early part of 1991, Operation Desert Storm was launched by the United States, and within one month Iraq's leader, Saddam Hussein, withdrew all his troops from Kuwait. Many magazines featured the news, and the people began to expect a similar event to unfold in Myanmar.

~

Then, something strange happened; on March 8 I was working as an intern at the emergency room of the Rangoon General Hospital and it was already a hectic day when a group of men in prison guard uniforms barged in and asked us to sign a death certificate, saying the body was outside. The doctor on duty in the ER asked them to bring the body in, but they adamantly refused to do so. The doctor then told me to bring a torch and follow her. To examine the body we had to climb onto a military truck, which was parked outside the ER. I had already worked out that the body must be that of a political prisoner, but it turned out to be someone I did not know well enough to recognize. We were only allowed to check his pupils and pulse and were not allowed to check anything else. The prison guards asked us to issue the death certificate as quickly as possible. I learned later that it was U Nyo Win; he was an executive member of the People's Revolutionary Party and husband of writer Ma Sann Pwint.

Another incident was far more personal. It was early June of 1991 and I was on night duty. My friend who was on day shift quietly told me before she left that the famous writer Maung Thaw Ka had been admitted that day after a heart attack. His condition was serious, and he was in the intensive care unit of the cardiac ward. In spite of the heart attack, my friend said, the patient knew what was going on and could answer all the doctors' questions. I was frantic with worry. That night I did not have a chance to see him as the ER was full of patients who had food poisoning, but my mind was racing toward the ICU. A doctor friend told me Maung Thaw Ka was cracking jokes. She was checking his eyesight and had asked him if he could see clearly. He had answered, "If there were an old man and a girl, he could only see 'that girl.'" It was a political joke, for it was strongly rumored that the top military men were dismissively referring to Ma Suu as "that girl" and at that time though under new military government, people still believed U Ne Win, then an old man, was still in power. Maung Thaw Ka's sense of humor was famous; I tried to tell myself that he would be fine if he still could crack a joke like that.

There are many stories about Maung Thaw Ka. I had followed him around when he was giving rousing speeches during the 1988 uprising, and I was also there when he would talk with other writers or editors about political activities. After he found out that it was I who translated Kipling's poem "If—" he could not stop praising me while giving me a thumbs up and saying, "Very daring indeed! Even me, I am still not courageous enough to translate that poem, but you did it. You have a lot of guts. You're a courageous one!"

During the NLD's campaign trips he had led and organized trips to Shwebo and Sagaing. On the way he had been very concerned when I was hanging precariously to the back of the truck. He nagged his nephew Myo Myint Nyein that it was not appropriate to let me perch so dangerously like that, even if they did not see me as a girly type. His satirical writings and a personal account titled "Gunboat 103"[15] were my favorites, and I had been hoping that I would one day read of his prison experiences.

After finishing my night shift I went home, took a shower, and went back to the hospital. I asked my friend who was on duty to help me see Maung Thaw Ka. On our way to the cardiac ward I was already miserable because this was the center of the protest camp in 1988, and Ma Suu had made her very first public appearance just outside of it,

---

15. About when he was serving in the navy and he and his crew were adrift at sea on a lifeboat for many weeks.

introduced by none other than Maung Thaw Ka. Now he was back at this very place as a patient. We found his room, and I noticed there were many MIs in civilian clothes standing around with some police and prison guards. We realized that it would be impossible to get permission to enter his room, but just then, a nurse brought a hot-water bottle and we quickly followed her in.

He was lying very still on his bed, surrounded by machines and with wires connected to his body. His clothes were spread out on top of his body and the blanket was dirty and ragged. The plastic utensils and bags that must have been his possessions in prison looked shabby. The only thing that sparkled was the pair of handcuffs lying on a dingy table. I had to force myself not to get too emotional and not to give in to despair while my hand was checking his pulse, but in reality all I could hear was my own thumping heart, not his. I restrained myself from calling him *Saya* as I usually did.

"How are you *Ahba*[16]? Are you feeling okay?" I could not believe I had said it—I had never called him *Ahba* as others did. I used to call him *Saya*; only army guys would call their senior *Abha*.

He opened his eyes when he heard my voice. I stared into his eyes and I noticed that the expression in them changed, and he gave me a thumbs up within my fingers, which were clasped around his hand. I too raised my thumb and pressed it onto his forearm so that he could sense it by the touch; all I remember of that moment is the silence around us.

By then, the MIs, police, and prison guards were in the room. I did not know when or how they had come in so quickly. The nurse was smart and broke the silence by saying, "It's all done as required, doctors," as if we were there just to check the care being given. One of them asked us why we were there and from which department we were. We said it was a follow-up for all patients that came through the ER, and left our names with him. That evening, I went to his wife Daw Hla Yin to tell her all I knew. I tried to see him again but it was impossible.

---

16. Elder Uncle.

Some nurses from the cardiac ward assured me that they were taking good care of him and told me not to worry. Everyone loved him, and the head of the ward also was keeping a close watch on his condition, so I thought he would be better in a few days.

However, on June 11, I heard that he had passed away after suffering a third heart attack around three in the morning. I ran to the cardiac ward but his body had already been removed to the mortuary. Some doctors and nurses told me as much as they remembered of his medical records. Although we were still under curfew, the ward's head doctor had requested permission to drive to the hospital from her home and had tried her best to revive him. Early in that evening, Maung Thaw Ka had remarked in a matter-of-fact way that "I started my (political) journey here and here it will end." The doctor was inconsolable. For me, it was heartbreaking beyond tears to recall his last look at me, with his upright thumb in my hand, and what it had meant. Nothing was more painful than knowing that we were now being deprived of his writing.

On the world stage, the year 1991 was dominated by the USSR's disintegration. In the domestic political landscape, the regime announced that insurgents were mobilizing around Bogalay in the delta and launched a military operation in which many Karen people, including women, were arbitrarily arrested or killed. However, news about their plight did not reach the world or even very far within Myanmar as there were no video or photographic records. On October 10 in that same year, Ma Suu won the Nobel Peace Prize. People were overjoyed and student demonstrations took place demanding that all political prisoners, including Ma Suu, be released. On December 15 the NLD, responding to pressure from the regime and fearing they might be declared an illegal organization, expelled chairperson U Tin Oo, general secretary Daw Aung San Suu Kyi, and U Win Tin and re-formed the Central Executive Committee without them. U Aung Shwe became the chairperson.

Chapter 6

"Normal" Life

Then, during our internships, we medical students got the announcement of our graduation ceremony. My childhood dream of graduating at the Convocation Hall was no longer of any importance to me, and instead of feeling excited I simply thought of how heartbreaking it was; without knowing where some of my classmates were or even if they were alive, I had no desire to attend the ceremony. Other classmates felt the same way, and no one even wanted to follow our universities' tradition of a dinner on the evening of graduation day or to produce a yearbook. I explained this to my parents and decided to get my degree through the post. My mother wanted to see me in cap and gown, as she was no longer sure my two young brothers would graduate, but my father understood my choice. Finally, some of my classmates and I agreed to simply hand in applications for our certificates to be sent by post. It was cheaper, too, without having to spend any money on new clothes. I took a passport photo wearing the politically-motivated *pinni* jacket to send with the application and a fee of fifteen kyat, after which I received my graduation certificate through the mail.

I was about to finish my internship and we were busy with new assignments, so I could not participate in the outpouring of joy in the streets over the news that Daw Aung San Suu Kyi had been awarded the Nobel Peace Prize and demands for her release. However, the MIs came for me, blindfolded me, and took me to an interrogation center for no apparent reason. I did not quite understand their questions, and it was not clear what they wanted to know. They asked me whether I knew this person and that person, and the problem was I did not really know any of those people. I could not even recall some acquaintances if we had not seen each other for some time. One of their questions was why I had not attended the graduation ceremony. I knew they would not believe me, but I said it was because of financial difficulties. They did not question me further. The next day, they told me they were going to send me home. I was blindfolded again and driven away. When they stopped and removed my blindfold, we were on the street at the back of the Convocation Hall. I felt a tug at the depths of my heart; such strange connections there were between this ancient building and me.

After finishing my internship I had to think about my medical career, since only the pop magazine was being published, and U Win Nyein was still recovering. Nonetheless, I did not wish to work as a doctor at the state hospitals; I did not desire to make money from being a doctor. I could not be sure I would be given the job even if I applied for it. I was also mistakenly accused of being involved in the attempt by some students to take down the photos of U Ne Win in various university buildings. My parents, knowing I would be using my own money to treat patients if I opened my own clinic, just wanted me to go for further studies. I had a bit more free time and as usual started to meet up with other political activists and do whatever I could. I had time to read more while preparing to sit an exam to study in the United Kingdom.

$\sim$

On Christmas Day of 1991, Gorbachev resigned as president of the USSR. In early 1992, another socialist country, Yugoslavia, disintegrated, and Slovenia and Croatia announced their independence. Boris Yeltsin became the president of Russia. The European Union was established in early February. The forces of the Yugoslav People's Army besieged Sarajevo, the capital city of Bosnia and Herzegovina of that time, in early March. On the full moon day of March, I heard that some of the people who were arrested in Ma Suu's compound in July 1989 had been sentenced to ten and eight years.[1]

---

1. For the past three years they had been detained in Insein Prison under Act 10 (A).

~

At the time, I had nothing much to do and thought I would write a novel. I also read Ma Suu's book *Freedom from Fear.* I wanted to write something about her not being able to attend the Nobel Peace Prize ceremony to receive the award in person. At the end of March, writer San San Nwe (Thayawaddy) told me that the journalist Hla Aung of the current affairs publication *Ahtauktaw* was seriously ill and that he might not last for long. Since there was no doctor attending him, I looked after him every day. I had once requested a favor of him, right after we had come back from the Ayeyarwaddy campaign, but we never met again after that; now I was seeing him every day. He was suffering from liver cancer and a specialist would occasionally come to check on him. As his condition grew worse, I was instructed to give him hydrocortisone every six hours—an injection given for cancer, particularly of the kidneys and liver. However, he passed away on April 7.

Citing ill health, SLORC chairman General Saw Maung retired on April 23, and Senior General Than Shwe replaced him. I thought from the very beginning that he looked like Yeltsin of Russia. On April 24, 1992, state media featured news of an amnesty for political prisoners who were of no threat to national security. Those who had been arrested in the NLD compound during the Nobel Peace Prize activities were released, as were the MPs who had been imprisoned for their involvement in forming a parallel government. I was as busy as ever when artists Ma Thanegi and K. Myoe as well as U Moe Thu, among others, were released. I waited in front of Insein Prison every day as groups of prisoners were being let out. Eventually, the number of released prisoners dwindled, and I realized the remaining detained NLD members would not be freed this time.

During this time, the former dictator U Ne Win announced that his photo must be removed from all government offices. I wanted to laugh, recalling that a group of us had once been summoned to see the rector, registrar, and other professors for allegations that we had demanded the removal of U Ne Win's photos from all public offices. I began to notice that our politics was being played out like a game of chess. In that period, writer San San Nwe introduced me to Dr. Khin Zaw Win, who introduced me to Vicky Bowman, who was then second secretary at the British embassy.[2] The day was May 27, the second anniversary of the 1990 elections. I was asked to assist Anna J. Allott,[3] who was compiling a paper on Burmese literature and for whom I wrote a 150-page analysis of contemporary short stories in Myanmar. The friendship between Vicky Bowman and me—who happened to have been born in the same year, 1966—grew as we had to translate Burmese text of the paper into English. With this translation task, the year of 1992 was my busiest time yet.

~

In June, Yitzhak Rabin became the prime minister of Israel, and Vaclav Havel retired as president of Czechoslovakia.

~

It was the end of June when the SLORC announced that they would be holding meetings in preparation to call a national convention. By this time, Dr. Tin Myo Win, to whom I had been introduced by U Moe Thu, was working at the Muslim Free Hospital,[4] which provided free medical treatment to the poor regardless of race or religion. Since I was doing many things for others without worry about status or position, U Moe Thu suggested that I should volunteer there as well. I hesitated, as I was not a close friend of Dr. Tin Myo Win, even when we were working at the NLD, but the idea of being a volunteer doctor was appealing. It was also interesting to see the way the hospital was run in order to help the neediest people. I became a regular volunteer there. At that point, my younger brother, who had just come back from Taiwan in 1991, left for Singapore. Then, the youngest brother, who

2. In her second posting she was the ambassador.
3. Teacher of Burmese at SOAS.
4. On Maha Bandoola Garden Street.

none of us knew was addicted to drugs, was arrested and jailed for three years. Through him, I gained contact with Myo Myint Nyein, who was still in prison.

From both of them I received news of prison life, which I shared with Vicky and some foreign reporters that she introduced; I was also able to send in special news to my friends. Because of my brother, I learned a lot more not only about the political prisoners but also about other criminals in jail. I tried to find time to write when I did not have to volunteer at the hospital, where I went only to do surgery. In the meantime, I taught science to eigth-grade children at a private school set up in a monastery, which provided free education to children from poor families. Through this I learned a lot more about the lives of these children and became good friends with them. I volunteered one day a week at a clinic at the Chan Myae Yeik Thar meditation center while doing other social welfare work. I did not have a paid job, but rain or shine I accompanied friends who were seeking employment, to keep them company or lend encouragement. Our family was doing well with the money my younger brother was sending from Singapore.

While being an all-round volunteer I organized some discussion sessions with the delegates who were about to attend meetings in preparation for the national convention, as I was not happy with the way it was being done. From this discussion group I became friends with U Saw Oo Reh from Kayah (Karenni) State and Daw Nan Khin Htwe Myint from Karen State. But still the urge to write a novel was inexorable. To get correct data for my novel, I followed a group of movie people around as they worked. My main character was a painter as well as an actress. The core of my story was about the challenges on set rather than about life as a star. I did not want to write this story in a conventional style so I needed to do a lot of research. I wanted to understand the nature of making movies—the sets, the equipment, and so on, so I asked actor Kyaw Thu for help through his wife Shwe Zee Gwet, whom I had known for a long time. I followed them around at work and either Ma Hmwe or my mother would come with me. Ma Hmwe and I were nine years apart, but we had been friends since

1988. Besides, Ma Hmwe was a good source of information for my book since my main character was a painter like her.

I began to write this novel, *True Color of the Sunflower*,[5] in late 1992 and completed it in the beginning of 1993, but the manuscript got stuck at the Press Scrutiny Board. When it was finally returned, it was full of crossed-out paragraphs and blacked-out lines. I had to edit it and submit it again. By this time, the national convention was already underway. As we thought, only one-eighth of attending delegates were elected MPs, and the rest were all handpicked by the SLORC. It was a mere show as all proposals had to be submitted and approved before being allowed to be presented at the convention, with no one allowed to question or discuss the matter.

~

In America, Bill Clinton of the Democratic Party became president in early 1993. In March, a huge bomb exploded in Bombay. North Korea pulled out of the Treaty on the Non-proliferation of Nuclear Weapons and refused to allow UN nuclear weapons inspectors into their country.

~

Around that time, my manuscript was finally approved and I was busy commissioning a cover illustration while at the same time working at the hospital, teaching at the monastery, visiting my youngest brother in prison, and smuggling news in and out of prison and the country. I closely followed the national convention progress and news. Then, friends from within Insein Prison smuggled out to me a prisoner's uniform shirt of white rough cotton with messages written on it, as well as a letter detailing conditions in the prison. I was to send this to the United Nations' World Conference on Human Rights, which was to be held soon in Geneva. I promptly handed this over to Vicky.

---

5. In Burmese, it is *Ayaung Sis Nay Kyar; nay kyar* means "sunflower," *ayaung* means "color," and *sis* has many meanings, including "true," "war," and "screening."

The shirt in fact was sent out through Zunneta Herbert, an English scholar who had been in Mandalay during the 1988 uprising and who had come back to Myanmar along with Yozo Yokota to compile a report on human rights. This shirt was displayed at the conference, and all who had written on the shirt were very happy, as was I. Although I knew it was dangerous, I kept on doing things like that as it was the most effective way of getting out the news. I stayed in constant contact with the political prisoners inside jail, the staff of Western embassies, and foreign journalists.

It was already mid-1993 when the first stage of printing *True Color of the Sunflower* was finished, and soon it would be ready for publication. Meanwhile, I applied to sit for an entrance exam for a fellowship of the Royal College of Surgery of London. I studied really hard; I had so many plans for the future and my dream was to open free clinics. In my dreams, I would use boats as mobile clinics equipped for surgery. I would go up and down the Ayeyarwaddy River to provide free medical care. I would also set up a printing press to produce and publish research papers that would be beneficial to readers, although I knew it would make no money. All my colleagues on this project would live together in a beautiful compound full of trees. We would adopt children who had been abandoned or orphaned. I did not want this to be like a normal orphanage—I wanted these parentless children to be surrounded with people they could call mom, dad, sister, and brother. This family-style orphanage would provide warmth, a secure environment, and a guarantee for a brighter future. As time passed my dreams became more colorful and elaborate. But sometimes dreams aren't able to stay so bright.

Chapter 7

A Black World

At the end of June 1993, some intelligence officers came to my door while I was out studying at a friend's place. Once they saw me coming back they entered and searched the whole house—especially my messy room, with things piled up everywhere. Most of what they saw was books; they confiscated some but not some others only because they had no idea what they were about. I had many rap music videos given to me by my younger brother Kyaw and forgot about the videotape of *Cry Freedom* mixed in with them. Unfortunately they found a piece torn from a T-shirt on which I had written some information meant to be smuggled into prison. The situation did not look good, but of course I kept calm and looked as if I was entirely unconcerned.

Just before this happened, my mother and I were planning to go to Pyinmana to pay our respects to the abbot of Letloke Mountain, who only allowed disciples to visit him two days a year. We planned to take the overnight train to Pyinmana, pay obeisance to the abbot, and come back to Yangon again by night train. My mother made two requests when they said they were taking me away "for a little while." First, she said she had to feed me since I had not had dinner. Second, she said I must be sent back in time to catch the train to Pyinmana, and they insisted they would do so. In those days, I was thin as a skeleton because I was too busy to eat well regularly. I told my mother that it was fine; I would just have some ice cream we had at home, which I did, and I grabbed a small bag, always kept ready for unexpected trips, containing my prayer beads and books of Buddhist sutras.

They did not blindfold me, so I could see I was taken to the upper floor of the Income Tax Office next to the YMCA building on Maha

Bandoola Road. Although I knew some Tri-Color young men had been taken in recently, I thought the situation could get a bit complicated since they did not know about the materials the MI found in my rooms. It was nearly eleven at night when I was brought into the interrogation room, so I asked for some time to do my daily routine of praying to the Buddha as it would become another day soon. They thought it was funny and said they could not allow me to do this. I adamantly insisted that I be allowed to, as this had been my routine since I was nine years old and that if not, I would not answer any of their questions. Some of them got angry and some just laughed. Finally they agreed to give me half an hour to do my religious routine. It was the best preparation I could manage since I did not know what was to come next.

They wanted to know about the underground journal the *New Era*. They said I had given a copy of it to the Tri-Color guys in custody. Since they had not found any copies of it in my room, I denied it at first, but since they seemed to know a lot more I changed my story, saying it was true that I had given the journal to them, but I had already gotten it back from them and returned it to the original owner. In reality, I did not remember what I had done with it as I was so busy. I remembered asking the Tri-Color group to return it to me but was not sure if they had done so or not. The interrogators kept asking me where I had gotten it and I said I got it in the mail, not wanting to implicate someone else. At that they openly admitted it was impossible, as they were opening all mail. I changed my answer again, saying I borrowed it from Vicky because by this time she had completed her tour of duty and was back in England.

They also questioned me about other items they had found in my room, and I answered all of their questions patiently—with my answers wrapped in a great deal of lies. They were amazed at how calm I was and said, "You look like nothing is happening to you. You only had some ice cream for dinner; we have not given you anything to eat and we've been questioning you for hours. You don't seem to mind not eating or sleeping." In fact, it was the adrenaline high from my nervousness that kept me going. Besides, for a long time I had been living on one bowl of noodles a day due to my lack of time, so I was used to going on without much food. I had not been sleeping or eating well since beginning to work on my novel; plus I was occupied with other things like the discussions about the national convention. Around three in the morning, they took me back but said they would come for me for another round of interrogations if they had more questions.

My family was delighted to have me back and said we should cancel the trip to Pyinmana. However, I wanted to go, and anyway, they would surely be watching me closely, so it was important to take this trip since we had told them we were going. I took a shower and then we left for the train station; I was exhausted all along the trip. My mind flew to many places while I tried to rest, wrapped in my mother's arms. I had heard the experiences of released political prisoners and I must admit I also wished to have this kind of experience. I told myself that even if I was taken again I would be questioned and then released, and if I ever got arrested the longest prison term I'd face would be maybe seven years. I came back to the present when I heard my mother saying she could no longer bear to see me like this. She begged me to stop my political activities and asked me to just go and study in England. Listening to the sounds of the train and swaying with its movement, I snuggled up to her and tried to sleep, willing myself not to think. We arrived at Pyinmana the next morning, went to Letloke Mountain, paid our obeisance to the abbot, prayed, and returned to Yangon on the night train.

The next day, I met up with Ma Hmwe and confided in her some important matters because I was not sure what was going to happen. As I expected, within two or three days they came back, and I knew this would be the last time they came to question me: I was quite sure I would not be sent home for some time as no one who was interrogated for the second time in a week could be released.

I thought of a way in which I could come out with the least harm to my colleagues and myself, since I knew there was no escape this time. I was not able to remain very calm when I was facing arrest in reality; I did not even have to pretend that I was scared and could not answer the questions when they asked harshly. The only thing I needed to remember was that I must lie when necessary, in spite of being scared, and look as if I was about to confess everything. They sent in different types of interrogators, doing a "good cop, bad cop" routine, and I would not even shake or nod my head if they sent in the bad cop—I simply stared at him with blank eyes. I gave some answers to those who addressed me respectfully as *Sayama* and spoke nicely. I told them, "I will tell you everything I know but please don't ask me any more after that because it will just be a waste of our time since you will get no more information out of me." Because of this tactic, they ended up only sending in the "good cop."

They were apparently confused after reading the books and papers from my room because among them were many on different types of "-isms." They could no longer stay silent and began to ask about the different ideologies.

"Who are you? What are they? Which ideology do you believe in? You are reading a variety of them. What is going on?"

"Nothing is going on. I read different types of books because I'm a writer."

"There must be one "-ism" that you believe in."

"Yes, of course—it's Buddhism."

They fell silent.

They already knew I would refuse to answer any question if I was not given time to pray, so they had no choice but to accept my answer. Then I said that I sincerely believed that the whole world would be much more peaceful if only we all believed in Buddhism—not just if we were born Buddhists but if we truly believed and practiced his teachings. None of them could argue with that.

Then they asked me about the piece of the T-shirt with messages written on it.

"It was an idea to include in an exhibition," I told them. I knew they would not believe me but I insisted I got this idea from the old-style calendars of a printed cloth hung between two wooden bars, and that I was testing it out to see if I could do the same design with a short story or poem. That stopped their line of questioning, so then they tried to decipher the messages, which had been written in code, but got nowhere. I responded to all their questions with a mixture of half-truths and half-lies, using whatever popped into my head; it was apparent they did not believe me but were nonplussed and did not know how to continue.

It was nearly 2:00 a.m. when they said, "All right, you can sleep now, we will continue later." I started to wind them up by saying, "Hey, don't stop now; don't leave things for the next day. If you have questions ask me all of them now. My parents are expecting me to come home and I am sure your families are waiting for you too. Wouldn't we all be able to go home quicker if we could finish this soon? It's nothing to lose some sleep—it's only one night. Please ask me as quickly as possible because I want to go home when we're done." They kept telling me to go to sleep and I kept insisting that they should continue. Then one of them got really annoyed and snapped at me, "Don't you realize we're human, too? We need sleep, too, you know. What is it—are you trying to torture us?" The urge to laugh at this was unbearable. I now knew exactly how to handle them. Finally, I accepted their suggestion and tried to sleep. I was not at all drowsy, but at least I could rest. I then tried to recall and memorize everything I had told them because they would be repeating the questions and I must make sure to have the same answers.

The next day, as I thought, they repeated some questions to test me and I bought time by giving the same answer again and again. I struggled not to give up any names and they threatened me and said if I did not give up names I would be the number-one culprit and would have to take all the blame. What could I do? I had already decided not to give up anyone; the case had to end with me. Many who had been arrested before me had already given up their colleagues, but from me they only got one—Vicky. I told them that the names on the piece of T-shirt they found in my room were the names of deceased relatives and colleagues from work. I had no choice, because it was not the case of the *New Era* journal that I feared but the prison shirt that we had sent to the UN human rights conference. I bought as much time as I could, and afterward I did not need to pretend to be extremely drowsy from sheer exhaustion. I was the one who had tried to persuade them not to sleep the previous night, but tonight it was I who could not even keep my head upright so they finally allowed me to sleep.

They got tired of that T-shirt issue and began to ask me about other papers and books and asked me for more names. As usual I answered cautiously. The food they gave me caused indigestion as the rice was rough and hard and the curry was oily, so I got sick and threw up. A policewoman on guard gave me some indigenous medicine made mainly from Kaffir lime, and I could taste and smell alcohol in my mouth after taking it. They looked startled as they stared at my face, asking, "What? What is it? What happened to your face?"

Sure enough, I immediately noticed a thickening sensation on my face as it began to itch; I was having an allergic attack, and red rashes broke out all over my body. I had already been on the verge of a reaction as I had had not bathed since arriving here, the room was dusty, and I was being interrogated for long hours. They did not say anything more but took me to a nearby clinic and allowed me to go to bed as soon as we returned. The next day, I felt revived by the night's sleep, and the rashes had gone down a bit as well.

During interrogations, I learned that they had been thinking there were two Ma Thidas—one a doctor and the other a writer—who were activists against the national convention. Only now did they begin to realize it was just me. Finally they stopped asking questions and just rewrote all their interrogation notes. They said they were sending me to Insein Prison, so I asked them to give my watch and a few belongings to my family and to bring back some clothes and food for me.

On the evening of August 5, 1993, I was taken to Insein Prison. Immediately I ran into a problem: I was a prisoner, so I was told to take off my sandals. Although it was not a big deal I did not want to do it. I argued that going barefoot in the dirt would cause an allergic reaction. They did not believe it and told me to try it first and see what happened. I was a bit unsure as sometimes I was fine after taking off my sandals during visits to monasteries or pagodas but now I had to test it. If there was no reaction I would have to go barefoot. But sure enough, my allergy and I have been close companions since my childhood, and now it came to my rescue: I had not gone ten steps when rashes appeared on my heels. Even I was surprised, let alone the prison authorities, who were speechless. It could have been the histamine, which is released in our bodies when we are nervous. Whatever the reason, I did not have to take off my slippers as I entered the prison's main gate.[1] My body was so fragile and sensitive that they even told the prison officers that I was sickly. I was put in a small cell in a cellblock in front of the office of the women's section where prisoners still on trial were kept.[2] My cell had a barred window on the outside wall, and the door to the corridor had a screened opening on its upper part with a wooden flap hinged at the top on the outside, so the flap could be propped up or let down as needed.

I was put in the cellblock where gay prisoners were held, which was in front of the office and was thus called the front block. Homosexual behavior in prisons was quite a problem so the authorities kept them, male or female, apart from the straight prisoners. Although I had always behaved like a boy, I am not gay—I just wanted to be a man of nobility as described in the Buddhist *Dhammapada*.[3] I did not want to be mistaken as gay, so I dared not even wear my usual *pasoe,* the male-style waist garment that my mother had sent me. I reminded myself that this place was temporary and that I should not live or behave in the way I would normally have followed outside of these walls.

So, although it was not easy, I taught myself to refer to myself with a feminine pronoun when conversing with others. I was not very familiar

---

1. Upon entering Insein Prison through the small doorway cut into the thick metal doors about fifteen feet high, detainees find themselves in a large, high-ceilinged room for the registration of new or released prisoners. A similar gate at the back with the same type of doors opens into the prison premises. The smaller doors in both metal doors are for people to enter and leave, set about eighteen inches off the floor. The bigger doors are opened only for vehicles or important personnel.
2. There were two women's sections in Insein Prison, one on each side of the main gates. The one on the right of the gate when facing out was where prisoners awaiting trial were kept. There was a large building for the general population and two secure cellblocks with individual cells in it for political prisoners, one on either side of the office. All three buildings are kept isolated from one another so prisoners from one building cannot see or talk to those in the other. On the left of the main gate is the women's section for sentenced prisoners, with its own buildings and a clinic.
3. *Dhammapada* is a Buddhist scripture ascribed to the Buddha himself and is one of the well-known texts of Theravada Buddhism.

with this as usually I called myself "daughter" with my family or older friends and a neutral but male-style first-person pronoun with colleagues and peers. As it happened, the person from the next cell started to flirt with me. She introduced herself as Po Chit (using the male name prefix "Po"), and tried to chat me up. In spite of it, I realized that what former political prisoners had told me was true—the physical and mental strains of prison were bearable compared to being interrogated, as I now had someone to talk to. She said she was on trial for dealing drugs. She was someone who could get in touch with my family for me when she had to go to court, so although I did not like her advances or her crime, I told myself I had to be nice to her. I did not have to worry about her getting physical with me since a wooden wall separated us. I called her Elder Sister Chit, and although she was not happy being addressed as female, she continued to talk to me.

During those early days in jail I just stared at the daily routine chart in my cell during the day and talked to Elder Sister Chit in the evening. At the beginning, the problems were about food, sights, and sounds. Through my interrogators my family had sent only snacks, so I had nothing to eat with rice. The soup given in the prison was made with chickpeas in the morning or unwashed leaves like spinach in the evening, so it was often mixed with earthworms, mosquito larvae, sand, and pebbles. The soups were a dingy color with a burnt odor. Its accompaniment, for lunch and dinner, was a bit of smelly, dark shrimp paste dotted with a few chilies. I had never eaten much of even good-quality shrimp paste, so it was impossible for me to swallow this down.

It was also because the future was so uncertain at that point that I had no appetite at all. But the worst problem I had was not food-related: it was the foul words used by quarreling prisoners and the guards who were trying to keep them under control. The dirtiest, most vulgar words spewed out of their mouths as if from a machine gun, words I had never heard before; I could not think of anything scarier than this. I was not that frightened during interrogations because I did not have to hear any words like this, but now my ears were thick with shame.

There were not only ugly sounds but ugly sights, too. Even in jail, some could live like barons no matter what kinds of hideous crime they had committed and no matter how serious a trial they were facing. If they could afford it they would get nice things and the best food from their families, which they could spread around and so become "saviors." Prisoners who were jailed for offences like drug dealing, fraud, or corruption could easily bribe guards, most of whom had no more than a primary school education. Even if they bullied others it was not a problem because bribery made them stars in this place. Those with no money and no one to visit them were oppressed and abused. A young guard who could not even spell her own name would abuse with obscene words a poor prisoner even if she was educated and in jail not for a crime she committed but perhaps for something like unknowingly buying stolen goods. Those were the things I had to bear daily in the prison. Young women being jailed for prostitution were asked to massage the calves of the female guards with their chins. The scenes of women prisoners being beaten mercilessly like cattle frightened me. I started to reconsider my wish to have a prison experience so that I could write a book and wondered how brave I would need to be in order to put these vulgar scenes into words.

While I was waiting for my trial to start, my overwhelming desire was to send word to my family about my situation. My youngest brother was in the same jail, so I assumed he had probably found out about me. If that was the case, my parents would have known about me by now. I felt devastated every time I heard the train's toot from the Insein Station, which was very near the prison; I was remembering the quick trip I took with my mother and how I had dozed in her arms. In fact, my mother's devastation was deeper than mine, as I was told only much later; she had fallen out of bed while crying uncontrollably. Besides, the request made to Elder Sister Chit to get in touch with my family did not work out. Luckily, I met a woman whose home was very close to my father's office, and I was finally able to contact my parents.

Through another prisoner who was on trial for dealing weed and who was helping out in the office of our section I was also able to send word to my family about my court date. Later I heard that hundreds came to the police lockup on Maha Bandoola Garden Street, thinking my "accomplices" and I would be brought there before being taken to court—a normal procedure. Every female prisoner going out to court told me that every time the waiting crowds saw a prison van, they asked if I was among them. My heart lifted at this news even though I had no idea how my case would turn out.

However, our trial was held at the special court in front of the prison,[4] and witnesses were called. Two witnesses whom I had never seen before gave evidence against me. I tried to answer all questions with as few mistakes as possible, knowing everything I said in court was more important and legitimate than what I had said during interrogation. The judge said my case would be heard on September 27 and a lawyer would be allowed if I could hire one in time for the trial. I secretly sent word to my parents to bring a lawyer on that date.

They found out about my getting in touch with my parents and on September 22 sent me into the cellblock behind the main building, called the rear block. They said it was too risky to put me among the ordinary criminals who could help me get in touch with the outside world. The political prisoners already in this rear cellblock were Daw Kyi Kyi (wife of Thakhin Zin, a communist leader who was killed during the civil war in the 1970s) and her daughter Ma Don, and Daw Khin Yee (wife of Bo Set Yaung, one of the group of thirty comrades of the independence movement) and her daughter Khin Hnin Yee. With them were Daw Ohn Mya, Daw Nyunt, and Ma Chuu, who had been involved in the beheadings of 1988 and were sentenced to death— later reduced to life and then to twenty years with the 1992 amnesty. I was put in an empty cell next to them; it was clean and airy. They all gave me food so it was even better. In prison, I was given luxury food by Daw Kyi Kyi and her daughter: huge king prawns and large strawberries that I had never even dreamed of eating before in my life. In the evening, Ma Hnin on my right and Ma Chuu on my left chatted with each other while the others listened. I also told them some things about myself.

---

4. Used as a military tribunal from 1988 to 1992.

Chapter 8

"Did You Say Twenty Years?"

On September 27, I was brought to the court and saw my parents with the NLD lawyer U Win Maung, who had prepared my defense. U Khin Maung Swe, the party's MP from my township, was there too. That I had managed to have my parents bring a lawyer despite not being allowed visitors was an unpleasant surprise to the authorities. U Win Maung was allowed to defend me as they could not find a reason to deny me this right. Nevertheless, I was not given a chance to talk to my lawyer. The ten others involved in my case were all men, five of whom I had never before seen in my life. I found out that one of them was also involved in the case against Dr. Aung Khin Sint[1]—this was the first time I heard he had been arrested. The prosecutor brought in fifty-two witnesses, and three or four of them were members of the NLD.

It was very complicated and I could not understand what it was all about. The ten men who had been arrested together were blaming each other and making it more difficult to comprehend. The case was being heard every two or three days and there were so many witnesses that the trial went on from morning to evening. Judge U Thant Sin made sure I was sent back before dark without handcuffs since I was the only woman in this case. My parents looked tired but did not seem downhearted. They had already gone through a lot and their endurance was strong. Ma Hmwe and some other friends came to my hearings

---

1. A medical doctor who led the strike of medical professionals in the 1988 uprising; also a member of the general strike committee. He became one of leading figures in the NLD.

to show their support; I heard from them that that my novel had been banned from publication.

The judge began the questioning by verifying my basic background information.

"Your name is Ma Thida. Isn't it?"

"Yes."

"You are twenty-seven year old. Is that correct?"

"No."

The judge looked up at me with startled eyes; the court fell silent.

"My twenty-seventh birthday has passed so I'm twenty-eight now."

I heard some faint laughs. Even the MIs smiled.

Then my lawyer U Win Maung was allowed to question me.

"The copies of the *New Era* journals that are on exhibit, were they taken and seized from you? Are they yours?"

"Since these journals are not marked with their owner's name, and since I only borrowed them, I cannot even say for sure if those were the ones I borrowed and then returned."

U Win Maung had not expected me to answer this way but he nodded at me and seemed satisfied. Then the prosecutor said that to reduce the time of the hearing he would not object if I wanted to give my testimony directly to the court recorder to be typed up and that neither he nor my lawyer needed to rewrite my testimony if the judge agreed to this. I then gave my testimony directly. Cross-examination of the witnesses failed to implicate me and if this went on I would have to be released unconditionally.

But the military regime's courts of justice were courts of injustice. On October 10, 1993, I was sentenced to twenty years in prison—seven years under Emergency Act 5 (J),[2] three years under Unlawful

---

2. Act 5 (J) was part of the Emergency Provisions Act passed on March 9, 1950, making it a criminal offense "to spread false news, knowing or having reason to believe that it is not true" and mandating imprisonment of "anyone who is considered to have contributed towards the diminishment of respect or disloyalty among members of the civil service or the military towards the government."

Associations Act 17 (1), and five years each under Unlawful Publications Acts 17 and 20.

Before our trial, most prison sentences handed down to members of the NLD and activists were just seven years. Only the writer Maung Thaw Ka had been sentenced to 20 years. I suddenly recalled a poem written by Ma Sein Bin, a female poet and political prisoner, for a collection of poems in honor of Maung Thaw Ka. The poem was titled "A Single Match" and its opening line was, "Did you say twenty years?"

I was not allowed to talk to anyone after sentencing, so from the prison van I gestured and shouted to my parents and friends that I had been given twenty years. Seeing the shock on their faces I tried to console them by saying, "It's not that long!"

As was normal practice for all sentenced prisoners, they arranged to transfer me to the other women's section where those sentenced were kept. On the side where I had been kept up to now, there had been so much talk of me being innocent and going free that the authorities were worried the news of such a long sentence might cause some anger among other political prisoners. I was not too depressed since I knew that anything could happen; my hopes were high because of last year's amnesty, and I believed I would not have to serve the full twenty years.

Once I entered the large upper-story hall within the section where all sentenced prisoners were kept,[3] the poet and political activist Ma Sein Bin greeted me with a shout: "Did you say twenty years?" quoting the opening line from her poem in honor of Maung Thaw Ka. As was customary with newly sentenced political prisoners, I had to spend one night in the hall where over five hundred prisoners slept, head to head and feet to feet in tight rows. The room was pungent with body odors and punctuated with an assortment of noises. The toilet bin had no lid, just like the one I had used in the cellblock, and was almost overflowing with everyone's business. I could not help overhearing

---

3. In this section there were two double-story buildings and a cellblock with ten cells kept apart and next to the office. The poorest criminals and those with children were kept on the ground floors.

the vulgar words from trustees who had been put in charge—such as the wealthier drug dealers—abusing what little power they had by bullying others; their revolting words flew around the hall like another kind of foul smell. For sure there were worse and more-frightening things to this room than just the four walls, locks, handcuffs, and shackles. My biggest problem was figuring out how to communicate with those kinds of people.

The next morning, five female prisoners who had been arrested on political charges took me to where they were housed on the upper floor of another building. I had to listen to their stories. I, who had just been sentenced to twenty years the previous day, had to listen to someone with only three months left to serve tell me how she longed to go home. Another woman whose family had a political background and was therefore no stranger to prison told me that criminals wanted the same rights in prison as political prisoners; she had replied to some of them that if they wanted to have the same privileges as political prisoners they should have only come to jail with a political sentence.

Someone asked me, "Didn't you know you would be arrested? Why couldn't you just be a doctor?" All I could answer was, "Yes, I knew, because I was not arrested for being a member of the Nursery Student's Union. I knew that I was going to be sentenced but I didn't expect this lengthy jail term. I don't have plans to be a privileged prisoner. I believe that my being in prison will not be in vain since the public knows that the regime jailed me unfairly."

Unlike in the cellblock, where I could bathe by myself, it was uncomfortable for me to bathe in a large group. Besides, we had to scoop up the water and pour it on our bodies in time with the shouted commands—"Scoop!" or Pour!"—of the trustee in charge. I began to understand why the political prisoners wanted the privilege of bathing by themselves and how those who were about to be released longed to go home. Nonetheless, I was not too upset by these inconveniences as I was getting a lot of material for my writing.

But then at about five that evening I was transferred back to the cellblock where I had been; everyone welcomed me back. Yesterday, the food I had taken with me to the other side had been packed in boxes by people who also gave me some from what they had there, so I came back with more possessions. They had also shared their food with me and I felt grateful for their kindness. They thought they had gotten one more member in their league but now I was back to my old place—in cell number three getting accustomed to standing next to the screened opening on my door and chatting with others from evening until the lights-out signal was played at 9:00 p.m.[4] There were only two other young women in this cellblock—Ma Chuu and Ma Hnin—but they transferred Ma Hnin to the other cellblock at the end of October after her mother finished serving her sentence and was released. With this, Ma Chuu and I became closer, but I found it was not easy as Ma Chuu, although young and beautiful, was rough of speech.

However, I still believed I would not be here for long, so I was willing to try to get along with all types of people. It was also my aim to use this time to concentrate on religious practice. Meanwhile, I was planning to tame Ma Chuu, who, although she was young, educated, and from a wealthy family, had rough speech and manner—but understandably so in light of what she had gone through. Another reason I wanted to help her was that Ma Chuu was just like me in always thinking up ways of using the guards to our advantage while not giving in to them one inch.

There was another woman in our block who was a little older than me, and I liked her but knew I could not make her my ally because the way she and I chose to face prison were very different. From day one she had been telling me, "Do you want to bribe the warden? I can hook you up with her. Do you want your cell door to be open from morning till closing time just like my mother, with the doctor recommending it for health reasons? We can use your allergy as an excuse to make it happen."

I refused delicately by saying, "My family is not rich enough to offer bribes, because it won't be just one person that I'll have to pay. Wardens are always being transferred as they too are civil servants, and I would

---

4. The wake-up signal was played at 5:00 a.m.

have to keep on bribing the replacements. Besides, my allergy is not as bad as your mother's heart condition. I'm a doctor so I don't want to ask another doctor for a false medical certificate just to have my door open all day." I really should have told her straightforwardly that I did not wish to encourage corruption, but having eaten their food I held my tongue.

Finally I was allowed family visits. Having to look at my parents through two layers of iron bars and wire mesh in a dimly lit room was bittersweet. I was not upset about my long sentence because I could now look forward to the certainty of seeing my parents every fortnight. I would be able to maintain my composure and pass the time in my cell, thinking about how after thirteen days I would see them again. The long visiting room, about six feet high, was divided lengthwise with two layers of iron mesh about a foot apart. On one side sat about fifty prisoners and on the other were their family members—maybe about a hundred of them. The two layers of iron mesh made it difficult for the families to find their loved ones; there were fluorescent lights but so covered in dust that they could only give out a dim glow. Body odor of the prisoners filled the whole room. So the mere fifteen minutes of meeting my family was like being in both hell and heaven—in this hellish room we all thought it was heaven on earth because we were looking at our families and getting the food parcels they had bought and other things like clothes, blankets, or plastic bowls. Even if what they could afford to bring was boiled duck eggs and fried fish paste, these were like divine delicacies compared to the prison rations of tasteless vegetable soup mixed with all types of insects, ash-colored chili, and almost-raw fish paste. I cherished these prison visits and the food, but every time I came out for family visits I got into trouble.

As a matter of fact, the unwritten law in prison was that the people with power always won against the weak—wardens oppressed guards; guards oppressed trustee prisoners put in charge of the baths, allotting sleeping space, and so on; and those uppity trustees with a modicum of power bullied the other prisoners. It was the law of the wild. The guards who inspected the parcels from family visits were just like the Press Scrutiny Board, always twisting the rules to their advantage.

In fact, the Press Scrutiny Board was a little better although it rejected or censored anything not in line with the regulations. But in prison, never mind the regulations; the guards inspecting the parcels simply took whatever they wanted by saying such-and-such was not allowed, true or not. If they wanted any permitted food, they just took some from it. To prevent the victim from complaining they would verbally abuse them at the same time. In searching for letters or any smuggled items, they used a single dirty spoon to stir the food, whether it was fish paste or sugar. So it was inevitable that I fought with them after every prison visit. I did not allow them to stir my food with their one dirty spoon and they said I was being arrogant when I demanded that they use different spoons for my parcels if they wanted to search for smuggled items.

When I was allowed to see my parents I could also see my brother who was in the men's side in Insein, in what is called "inside visits" (as opposed to "outside visits"), when family members in the same jail could see each other once a month. In this way I was also able to learn the living conditions of the men. We could also exchange food although it was only I who gave him some and never he who gave to me. Most of our conversations involved me urging him not to use drugs anymore for the sake of our parents. I begged him to try not to burden them anymore and to understand how much they love us. I did not learn much about my colleagues because there were no political prisoners in his building and I got only some rumors out of him. Although I did not believe it did any good to incarcerate junkies or that they deserved it, I could do nothing to change this system. I tried with all my heart to make him understand and choose to change his life.

Eventually, he told me how some of his friends and even some of our relatives had been encouraging his behavior by telling him how we, his family, treated him badly and looked down on him, and that was why he had never listened to us. He only realized now that he was in prison that it was we who really loved him and were taking care of him as much as we could. He began to see this when I was sharing a lot of my food with him. Although things got better between us I still faced annoyances after my family visits.

One time, the guard inspecting my food parcel was about to take a sip from my plastic bottle of orange juice, saying some people had been smuggling in alcohol. I immediately snatched the bottle from him and said, "What are you trying to do? Hold out your palm to me if you want to taste it." I was so angry that my voice was harsh. All the prisoners standing nearby and the other guards were stunned into silence as they looked at us. The guard in question was about twenty years older than me, but dazed by my reaction he held out his open palm. Still angry, I poured a few drops onto his palm saying, "You can sip from your own palm." He then regained his composure and with a red face told me I could keep the juice bottle.

During the next weekly inspection by the male senior wardens when we had to sit in the standard lineup position in our cells,[5] we could report anything we wanted. I did not want to say anything but sat there with a stern look on my face—I never sat with arms folded as required but with my hands on my lap with the palms up. Our warden later admitted to Ma Chuu that it was the guard who was in the wrong in trying to sip my orange juice. This guard came to apologize but asked me not to yell at him in front of others. After that, no one searched my bags anymore. The guards were mostly uneducated and in their whole lives had known only prisons and prisoners. They yelled and shouted at the prisoners and their subordinates all the time, so they did not know how to react when a prisoner did the same thing to them. After this incident, I was considered untouchable by the guards, and I was surely on their troublemaker list.

As a result of my problems with the guards, Ma Chuu became the most important person for me during my incarceration. Although she was under a death sentence for her part in the 1988 beheading of someone accused by the mob of poisoning the water tank of the children's hospital, she was an educated person, came from a wealthy family, and was kindhearted and sensitive. Moreover, she was very beautiful and

---

5. The standard lineup position for women was to sit in silence with legs tucked under, arms folded across the chest, and head bowed. Sentenced prisoners had to wear a white uniform (the color has since changed).

generous, so the more honest guards were fond of her and did not hesitate to help her if she ever wanted to smuggle in books. Her family also paid handsomely for these privileges. As for me, no guards wanted anything to do with me, let alone to offer help. Luckily, any book or magazine that Ma Chuu received I could read as well. Moreover, our fathers had been only a year apart at Rangoon University and knew each other. I asked my parents to give all the books I wanted to her parents and so we were able to read monthly magazines as well as religious books.[6]

We had to be very careful not to let two older prisoners in our block know about this because they both preached at us often to adhere to the old adage "When in Rome, live as Romans do"—that is, obey the rules of prison. In the meantime I was able to revive Ma Chuu's gentle and polite nature from underneath her rough manner, which was the result of past trauma. She was three years older than me but was still like a little girl, not knowing much about the world. Some prisoners criticized her as arrogant and getting her own way because of her wealth. The truth was that she would sometimes say insensitive things to poorer criminals but at the same time share a generous amount of food with them. As I got to know her better and saw her true nature I became fond of her. She asked my opinion of the beheading, and I told her not to dwell in regret but starting now to strictly and daily keep the Five Precepts. She was happy with my advice and we have been good friends since.

In late 1993, a warden who had been fired and jailed for corruption was put in the cell next to mine. We learned many stories about prison from her, one of them being that the two older prisoners who were always telling us to "live as Romans do" had bribed her handsomely; nonetheless, we continued to maintain our friendship with them. Two Karen women were temporarily put in our block but there were no other

---

6. At the time, only small booklets with Buddhist verses or sutras were officially allowed in prison, but later the International Committee of the Red Cross made it possible for prisoners to legally receive and keep books and exchange letters with family and friends..

changes besides getting a new warden. She was arrogant, proud, and seemed to be of Chinese ancestry. In early 1994 she and Ma Chuu got into a dispute, and I fully supported Ma Chuu since she was in the right. As a result, Ma Chuu and I became closer and everyone noticed this. Then the new warden, who did not like my being friends with Ma Chuu, approached me in a friendly way; we found out that she and I had gone to the same school and had in fact taken the same school bus. Only then did I remember her and her sisters rushing to wash their faces only when the school bus was in front of their house. Her younger sister was one grade lower than I, but we were friends. Despite that, she did not help us out much. At that time I was not very healthy and would often have stomachaches. I had to ask Dr. Lei Lei Win, the medical officer for the woman's section, to write a prescription for the medication I needed and then have my parents send it to me. My long neglect of regular meals, plus the hard rice and unhygienic prison fare as well as the dried and deep-fried foods of my present diet, was making things worse.

One morning, we were told that a minister was coming, and we had to sit in the lineup position from early morning. The prison-issue *htamein* was so short that it barely covered my knees; besides, all prison-issue uniforms were stained and grimy after years of use, so most of us asked our families to send in new ones. Sometimes important personages like this came without warning, so to make it easier to change into whites Ma Chuu had a plain white top made like a baggy T-shirt that she could quickly pull on over what she was wearing, and I copied her idea.

I usually sat cross-legged without folding my arms or bowing my head, like a kindergarten kid. Once a new guard asked me why prisoners had sit in this position. I said, "This procedure was introduced during the British period.[7] The main reason, I think, is that it is easier to count prisoners when they are in this position, seated in rows in the buildings. It is also not easy for them to attack the guards from a sitting

---

7. The prisons are still run according to the jail manual introduced in colonial times.

position. Another reason is to show that the prisoners are well enough to sit up. But we in locked cells, we have no way of attacking anyone, and no matter how we sit the guards will be able to count us. It is good enough for them to know the prisoners are well enough and still alive. That's all." And I continued to sit as normally as possible without being disrespectful.

This lineup procedure meant piling our bags of clothes or food in a corner of our cell so that they could not be seen by anyone looking through the screened opening on the door. Those in the halls had to sit in neat rows after they had piled all their belongings in one corner and covered them with blankets. Before the departure of the important visitor, no prisoners could get anything from their bags including food. No one was allowed to eat as the visitor might come during the meal. That day he did not come at all so the lineup was finally dispersed at three in the afternoon. Everyone was starving, including the staff; rice from prison hospital[8] arrived, and only after that were we allowed to break ranks. Although those of us with food in our cells could quickly have some snacks during the wait, when we were hungry we only wanted to eat rice. We all sent out loving-kindness[9] to the visiting official who never showed up. The whole day was wasted this way and it was already time to sleep.

In the following days, there were rumors that some foreign visitors were coming and that the minister was escorting them to prison. In prison anything could be news, and it seemed nothing ever came true so I forgot all about it. On the morning of February 10, 1994, we were told to sit in the standard lineup again. Just like before, the rumor was that someone from the Department of Corrections was coming. So that day I was in whites, lying on my back on the bed, which was a wooden platform about four inches high, my legs up in the air; I sat up only when I heard the jailer shout out, "Line up!" Then her face suddenly appeared at the opening in my door so I lowered my legs but remained

---

8. Those in the cells receive better-quality rice from the hospital kitchen.
9. Sarcastic idiom.

on my back. She gestured for me to come closer, only to confuse me by saying, "Er . . . never mind," before she left. I wondered if something was up but did not think too much about it.

After a couple of hours, two guards came and said, "The minister wants to see you, Ma Thida." Even then I did not think much of it and followed them. Ma Don urged me to wear a proper women's top instead of the sack-like shirt; I did not have one so she lent me hers. I went past the building for the general population and reached the office just behind the main entrance.

There were prison authorities, Military Intelligence, and the chief, deputy chief, and director of the Department of Corrections in one office; rather unusually, they were all smiling. I began to think something very strange was afoot as I was led into another room although I could see nothing because of the strong video-camera lights directed at me. There was a big empty chair in the room, and right in front of it was a table with three foreigners seated behind it. A Burmese man stood next to the table and I could see several uniformed people around that table. I saw cameras and flashlights. Two of the foreigners greeted me as I was about to sit down. Then the man standing by the table asked me whether I would talk to them by myself or wanted him to interpret. My English was not very good but I was concerned that the interpreter might not be trustworthy, so I said I would talk for myself.

The foreigners introduced themselves and told me who they were. It was happening so fast that first I did not catch everything they said but I noticed that the minister was not near us. All I could understand was that one man was a US senator, another was from one of the United Nations agencies, and the third was a journalist, but I could not remember their names. The senator started telling me that although they had planned to come the other day they had to go and see Daw Aung San Suu Kyi, as they had suddenly gotten permission to see her that day. I got very excited on hearing that and blurted out, "Oh, you're so lucky! Is she well?" He said she was well, that she sent her love to me and told me to be brave and strong, and that they had come to see me because she told them to. They also told me that I could send a message to her as they were going to see her again. I got so excited that I forgot all the officials around us and unloaded all that I was feeling. I answered fully, leaving nothing out, when they asked me about my experiences in prison. I told them not only about those of us who were in the cells but also about the prisoners in the halls and how we were treated by the guards. Then one of them told me to state my own situation rather than that of other prisoners.

Then we talked about politics. They asked about my opinion on the national convention, which was currently taking place. I said it was not an acceptable political process since they ignored the 1990 elections' result, and besides, only 12 percent of those elected MPs were allowed to attend. I said that parliament must be convened first, and only then could a national convention be held to draw up a constitution. We also talked about political prisoners and agreed that we could have true national reconciliation only when all political prisoners, including Daw Aung San Suu Kyi, were released. Their next question was what the political solution could be. I did not have a lot to say to that question apart from "dialogue is the answer." They also asked whether I was all right in prison and I said, "This is a prison, not a hotel, so nothing is alright." I sent a message to Ma Suu that she was in my thoughts at all times, to take care of herself and not to worry about me, that I remained as strong as ever for the cause, and with this spirit I was always with her.

Soon I sensed that the uniformed people were becoming restless. The visitors said goodbye and the senator gave me his name card. The warden of my block approached me: time was up. I was to be sent back to my cell. At the gate, she asked me to hand over the senator's name card. I said I had not even looked at it yet so she quickly murmured, "It's Bill Richardson, Bill Richardson," and snatched the card out of my hand.

All the way back to my cell, her face was clouded and she grumbled, "You talked too much. You could have just talked a little bit."

"Well, too bad. It can't be undone. I had to tell of my feelings and experiences truthfully," I answered.

Everyone in the cellblock wanted to hear all about it, yet they were still sitting in the lineup position. Even the guards wanted to hear so I said loudly, "It wasn't the minister. It was a US senator. They didn't

US senator Bill Richardson and New York Times correspondent Philip Shenon meet Ma Thida inside Insein Prison as Aung San Suu Kyi had suggested to them on the previous day.

Ma Thida during her meeting with Senator Richardson.

want me to be prepared for what to say so they lied to us about waiting for a minister."

In my mind, however, I was delighted to have received Ma Suu's message of love. At the same time, I wondered what would happen as a consequence of what I had told the senator. I overheard from some guards that the senator also met with U Tin Oo, U Kyi Maung, U Win Tin, and Min Ko Naing,[10] all in Insein.

As soon as the lineup was over, Daw Kyi Kyi came to see me. Everyone was itching to know so I tried to sum it up for them. Later that evening I heard some reports of the day's events—Daw Kyi Kyi and her daughter, Ma Don, spent a lot of money to get information from the guards and in this manner the news came back to us. Apparently, the chief warden of Insein had asked my warden to tell me not to say anything bad about the prison or to lie about its conditions. That was the reason she came to my cell this morning but seemed to be confused about how to say it, for she knew I would not obey. She thought it would be worse if I knew a US senator was coming, and so she had decided not to ask me anything. They had thought that I would not be able to answer capably in English with such short notice. They were shaken to find out that I was not only able to answer all the questions but also to relate in detail all that I wanted to say.

I heard what the chief warden had said about me: "She's a mastermind and we have to be careful next time. I don't know how much she would have said if she knew in advance the senator was coming! Unbelievable!" The next day, all guards in the women's side were summoned and told to sign a pledge that they would not talk to me or to Ma Chuu. The real reason was that they feared Ma Chuu or I might ask the guards to contact diplomats on our behalf. It made me laugh.

Yet it did not stop there. I told my parents about meeting Bill Richardson on their next visit. Previously on every prison visit a guard sat nearby and eavesdropped on us. Now it was not just eavesdropping—she even wrote down what we were saying. Sometimes my

---

10. Min Ko Naing was a prominent student leader and is a well-known democracy activist who spent more than nineteen years in prison.

parents and I used English to share information; the week following one such conversation, Ma Chuu came back from her family visit and said that there was a new rule: no one was allowed to speak any language other than Burmese during visiting time. Prison visits and I were never far away from problems.

Chapter 9

Secrets and Daily Doings

At that time, Ma Chuu and I were able to read books, but mostly we read literary magazines. Her family bribed a guard so generously that she smuggled any book or magazine she wanted. The guards did not know I was also reading the books, because the wall between Ma Chuu's cell and mine had no holes. The backs of our cells were about three feet away from a high galvanized iron wall, and beyond that were the men's compound with an empty plot, a farm, and the men's death row. Thus, no one walked past our windows on that wall during the night. Usually, we hung our washed plastic bags to dry on a string looped between our windows, a string we had woven from old plastic bags; we recycled a lot in prison. We also used this string to pass books to each other, tapping on the wall between us to signal when a book or magazine was in a bag and hung on the string, ready to be pulled either way. I could finish reading a magazine within three or four hours and then I would return it using our cable. Ma Chuu and I would stay up at night to frantically read as fast as we could; we were so hungry to know what was going on in the world.

~

It was September 1993 when I was arrested and during that time Palestinian leader Yassir Arafat and Israeli prime minister Yitzhak Rabin signed a peace treaty. In October China tested its nuclear weapons. By early November the European Union had become well-known among people in Myanmar. In December the UN General

Assembly assigned a human rights rapporteur for Myanmar, and January 1994 marked the end of the Cold War.

～

Reading was our most important secret, and we had to find chances to discuss what we had read, share news, and so on, although it was hard enough to even see or say hello to each other. I would wait near the screened opening for her when she was allowed out for a walk and she would do the same when I was out, but we would not walk—we just stood talking. We were only allowed a total of forty-five minutes each for walking up and down the corridor—half an hour in the morning and fifteen minutes in the evening.

We could shave a bit from our bathing time by washing quickly so that we could talk before or afterward. However, we could not even do this if the guard on duty was grumpy. Sometimes, from our windows, we would talk in code but it was more like shouting as we could not hear each other easily, so we could not do this after the 9:00 p.m. lights-out signal. We referred to our reading material as "tonics" and would ask each other whether we had taken the tonic and tell each other, which made us stronger. We discussed world news as if it were history, but as Daw Kyi Kyi and her daughter—who were both well-educated and informed of news by visiting family members—might understand that we were talking of recent events, we used cryptic terms. We had to change the subject if a guard came our way or if we suspected someone was listening. Another wonderful escape for me was to hear Ma Chuu singing. She had a very good voice and sang very well—as good as a professional. She would tap on her door for rhythm when she sang and would entertain us nonstop the whole evening. Everyone, including the staff, liked her singing. In this way I passed 1994 by taking "tonics" and listening to Ma Chuu's entertainment.

Not long after being arrested, notifications and timetables from England arrived for the entrance exam; my dream of obtaining an MRCP or FRCS qualification[1] from the United Kingdom was alive and well up to then, so in February 1994, I demanded the right to read in prison. I officially requested that I be allowed to read the necessary textbooks for the exam, as well as religious books. In April, they said they would allow me to read religious books but not medical books. So I asked my parents to send me some religious books and after going through an inspection period lasting over a month, three books reached me. My parents had sent five but they said I should read these three first and they would give me the other two later. Although I had already read these books, the experience of reading them again in prison was very different, and they were an immense help when I began to do Vipassana meditation in late 1995. The problem, however, was that no more books were allowed after those five. The punishment for my complaints during the meeting with Senator Richardson was that I was not allowed to read. I did not continue my demand for more books, as I was able to read magazines from Ma Chuu.

Soon after receiving these books I came down with a fever that would not go away. At the time I weighed less than one hundred pounds and I did not know why I could not shake off this fever, although I was not too worried, as I have never been fit. Finally, Dr. Lei Lei Win diagnosed it as typhoid. My heartbeat was not very fast and I had a high fever, so I thought that seemed possible. I went on a liquid diet, but it was not easy since we did not have a wide choice of food. I needed hot water to make malted milk drinks like Ovaltine and Horlicks. According to prison routine I would get one cup of hot water in the morning when the hospital sent around our rice and another cup at three in the afternoon. We were not allowed vacuum flasks so it was almost impossible to be on a liquid diet. Luckily, Daw Kyi Kyi was allowed to have one and she filled it up every afternoon to share with me. As a result, I passed two weeks on a liquid diet with Ma Don making me chicken soup from stock cubes as well as malted drinks. I lost a lot of weight but the fever went away.

---

1. Member of the Royal College of Physicians or Fellow of the Royal College of Surgeons.

One certain thing was that I did not completely recover from my illness. After I arrived in Insein, for seven or eight months I did not have my period; I knew that my general weakness combined with stress had caused a hormonal change, so I was not very concerned about not having a regular period, and besides I suffered from cramps every time. Yet when it came, it came with a vengeance, and the excruciating pain it brought lasted for ten days a month as I was getting cramps even during the ovulation period. Although I was already accustomed to this pain, it was worse in prison. I was hoping to begin meditating, but because of this pain I could only recite sutras and count my prayer beads. I thought it could not get any worse, but I began to lose weight and was again feverish while the painful cramps returned every month.

Meanwhile, I took my "tonics" every night—and sometimes all night—to keep myself at pace with the outside world, and in this way tried to endure my pain. I wanted to be a man even more so because I knew there were more of them in Insein as political prisoners and I had heard they were holding debates, forming reading groups, and secretly producing handwritten bulletins and had even smuggled in a shortwave radio to listen to so they could spread news from the BBC and VOA to other political prisoners. As happened often enough, rumor of an amnesty again spread throughout the prison. I tried to stay out of trouble while reading magazines and keeping alert for news of our political situation.

During those days, Ma Chuu and I tried to negotiate with the guards to keep our cells open from 10:00 a.m to 4:00 p.m. We agreed that they could lock us in whenever higher officials came, and this was no problem since the guards had to shout, "Line up!" when officials entered our gate, at which point we would quickly slip back into our cells. Daw Kyi Kyi and her daughter did not need to be involved in our negotiations, as their cell was always kept open already. We were able to negotiate with guards who were sympathetic, and in return, we shared our food with them. We then had a change of warden; the new one was sympathetic so we made our request to her directly. We tried to increase what little freedom we had in the prison by promising that we would not go anywhere and would not break any rules. We ran into all sorts of trouble for this; sometimes we got what we wanted and sometimes what few rights we gained simply vanished. We never abused any rights we got through asking for them.

We also befriended new arrivals to our block who had some education and interest in politics but were there on criminal charges like manslaughter or fraud. Mainly we befriended the guards, and most of them also showed a soft spot for long-term prisoners. As time passed, friendship between guards and prisoners grew. Besides, they spent most of their time in prison—from five in the morning to about eight at night, except for a lunch break. Their salaries were never enough, so they were used to doing anything they could to earn extra income or food, including being kind. If they turned a blind eye we could talk to prisoners who carried in the rice or hot water into our cellblock, and they too wanted to befriend us out of respect for our being political prisoners.

Others we tried to befriend were women who had been arrested for prostitution, vagrancy, and drug dealing; sometimes these young women could be depended upon to get information for us. News of my meeting with Senator Richardson was featured in the state newspapers, and everyone in prison knew about it. A young woman who was on cleaning duty for my cellblock saw my photo in the newspaper while she was out to face trial, and as she was illiterate asked someone to read it to her, tore out that part, and smuggled it in. She gave it to Ma Chuu to give me because she knew guards were quite strict with me; it was not just once that these young women helped us. On September 20, 1994, Daw Aung San Suu Kyi was driven to a government's guesthouse to meet with Senior General Than Shwe, General Maung Aye, and General Khin Nyunt. The tide of rumors about an amnesty rose to its peak. That news was featured in the state papers, and a clipping also reached us. This time, another young woman also on cleaning duty smuggled it in.

We got a lot of help from them as well as from some guards. Between our cellblock and the hall nearer to the front where the criminal population was housed was a roofed, open shed with wooden benches for guards to sit. On hot summer days, some criminal prisoners who were friendly with the guards would come here to escape the heat.

Some would bribe the warden to get positions as overseers of the cleaning group. If they had a bit of education and were from middle-class families, it was good for us in the block because they understood who we were. From two of the cleaning women we even learned some Chinese and Shan, and I was able to talk to my father in both languages as he knew a few Mandarin words and could speak Shan fluently. Thus I did not feel isolated at all during my incarceration, although I wanted to be free. My health was not too bad then so I spent most of my time learning other languages, reading whatever was printed on packets of snacks, taking "tonics" whenever we managed to get some, memorizing the sutras, chanting some Buddhist scriptures, counting my prayer beads, keeping my cell clean, and going over and over in my mind the procedures of surgical operations—from the time the scalpel touched the skin to the final suture—so that through all the hours of the day I was never bored.

Having to manage with my personal waste was a big deal. There was no toilet or drainage hole in our twelve-by-twelve-foot cell. We were each given two terracotta water pots, one for drinking and one for general washing, kept filled by different water carriers, as well as two glazed earthenware basins—one to discard water after washing our faces and our dishes, and another for relieving ourselves. The reek from it was a problem but we were allowed to bring in a cover for it or to legally bring in plastic commodes with lids so it was bearable. The biggest problem was about my personal hygiene; we were not allowed to use tissues after the toilet and I normally use a lot of water to clean myself, but neither the glazed earthenware basin nor the commode was anywhere near big enough. So I asked the doctor to write a prescription for a roll of cotton wool and a bottle of Dettol antiseptic lotion, not only to clean myself with but also to sterilize the area around the waste basin. In this way, with several applications of Dettol each day, I kept my cell clean. The cotton roll was useful not only for cleaning but also for other reasons; we were not allowed or given pillows so I wrapped a spare roll in a towel to use as one. If I really thought about it, being in Insein Prison was like being a modern Robinson Crusoe. I rolled a sheet of plastic into a tube to use as a gutter—some days I might use a lot of water, and if the waste basin was near overflowing I poured out the water through it. I managed to survive in that twelve-by-twelve-foot cell like a Stone Age woman.

Up to that time I had not turned to religion more deeply than simply doing my everyday routines. Thinking like a writer, I was swimming fearlessly in my new experiences and gathering material for a book; the desire to become a writer still dominated my thoughts. Being a doctor also, I gave treatment to whoever needed it and whenever possible. I was not concerned about getting along with the warden or guards but about maintaining my principles, so I did not care when they criticized me.

I had publicly stated my view that according to a traditional saying, it did not matter if ten thousand sinners criticized you because praise from one good person would erase it, and since jail is full of sinners I did not have to take notice of any criticism there; in fact, I even feared to be praised. As a result of this attitude, I had only Ma Chuu to help me when I needed something. I gradually became an untouchable in the prison, but this untouchable was one who took refuge in the Buddha and the Buddha's dharma. In fact, it was through the Buddha and his dharma that I am still alive and living with peace of mind.

Spider webs hung from the ceiling of my cell in thick clusters. Pigeons, sparrows, and crows came to the back window in search of food. There were different kinds of ants: some were dark and tiny and others were big and reddish. Ants were what I feared most during my imprisonment, as whole armies of them would march in if they smelled food. I only had a few plastic boxes and bags for storing my food, and these were placed in a corner on the floor where ants could easily invade them. The black ones could be found in the sugar bag and red ones in the curries, and nothing could be done to keep them away. Thus, I had to compromise with them by putting some food near a spot where they usually came out so that they would not march farther into my realm. Although I did not feed pigeons, sparrows, or crows I was providing regular meals for ants.

Two other problems were bedbugs and the near-foot-long, grayish striped geckos.[2] The wooden platform in my cell was only a few inches high, and bedbugs would take refuge in the cracks. I had to launch an elimination attack on them, using both Dettol and camphor balls. The biggest shock I faced was when a gecko crawled into my cell through the window before I had completed my anti-bedbug mission; both the gecko and I were frightened out of our wits upon catching sight of each other. It ran amok around my cell leaving its gummy mucus along its path while I was jumping up and down on my bed with terror. After it escaped through the window, I was again attacked by bed bugs, so I could not even think about the hordes of mosquitoes trying to suck my blood. By then I was quite used to having the red dots of their bites all over my body like a scattered tattoo, since we were not allowed to have mosquito nets. I was, however, able to avoid face-to-face meetings with occasional visitors like snails and centipedes. Fortunately, the fat field mice we often saw around our block could not come in as the four exterior walls of our cellblock were brick. Because of these guests, I could answer honestly when asked that no, I was not in solitary confinement; if I had to include the army of ants, the population in my cell would have been in the thousands. Also, I was able to communicate in some manner with inmates from the other cells, which was another factor that kept me from feeling isolated.

---

2. It is strongly believed in Myanmar that these lizard-like creatures have such strong suckers on their feet that if they land on you nothing can remove them.

Chapter 10

Ill Health

It was over a year that I had been sleeping on the wooden bed with just one layer of blanket as the mattress when, in early 1995, my back began to hurt. I ignored it at first thinking I might have slept in a wrong position, but then the pain got worse and was hurting even more when I breathed. I thought something was up as I also had a fever in the evening, although the following morning I would be fine, as if nothing had happened. Yet around three in the afternoon, I would again become feverish and quite ill. My body temperature was ninety-nine degrees Fahrenheit (37.2°C) and the pain in my upper back got seriously worse, so I began to worry. Although I was not coughing, I lost a significant amount weight and thought this had to be tuberculosis.

I decided that it was no longer working to take paracetamol for the fever and asked to see the medical officer for women prisoners, Dr. Lei Lei Win. She did not believe my diagnosis and told me to take antibiotics. Yet the pain in my back got so bad that I was also finding it very difficult to breathe. The next day my request to have my lungs x-rayed was rejected. She was the wife of a military officer and was only familiar with hospital administration and conventional treatment but had no experience in diagnostics. The problem was that she was the doctor and I was the patient. Finally, she asked the opinion of the current head of the prison hospital. The previous head was a Karen man and I had a lot of respect for him. The current head was my lecturer who had taught anatomy during my second year at med school.

After listening through the stethoscope and learning that I was not coughing he said, "It might not be tuberculosis at all. It could be accessory nerve neuritis. Take a full dose of dexamethasone." This disorder is a swelling of a major nerve within the core nerve system and it happens to one out of one thousand people. What made it worse was that the medication he prescribed lessened the swelling of the major nerve by deliberately suppressing my immune system. This medication would cause more problems and increase the risk of spreading infection if what I had was tuberculosis, so I did not dare to take the medication he prescribed.

Although my experience as a doctor was merely two years, I could tell that it was definitely tuberculosis; however, I had no evidence. After three or four days, I informed them that my fever had not gone down, the pain in my back was still there, and I was still getting a fever in the evenings. My whole head would be soaking wet with perspiration all through the night, and I was losing weight at an alarming rate and had difficulty breathing. Finally, they promised they would write a report and send a request to higher authorities for me to have my lungs x-rayed.

The prison administration office was a ten-minute walk from my cell but it took them two weeks to give permission for me to have a lung x-ray at the prison hospital. Having suffered from a fever and pain in my back for such a long time, it was extremely exhausting for me to walk even the short distance to the hospital. I asked if I could see the x-ray but was not allowed to. "We will send it to the specialist at Insein General Hospital's x-ray department, and you will be told the result when it comes back," I was informed. I was sure I had tuberculosis and did not want this disease to be prolonged. I would have even preferred to find out that it really was accessory nerve neuritis. Yet I had to wait. I kept taking paracetamol and other painkillers to reduce my fever and pain and had to wait another ten days.

"We got the x-ray result back—you're right, it's tuberculosis. That's very strange because you're not coughing at all. Anyhow, here's the prescription so you can ask your family to buy the medication. We will talk more when you get it," said Dr. Lei Lei Win. By the way she talked it was as if it was not their fault for the misdiagnosis but mine, since I failed to cough. She did not seem happy that I was right. She was not even aware that I was hoping to be wrong. Yet I would have to wait longer to get the medication as my family's prison visit—when I could give them the prescription—would not be for another ten days. They would then come back the next day to the prison office to deliver the medicine. The prison administration's view was that since it was my fault for getting infected, it was the responsibility of my family to take care of it. The prison could not even provide enough of the cheap, made-in-China paracetamol, let alone something like tuberculosis medicine. I passed more days with evening fever and pain before the medicine reached the hand of the doctor.

"Here's your medicine, but you can't take it right now. You have to take tetracycline first for two weeks. I will take this back for now," she said, holding up the packet of tuberculosis medication which my parents had brought to the prison on the same day as their visit. Normally I would have snatched that packet from her but there were other women prisoners nearby who were enjoying privileges from this doctor to have their cells open the whole day on her recommendation that they were at risk of stroke if locked in the whole time, so they would have been ready to protect her. I tried my best to talk to her in a normal tone but I knew it was icy when I said, "The modern treatment for TB is to take the medication right away, to take tetracycline before that is an old-fashioned method. I have the right to keep this medicine and take it because it was my parents who sent it and I know how to treat TB as I am also a doctor." She did not back off even then and took the packet away, saying she had not entered it in the list of items sent in from outside. I was able to start my treatment for tuberculosis only over a month after knowing for sure I was infected.

My fever did not go down, maybe because I had gone too long without proper treatment. In prison, those who wanted to be free and would try anything to get that freedom were dubbed "freedom loony." There were prisoners who acted out in various ways in their desperation to be freed, or those who feigned all sorts of illness to get sympathy, privileges or attention, so the doctor and some guards wanted to show that I belonged to this category. But I really was losing a lot of weight, my complexion was ashen, and I was panting for breath—it was apparent I suffered most from shortness of breath. Since I was never very healthy I used to ignore it, but this time, my fever would not go down despite my taking medicine. The prison matron and nurse took my temperature, yet they seemed disbelieving. I was left exhausted after making the slightest movement, so Ma Don and Ma Chuu had to help me when I could no longer wash my own clothes. Also, I could no longer stand by the door for the nightly chat with Ma Chuu.

Our nightly chats had taken some effort as we had to almost shout, but before I fell ill we had faithfully stuck to this routine. Ma Don sometimes joined in, but mostly she listened. We talked about our childhood, relatives, movies we had seen, and books we had read. Ma Chuu and Ma Don continued after I could no longer join in, but I would lie on my bed and listen and say something if I wanted to. They were worried about me but always happy to hear my voice. I often tried to crack a joke, so Daw Ohn Mya and Daw Nyunt even teased, "Aw, our sickly patient can still laugh." I responded, "Don't you know? The main character of Ekyar Kway[1] is named Frail Hercules!" My mind was still strong like Hercules but my body was feeble, like a wet rag.

Despite taking medicines, I grew worse, but getting "tonics" from Ma Chuu still kept my spirits high. I felt very bad for my parents, because in their old age one son was abroad while the other son and their daughter were both in jail. On top of this, I was sick. They were exhausted both mentally and physically, yet they would without fail make the long trip on a crowded bus, weighed down by heavy loads, to visit us. They never showed how tired they were but tried to lift my spirits with their encouragement. They still did whatever I asked of them and my spirit remained strong like "Hercules" only because of them. I told them that my prison cell was like my mother's womb, and I was waiting for freedom, or birth from this womb, while I was surviving from day to day on the nourishment they brought. The prison visits were like an umbilical cord that supplied me with all I needed, including their deep love. Although that womb was rather small, my heart and spirit grew in strength because of them.

---

1. Ekyar Kway is a writer who usually writes comedy and satire.

In February 1995, the former Prime Minister U Nu passed away and some students were arrested and sent to Insein after participating in some protests at his funeral. On March 15, U Tin Oo was released. Then Daw Kyi Kyi was taken out to be questioned and there was hope that she would be released, and some were hoping I would be too. I longed to be freed, but my biggest wish was to get well, as I was getting very weak: this Hercules could not even walk the five minutes to the visitation room to meet her parents. By the time I got there my chest would heave like ancient bellows, and I would be unable to utter a word. My parents were heartbroken to see me like that so I asked to be brought out ten minutes before my parents came in. Later, it got to the point where two female prisoners had to carry me to see my parents. Even then, I would still be breathless when I got to the visiting room. The tuberculosis bacteria had had plenty of time to grow inside me, so the medication was not able to fight the microbes off easily. I had to entreat my parents not to worry about me. I even thought it was good that I got tuberculosis while in prison and not outside because if that were the case I would have had no time to spare with all the things I needed to do—I might have to take a leave of absence from the hospital, I would not be able to write, and my parents would have to tend to me constantly. In prison, at least I did not have to worry about any of this. Although I had to trouble Ma Chuu, Ma Don, and others who were near my cell, I thought it was not so bad after all. The only downside was that I was completely sick.

At that time I started to occasionally practice Vipassana meditation. Before, I did not allow myself to be idle and would chant sutras, count my beads, and reflect on the teachings of the Buddha. I now realized that I was not at peace no matter how much I chanted because I could not help but be aware of my suffering. I would notice the pain and then my mind would go back to my chanting. It went back and forth like that, so I decided to practice Vipassana meditation since it was all about awareness. I had done Vipassana meditation only a few times before and did not have any set goal; the only thing I knew was that this would give me peace of mind, and my only intention was to ease my suffering through it. The truth was that I was trying to take a shortcut without trying to understand the pain and suffering I faced. Besides, I had the attitude of never giving in, which I had gained by taking "tonics." Also it was a place where unless I was resisting something, nothing would go my way, so I felt no self-pity for what I was going through. In other words, out of the necessity of the situation, I *had* to be tough.

Increasingly it began to seem like I was married to the fever. Normally, I would have stopped the two types of medication after two months and changed to another two. The problem was that even after two months, my fever would still not go down and the pain in my upper back returned as soon as I changed the medication. This time the doctors readily agreed to have my chest x-rayed and the diagnosis was "reactivation of pulmonary tuberculosis." Great! What could I do? I stopped the medication I was on and ordered another dose of quality medicine from a reputable company. A physician at the Insein General Hospital decided that I should take a cocktail of four different tuberculosis medicines for a month. However, I got another problem: my period became irregular and I began to get cramps, too. It looked like the hormone level in my body was being altered.

I could not even take good care of myself, and my period seemed to come and go at its own whim, either gushing out or stopping completely, so I again had to see the doctor. This time too she did not accept my explanation that I'd had an ultrasound taken before I was arrested and that the diagnosis was endometriosis—a growth of abnormal tissue outside the uterus. She asked me to show her that ultrasound result as proof and said she would only believe it after seeing it. My parents tried their best but could not find that piece of paper (which was only the size of the palm of a person's hand) as the MIs had already ransacked my room, which had been a mess even before that. So again I was thought to be making scenes just to get sympathy or attention. Yet everyone in my cellblock could see the pain I was suffering during my periods.

Actually the doctor had hinted through a guard that she would make my life easy if I bribed her. I replied that I had resisted corruption all my life and that I was not prepared to bribe anyone in prison either. Thus I got no consideration of my condition from her and I continued to wrestle with my pain. I was not the wimpy type to be calling for help when I got sick, but they could all hear or see me burping continuously and could see I was in a serious condition. Everyone who came to look at me knew exactly what I was going through, and the guards also became very worried. Only then did the doctor say she would write a letter to the authorities to have me checked by a gynecologist from Insein General Hospital. It was yet another waiting game.

In about ten days, the gynecologist came to see me in prison and advised me to have hormone replacement therapy after we discussed my condition. I thus started to take Primolut-N (norethisterone), yet my period was still irregular and I was still feverish. After a month of it, my condition became severe; I threw up whatever I ate or drank. Then I thought of liver damage, which could be a side effect of the tuberculosis medication and could also be compounded by the hormone treatment that I was on. I noticed that my liver was not functioning well and thus I was vomiting most of the time. While working at the Muslim Free Hospital I had seen patients with the same symptoms, so I appealed to the women's doctor-in-charge that I first needed intravenous feeding as I could no longer eat orally—otherwise I would not survive if I kept taking these medications without enough food. Second, I wanted to have a liver function test at a lab outside and would ask my parents' help for it: the prison need not arrange it or pay at all but they had to get my blood to my parents; then I would discuss and revisit the treatment with my general practitioner and gynecologist after the results came back.

Then, a bigger problem: the doctor thought it could not be my liver because she said my skin was not yellow, implying that I was lying. Soon after, it took me a while even to go to bathe because I was vomiting all the time. I often had to stop on my way back and lie down on the bench in front of our block before walking to my cell. Only then did she decide to have my blood tested—but in the prison lab, so there was no liver function test. I could make out by looking at the little long tube in the nurse's hand that it was for HIV. It was natural for any doctor to have a patient whose fever would not go away tested for HIV, but it was not accepted procedure and not ethical to do so without my knowledge and consent. I did not say anything since I had very little strength to protest, so I simply indicated that I knew what it was for and waited for the result.

Chapter 11

Staying Alive

My condition could not wait for the HIV result, as my health deteriorated further in early June. Still feverish and vomiting, I began to see the prison cell as hopeless as a desert I had to cross. I asked for someone in my cell block, whatever they might be—prostitute, murderer—to care for me just so that I could have someone to nurse me during the night. I said I would take care of food, toiletries, and other necessities for her. The test results came back in two days—negative. Two benches were put in front of my cell for a guard and a nurse to sleep on in case something happened during the night, though the key to my cell was kept in the main office, which was a fifteen minutes' walk away.

I moved the waste basin nearer to my bed. The guard and the nurse could just look on with pity when I was vomiting into it during the night. Once when they could only see the whites of my eyes (which I only learned later as I was no longer aware of anything by that time) as I was near passing out, they were asking anxiously, "Should we go and ask for key from the office? Should we call the doctor?" Ma Chuu and Ma Don urged them frantically to do something and were constantly asking them about my condition. I had decided by this time to let it be and just shook my head at whoever asked whatever question. Reaching for drinking water or cleaning up after I threw up became a huge battle that I had to struggle to wage. It did not matter how others looked on with sympathy; it no longer made a difference to me.

It helped to know I could not rely on anyone but myself for survival. I had to find all the strength in me to get myself out of this danger. My only pride as a political prisoner at that time was that I would survive and live by my own principles. I was determined not to betray myself and to continue fighting for my political ideology and beliefs; I would resist as much as I could to find a solution through discussion and dialogue if the authorities rejected my demands, but I was certain that I would never surrender. I valued freedom, including the freedom of expression, and wanted to live my life without having to rely on anybody and without fearing anyone. Thus the only thought I had was to rely on myself and no one else.

On June 7, my condition got so bad that my fever was high, I was either vomiting or belching, and there was also spotting even though it was not time for my period yet. With the cleaners' help, I placed the drinking-water pot, the washing-up basin, and the covered waste basin around my bed; it looked like a Burmese drum circle. Then, some guards arrived at my cell, started to pack my belongings, and said they were going to send me to Insein General Hospital. At that time, in my mind I could only think of the writer Maung Thaw Ka who was sent to Rangoon General Hospital in early June 1991 and passed away on June 11. Ma Chuu and Ma Don were happy to hear that I would be sent to the hospital; Ma Chuu asked me what she could do for me so I said, "Ma Chuu, sing Khin One's song 'I Am Leaving Now' because just like that song I am going now. But I don't know when I will come back here." Ma Chuu sang that song for me while half crying: "I'm leaving now . . . as the road carries me away . . . far . . . away . . ."

Although I was still in the prison compound, I was on this road leading to the outside world, so it was good enough to make me feel as if I were already beyond the prison walls. It was dusk so there were no visitors around. The truck I was in passed Insein Market and headed to the hospital. I could not even feel anything special about the air or smells, as I was extremely nauseated. It could well be because this was not a trip that would set me free from prison, but I hoped that it would set me free from my very real pain. We reached Insein General Hospital in the dark. There would not be any chance for me to know a taste of freedom as I was still in the white prison garb upon arriving at a familiar environment where I used to be in a white duty coat with a stethoscope draped around my neck. To strangers who saw me in prison garb and escorted by guards, I was only an ill criminal coming for treatment at a public hospital. I walked in feeling embarrassed to be seen like this but also wondering why I should care, while bearing my pain with every breath. I also pulled my mind toward the Buddha, the dharma, and the sangha as I walked slowly to where I was led. So my mind was strained in many different directions.

I was registered and the prison staff handed me over to the policewomen, as it was no longer their jurisdiction. I was admitted to the gynecology ward and was to be given an IV drip by the two nurses on duty, who were quite friendly. When the two nurses left me for about ten minutes, I quickly communicated with patients near me by using hand signals and gestures and gave my name and home phone number so they could contact my family. By then, they already knew I was a political prisoner as well as a medical doctor. All gestured back to show their willingness. After months of having been robbed of meeting "normal" people, their smiles already made me feel better. Not long after that, the two nurses returned and prepared to handcuff me to the hospital bed as they were going to have their meal. A young lady doctor stopped them from doing it and said, "Oh, wait! There is a private room available. Although we can only move you there with the Medical Superintendent's approval I will explain it to him, so go ahead and put her there. You can just lock the door when you go to eat and so there'll be no need to handcuff her." The two policewomen readily obeyed. I was thinking I could have communicated more with the others in the public ward, but I was glad not to be handcuffed. As I left, all the patients in the ward gestured to me not to worry. I felt better after the IV and was able to sleep that night.

I woke up quite early the next morning—probably because I was accustomed by now to getting up at 5:00 a.m. I tried to make friends with the policewomen while I went to wash my face and freshen up. Like any other public hospital, the baths and toilets were extremely old but smelling of antiseptic. On my way to the toilet, other patients showed their support and gave me smiles and nods as if they were saying, "Get well soon." Some gave me a thumbs up.

I felt as if my whole body were lifted up with delight when I heard "Good morning" from a couple of nurses as they walked past. "Good morning" was the greeting that I had heard many times each morning when I was volunteering at the Muslim Free Hospital. For nearly two years I had not heard this greeting, a normal practice between nurses and doctors. The words sounded so fresh and joyful to me now, like a blessing: I was revisiting the experience of good mornings in freedom while I was at Insein General Hospital, and not as a doctor. Immediately I replied, "Good morning," with rising happiness. Then I was overcome with tears when another nurse said, "Good morning, Doctor." Emotions of both joy and yearning overwhelmed me; I felt that the "I" who said good morning in reply was no longer the "I" who was locked up in cell number three in Insein Prison. I was surprised to hear myself saying good morning as if it were a habitual event, but I did not know that this would end sooner than I expected.

On the way back to my hospital bed I bumped into an old classmate, Dr. Thida Oo. The policewomen who were escorting me did not say anything while I chatted with her. Although she was rushing to see her younger brother who was about to have his appendix removed she asked me what I would like to eat and said she would come back right away. At about half past eight gynecologist Dr. Daw Khin Than Tin arrived to examine me; she was my lecturer when I was in medical school. I explained the whole history of my illness and what was happening now. We mainly discussed the blood test I needed for my liver and what to do next if it was not functioning well. We also discussed my fever, which had lasted for nearly six months. Then a phone call came for her: it was from the medical superintendent of the hospital, to whom the chief warden and Dr. Lei Lei Win had come in person to demand that I be discharged immediately and taken back to prison. We could not understand this and were surprised as well as disappointed. Dr. Daw Khin Than Tin explained that she had not even checked me yet, but the superintendent asked her to just do it quickly and have me write and sign "Discharged by Request." The medical superintendent could not resist the demands from the chief warden and the prison doctor. I had no wish to say anything more; I assured my teacher there was no need to get upset and just requested that she check on me in the prison.

As I prepared to pack up my belongings, my parents along with their friend Aunty Yin arrived with packets of food for me, their faces full of worry. My mother nearly broke down when she learned I was to be returned to prison, my father looked very dejected, and Aunty Yin looked anxious. A prison truck was ready to take me back, and standing around there were the chief warden, the women's doctor-in-charge, and a person I thought must be the medical superintendent of Insein General Hospital. The policewomen on duty were there, too, looking confused. All the women patients from the wards were looking out at me with sympathetic faces but did not seem to realize what was going on. In the middle of this, my friend Dr. Thida Oo came back with packets of fried noodles. On seeing that, the faces of the chief warden and other officials lost their composure, and the women's doctor-in-charge looked very upset. I said farewell to my mother, father, Aunty Yin, and Thida Oo, telling them not to worry.

Then, with strength rising out of adrenaline, I turned to the chief warden and women's doctor-in-charge and said, "It's your wish to take me back to prison without getting any treatment. Therefore, whatever happens to me will have nothing to do with this hospital and doctors, and nothing to do with me, either: it's all on you, completely. I warn you, this is your responsibility. Remember that!" I climbed up the steps of truck with all my bags. I waved to my parents and said, "Please come and see me as usual on the next visit day." There were only the lower-ranking staff and me in the truck. The chief warden and others followed in an air-conditioned van.

Back in the prison, Ma Chuu and the others could not believe their eyes when they saw me, looking deathly sick but angry, back in prison less than twenty-four hours after saying goodbye. I took a much-needed rest after putting away my things; I had no strength left to explain. Before I could fully regain my breath a nurse came to tell me that I had to keep all my medicines in the prison clinic. They would not accept my refusal. Then the matron came over and told me that this order came straight from the women's doctor-in-charge. She also told me that they would bring me the medicine whenever I needed to take it. I could not accept this; my parents bought these medicines for me and I often shared them with others in my block. I could not accept that I must put all my medicine in their hands, because they had not even given me any effective treatment.

Then the women's doctor-in-charge herself came and told me sternly that since I had said it was their responsibility if anything happened to me, she had the responsibility to be in charge of my medicine. They forcibly tried to pry away my medicine basket from my grip, and I used all my strength to hold on to it. When a guard approached me, I said her, "Confiscate these medicines if you dare. Then I won't take any medicine, I won't eat, I won't even drink. And I won't stay in that cell. Just try, if you dare—let's see how much a person like me, who's had a fever for straight six-months and weighs eighty pounds, can take it." So saying I stalked out of my cell, my steps swift with anger and my body shaking like a leaf, while Ma Chuu called out anxiously to be careful. I went out and lay down on the guards' bench. Both the doctor and guard fled back to the clinic without saying anything more. When the cleaners approached me I told them to leave me alone.

I immediately tried to do Vipassana meditation, which I had not been doing regularly for some time. The main thing was that I wanted to prepare myself, as I knew I must not face them again with this boiling rage. I needed to be calm and tried to be by focusing on the feeling of touch at the tip of my nostril as I breathed in and out. Vipassana had often rescued me from situations like this. Just as I expected, within fifteen minutes, I heard the sound of "Line up! Line up!" I sat up on the bench. The iron door of our block swung open and a few uniformed men walked determinedly toward me. Some wore stern looks as if stalking prey and some wore friendly looks as if to manipulate me. There were many stars on their epaulettes; it looked as if all the high-ranking officers of the prison were coming to confront me. Among them, I saw the head of the prison hospital, but I did not see the women's doctor-in-charge.

"What do you want?" asked Chief Warden U Tha Oo.

I bluntly answered, "One, I can't allow my medicines to be taken away. Two, I won't take any treatment from the women's doctor-in-charge and would like my case to be handled by another doctor."

They then told me the same thing—that this was the result of me saying that whatever happened to me was on them.

"It's nonsense. I was at the hospital but got no treatment whatsoever."

"It's an order from above. We can't do anything."

"Then what is this about taking my medicines away?"

My voice was still harsh despite the fact that I was trying to control my anger. I pulled all my attention again to the tip of my nostril to concentrate on my breath, and tried harder to calm myself.

"That's because you might use these medicines to kill yourself. You could do it, too, because you understand everything about medication," said Deputy Chief Warden U Ohn Lwin in a gentle tone.

Good, I thought, *I have finally found someone I can talk to in a civilized manner.*

"Oh gosh . . . no . . . Uncle." I deliberately addressed him as uncle as I wanted to get on informal terms with him. I wanted our interaction to be friendly and thus gain his empathy.

"If I wanted to die, even if you left me, pardon me, naked in my cell, I could still keep hitting my head against the wall to kill myself. My problem here is to stay alive and well, not to kill myself. I don't want to die. Having had no effective treatment for my illness, I am asking for these two things in order to live, Uncle." My voice became calmer.

Suicide is illegal by law, and according to the teachings of the Buddha the consequences of this act would end a single life but would not release me from samsara, the recurring cycle of life. I had never even thought of doing so and would never do so, ever, and I was astounded at how they had come up with this idea.

"Actually, what you are putting me through will surely kill me, Uncle. That's why I said that the prison must take responsibility for any consequences of me not getting treatment."

"Don't talk too much. You're not well," said the head of the prison hospital. I felt sorrow creep up on me.

"Please understand—have you ever had a fever for six months? Have your children ever suffered like this?" Tears filled my eyes as I said those words. I thought, *No, no, I must remember Vipassana. I must remember!* But since I was not in regular practice I could not remain strong and in no time tears were rolling down on my cheeks.

He tried to console me by saying, "Oh, my dear, there is a state slogan: 'Everyone must be healthy by the year 2000.' You'll get better."

My tears dried up completely.

"That's not right. It's an incorrect interpretation. The original phrase is 'Health for all by the year 2000.' It is impossible for everyone to be healthy. It's obvious even from a mentally handicapped person's point of view. The real meaning is that everyone should have health services and proper care by the year 2000. 'Everyone' means rich or poor, any race or religion, and prisoners or whoever they are—they should all have access to good health care. The only thing I am asking of you is to give me proper and systematic treatment. I think you can all understand that a doctor like me would not want to go to a hospital as a prisoner. If I get proper treatment here in jail, I have no reason to complain. If I can help it I really do not want to go to any hospital. The problem is that a doctor like me knows very well whether care given in this prison clinic is enough or not and proper or not. I know how to treat myself to be alive. That's why I am asking you to give me that kind of treatment."

I sounded like a lecturer talking to her class.

"Alright then, we understand that, we won't take away your medicine. However, why do you have to refuse treatment from women's doctor-in-charge here? She's crying over there—she's really upset," said the deputy chief warden. The other officers were also beginning to relax.

"Please think about it, Uncle. It is very upsetting for me as a doctor to refuse another doctor's treatment, but this is a matter of life and death. Her treatment is seriously risking my life; she has never accepted my diagnosis, so if we go on like this I won't be alive for long. Hear me out. Uncle, can I ask you this—what would you do if your doctor said you had only six months to live?"

By this time all of us were at ease and the situation was no longer tense.

U Ohn Lwin responded lightly by saying, "Oh, who, me? I'd go to all the places I'd like to go and eat everything I like." They all had slight smiles on their faces.

"If I were you, I wouldn't do that." I smiled, as if about to disclose a secret.

"Why, what would you do?"

"I would ask a second opinion from another doctor. That doctor may not tell me I will die in six months."

I heard some subdued laugher from the others, but Deputy Chief Warden U Ohn Lwin burst out laughing.

"That's all, Uncle. I would like to get a second opinion from another doctor who won't say I am going to die in six months. Let's do it this way," I turned to the head of the prison hospital and continued, "You'll be the one to continue checking my condition. If so, I will accept it."

"Let me say, Ma Thida, you're the one who's free." The deputy chief warden uttered these words with his eyes lowered, and sighed softly.

Ma Thida, you're the one who's free. Ma Thida, you're the one who's free. Those words echoed in my ears. Although I knew what he meant I asked anyway, "What do you mean, Uncle? Are you saying I—locked up behind these doors in a twelve-by-twelve-foot cell for twenty-three hours, fifteen minutes a day—am the one who's free?"

"You can say what you think, but we are civil servants. Please understand us." His voice faded as he spoke. The others were so quiet one could have heard a pin drop. I knew I should not push further.

I turned to the head of the prison hospital. "I would like to make a request. Can you write an official report saying that a female prisoner is concerned that her life is in danger and has refused to get treatment from the doctor on duty and instead requests that you treat her . . . and therefore you will be taking up this matter . . . something like that?"

"Alright, I will do something about this. Right now, *thamee,*[1] you're tired. You should eat and then rest. We are all tired as well, so let's go."

---

1. *Thamee* (daughter) is a term of politeness used by older people even toward strangers on the street.

"Yes, I agree. But meanwhile I will not consult the women's doctor. When I see the official letter from you saying you have transferred my case to yourself, I will only consult you and other doctors, not her."

"Alright, alright!"

And with that, they all left.

The guards looked relieved. I wanted to share the food my parents and Thida Oo had given me. My fellow inmates wanted to hear my story of that short period of freedom in the outside hospital. But for me, I could not wait to share my other kind of "freedom" with them: *Ma Thida, you're the one who's free.*

Remembering the deputy chief warden's words, I realized that I had never let go of my freedom of expression in jail.

Chapter 12

Birthday Parties and Other Things

The next day, the results for my liver and HIV blood test finally came back. The HIV result was negative and the liver's bilirubin reading was twenty-three times higher than normal. Only then did the whole medical staff of the prison understand and realize their mistake; they had thought it was not my liver as I did not turn yellow. I felt calm at last, as my diagnosis had been accepted. The next day, Major Soe Nyunt from Military Intelligence came to ask about my health. I told him everything, including the blood test results I had received the previous day.

He then asked, "Is there anything else that you're not happy with?" I replied, "This is prison, not a hotel. Since the day I entered the prison gate up till today there is nothing to be happy about here." So he just walked away. In fact, "this is prison, not a hotel" was a phrase used by the prison staff every time a prisoner complained about anything; all I did was throw it back at them. After all that drama, I was given an IV every day, and the gynecologist Dr. Daw Khin Than Tin visited me in the prison. She decided that I should stop hormone therapy temporarily due to my liver problem. We agreed that my immune system was very weak and that taking all these medicines could completely stop my period. The physician also stopped giving me one of four medicines that I was taking for tuberculosis as it was giving my liver too much trouble. Though still feverish, I started to feel better. On June 29, the official letter about the transfer of duty from the women's doctor to the head of the prison hospital was issued. I heard that on the same day she submitted a request for transfer to another place. I felt sympathy for her.

At that time, a young university student who was in prison for drugs was put in a cell near mine as punishment[1] as she always came back drunk or high from her court appointments. She told me how easy it was to buy drugs at the police station where they were kept and how she sneaked them into prison. She even told me she'd never had any intention of stopping her drug habit since the first time she took them but it had turned her into someone who would do anything and everything to get money to buy drugs. She was not there for long. The next one to be put in that cell had been charged with fraud and was from a prison in another town but was brought to Yangon to be a witness in a corruption case against prison staff there, as she was the whistleblower. Naturally, the staff disliked her. Here, I was getting a chance to learn about various people with different characters and manners. However, I can only vaguely recall those I met during the time I was ill.

I began to feel better and I also cut off my long hair with the warden's permission as it was getting difficult to shampoo. Prison does not easily allow for changes in appearance and we did not know who reported it, but the warden was asked to submit a written explanation as to why she had allowed it. Since my request was rational, she had allowed it and even brought me a prisoner who knew how to cut hair. I felt bad for her situation, but for me it was fabulous as my head was lighter and I felt freer with my short crop. During that time, an astrologer who was being charged with fraud—for her role as an accessory in someone's case—became a cleaner in our compound. She said I should be careful with what I said or else my time in prison could be longer, but I did not take her seriously.

Every year on July 7, no guards were allowed to go out during their shifts and they were all on alert: that day is the anniversary of the student uprising of 1962, when many students were killed and the Students' Union building was blown up. This year, strangely enough, two criminals under a combined sentence of one hundred years for murder and many other felonies escaped on that very day.

---

1. Prisoners living in the general population hall are sometimes put in cells as punishment.

Over the space of many days, they had rubbed salt and fish sauce over their shackles and the bars of their cell, which in time became rusty and corroded. That morning, while working on the prison farm, they had broken their shackles just enough that they stayed on but could be removed easily later, and had escaped early the next morning around 4 a.m. The whole prison was in turmoil, and everyone was worried that salt and fish sauce would be banned. Whenever rules were broken or anyone came down with a sudden illness, a blanket order would be issued—for example, banning the type of food that the sick prisoner had eaten, disregarding the fact that the same type of food had come from different kitchens. However, in a place like prison where you have no rights, everyone had to bear the consequences of any wrong that others had done. Nonetheless, we in our cell block would not have been able to use salt and fish sauce to break out since our cell doors were made of wood.

It could well be that these cells had wooden doors because they were meant for women prisoners who were not considered strong enough to break out. Yet I heard of how a prostitute with some mental problems had battered the door down with her body; I had seen the repaired door. She was in and out of prison, so she knew everything about the guards. If she thought they were going to do something to her she would strip off her clothes right in front of everyone and yell out—in colorful language—personal details of the guards. The guards usually gave up at that point and left her alone. Actually, she was just trying to protect herself in the best way she knew in a place where injustice was normal. Prisons become places where criminals are made to think that to defend their rights and protect themselves they must do anything possible, even if it is wrong or unfair.

On the morning of July 10, Major Soe Nyunt from the MI came. As soon as he saw me he asked, "Your family submitted an appeal for you, didn't they?"

I was caught unawares, not knowing what my mother and father might have done without telling me. I was appalled at the thought of it, but I found out later that my parents had actually done no such thing.

"I don't know anything about it, but since I am still under their care they have every right to decide for me. I can't tell them what to do and what not to do. As for me, I can't give any promises," I responded promptly.

Then he said, "Is it correct that you are sending letters to embassies from prison? Did you ask the guards to do it for you?"

It was unbelievable; so I said, "Yeah, really? Ask your own guards. Ask them what exists beyond Insein Market. Even if I asked the chief warden he would not be able to do it properly." He laughed uneasily at that, and although he seemed somewhat upset at my answer he knew it was true, so he was just nodded.

I did not say this without reason. Once, a guard who was a few years younger than me said, "It was so embarrassing; the other day I was assigned to escort a prisoner to a public hospital. To tell you the truth, I virtually grew up in Bago Prison as my father was working there, and then I got this job here in Yangon. The only places I know are Insein Prison and the market. I was so happy to go out, so I was gawking at everything I saw. Then I saw this huge house with so many clothes hanging on the veranda. I said to the sergeant who was sitting next to me that this must be a very rich person's residence, they have so many clothes. Then the sergeant said, 'That's Bogyoke Market,[2] not a house.' The prisoner with us also laughed at me. It was so embarrassing that I didn't even know Bogyoke Market."

Next, the major asked, "What will you do if you are released? What do you want to see happen?" He tried to wind me up some more by acting as if he were truly interested.

He sat up straight when I said, "I want to be more than a doctor." He relaxed and sat down when I continued, "I am also going to be a writer, and I want to be a surgeon and get a post-graduate degree in that field."

However, he was not fully satisfied. He asked bluntly, "Would you continue being a political activist?"

---

2. The biggest market in Yangon, also called Scott Market.

He frowned when I answered, "I believe that even when a woman is cooking in her kitchen she is involved in politics, so how can I answer your question?"

Then he asked me abruptly, "What is your political goal?"

I said, "I just want to be a good citizen—nothing more, nothing less." He looked puzzled at first, but then he smiled.

After that he just asked trivial questions like why I cut my hair, and then left. I told Ma Chuu all about it when I got back to my cell. The next morning I learned that Ma Suu had been released from house arrest the previous afternoon. I then recalled the astrologer's words warning me to be careful of what I said or else I would have to stay longer in prison. What could I have done? I had no psychic powers and could not have foreseen it. I did not realize he was sounding me out. How careful was I at saying things? Before he had even asked anything of me I had declared firmly that I couldn't promise anything. How much did I want to practice my right to express myself freely? How far had I gone with this right, without any fear of having to serve my full term? Fearless me then began to embrace one fear, at last.

∼

At this time the world was in chaos. A massive genocide took place between the Hutu and Tutsi races in Rwanda. In South Africa, however, there emerged the very first elections in which all racial groups were able to participate. Nelson Mandela, who had been imprisoned for twenty-seven years, became the first black president of South Africa. Israel and Jordan signed a peace treaty, and in early August the people of Cuba began to protest against Fidel Castro's government, which had held power since 1959.

∼

After Ma Suu was released from house arrest, hopes were high for other political prisoners. Yet in my heart I had no hope for myself since I knew I had already settled my fate. The most important thing for me was my health; my fever began to go down in August, I stopped vomiting, and my breathlessness got better too. However, my period stopped completely after I discontinued the hormone treatment. The doctor and I also decided that I should be taking two types of tuberculosis medication for another four months. Around that time, it became harder to smuggle in reading material, so Ma Chuu and I turned to religious books. It was the time of the diamond jubilee of Rangoon University, and my urge to write grew stronger; I wanted to write about the relationship between the Convocation Hall and me. I smuggled in papers and ball-point pens with Ma Chuu's help, and finally I wrote it and smuggled it out to my family with a message to keep it safe at home.

In early September, my father told me that one of his friends had asked him if I was living in China, and my father had said, "No, she's in prison." My family and I thought it was funny. However, I received very different news in connection with China in a week's time, when Ma Chuu had her visit: my twenty-ninth birthday was celebrated at the Fourth World Conference on Women in Beijing.[3] I was not sure whether to believe it or not; I felt happy and sad at the same time but learned nothing more. My parents also heard about the honor, and that the delegation members from Myanmar were all men. I did not know whether to laugh or cry when I heard that; the government always sent men to attend any seminar, including even this women's conference. What a joke!

I thought of how my birthday party was celebrated by the international community while I was sitting in a twelve-by-twelve-foot prison cell under a dim, orangey light. They had not forgotten me! It was bittersweet. What was made more certain to me was that my time in prison was not in vain.

About that time, a young Thai woman was put in our cellblock. Her name was Pan; she was born in Phuket to a Burmese father and a Thai

---

3. After my release I learned that the Chinese government had not allowed them to order a birthday cake and that I also had received three sheets of paper wishing me well and signed by all nongovernmental representatives attending the conference.

mother. She was arrested after her father brought her into Myanmar illegally because she wanted to go to the Shwedagon Pagoda. We told her she could pray to the Shwedagon from the plane as we all knew she would be deported. She was about sixteen years old and had been sentenced to six months in Meikthila Jail; after serving there for five months she was brought to Yangon. Meikthila Prison did not provide sufficient water, so she was suffering badly from scabies, especially on her arms. If she had to scoop up water by dipping her hands in the water it might infect all of us, so I got busy bathing her and applying ointment.

Eventually she got better, and she said I could become rich if I wanted to practice in Thailand. She had learned a bit of Burmese while in Meikthila Prison, and often request Ma Chuu to sing by saying, "Elder Sister Chuu, sing, sing." Her favorite song was an original Burmese tune, and she even learned to sing it. I learned some Thai from her, too. About a week after that, another Thai girl was put in her cell after the evening lineup. I passed some food to her through a cleaner of our block. My door and theirs were near, so we did not need to shout. I then heard a knock on my door and it was Pan; I wanted to laugh when she asked "Elder Sister, who do you like more? Me or her? You have to tell me or I will not give this food to her." Every time I asked Pan what she wanted to do when she grew up she would reply, "I want to be Miss Thailand." She also liked to wear the Burmese *htamein*. Before she left, she felt terrible when she saw I had been infected with her scabies, but she would also tease me about my skin condition as hers was completely cured by that time.

Depending upon the goodwill of the guard on duty I could give necessary treatment to my fellow inmates with the medication that I had gotten from my parents. I especially took care of those who were on cleaning duty as they were jailed for prostitution or theft and had no one to visit them. They had nothing to eat except prison food, and some could not even take a bucket bath as they had no extra clothes to bathe in, so we shared our food or gave them clothes, and I was able to do extra good work by giving them some health care. There were no protective gloves so I had to use plastic bags instead while carefully and thoroughly cleaning their sores with spirits and Eusol before applying ointment. With tears in their eyes, they would thank me for not only giving food and clothes but also providing treatment. One of them cried with happiness as she had never been cared for by anyone before. Other women who were onlookers when I treated these women could not believe it; they said they had never seen any doctor like me before. That made me consider what had happened to the role of doctors in my country. I felt choked with the thought that there could be many people who had died without getting medical attention.

Daw Ohn Mya's complexion began to turn yellow. I was worried that at her age, if it were not inflammation of her liver, it could well mean she had gallstones. I wanted her to have an ultrasound since she complained of having pain in her stomach too. However, the female medical officer decided to have her chest x-rayed so that she could see the position of the diaphragm over Daw Ohn Mya's liver and whether the liver was enlarged. The position of the liver could be felt by an external examination, but if there were gallstones, only an ultrasound could show if they were present. I was not happy that the doctor decided on an x-ray, since she would not see anything relevant from it. I realized this was not about incompetence but about avoiding the extra paperwork since an ultrasound had to be done outside. I tried to intervene but was not successful since I had already had serious problems with this doctor. Later the problem was put to rest when Daw Ohn Mya got better.

However, the way some matters were "put to rest" was very upsetting. The prison trustee put in charge as a medic in our block was a former schoolteacher in jail for fraud; and she had bribed to be in this privileged position. She was the one tasked with solving medical issues during the night despite not having any knowledge of medicine. One night, a pregnant woman began to have dyspnea, or impaired breathing, so this medic checked her blood pressure—as far as she knew how—then declared the pulse rate too fast and gave the patient four 40 mg Propranolol pills to slow it down. Apparently the woman was dead within minutes. As she was a vagrant and thus not at all important, her death went unnoticed without anyone being investigated. I found out about it much later and wondered how many people had died unnecessarily from incorrect treatments. This kind of case had nothing to do with the authorities; it had everything to do with each and every person needing to take responsibility, be accountable for their actions, and be good at what they do.

While in prison, to keep myself from forgetting, I often imagined surgical procedures step by step. During my incarceration I found myself missing my medical practice so much, especially doing surgery and caring for patients. I missed using my scalpel so much that I would take my time in carefully and neatly cutting up onions, cabbage, and roasted meats as if I were operating, using a small cutter which Ma Chuu, some other prisoners, and I had smuggled in. I practiced making knots, suturing, and threading whenever I got hold of a piece of cloth from which I could pull out threads. I could almost smell the hospital atmosphere while I was going through imaginary operations. In times like that, I could also hear noises and the voices of doctors and nurses comforting or reassuring patients and teasing one another as we went about our duties. I recalled some of the experiences in the ER. I chose to be a doctor and could never stop wanting to one wherever I am.

During that period, Madeline Albright, the US ambassador to the UN, came to see Ma Suu and met with the military leaders on her return from the Beijing conference. As usual, hopes were high in prison, but days passed and there was no amnesty for anyone. By October, the Buddhist Lent had ended yet Daw Kyi Kyi from our block, who had been interviewed early in the year, was still not released. Nothing changed. That year, we covered our windows and the opening on the door with pieces of mosquito netting as hordes of these creatures would fly in at dusk to torment us the whole night. We were not allowed to use mosquito nets, and this was the only alternative. The guards could still see into our cells—although not too clearly—so they did not object, and that gave us better chances to read. Compared to the tricks our male colleagues-in-prison were getting up to, what we were able to manage was nothing, but we still felt pretty good about it. However, Ma Chuu and I were extra careful since I was under watch as a troublemaker because of my incident with the doctor.

We had a small problem about a vacuum flask. My request to keep one in my cell was granted when my health got worse and I was having frequent stomachaches. When my family sent one in, the guards said I could not keep it with me, so I said I would stay right where the vacuum flask was put and would not go back to my cell without it, because I knew that another in our block had been allowed to keep hers. Only then was I allowed to keep it. The matter was solved smoothly because the new warden intervened; she was rational and humane. I was happy to meet such a person in this position. Her name was Daw Khin Khin Win and she ruled over her charges with equal fairness but was regarded by some as too soft because of that; they claimed that the prisoners circumstances varied from one to the next and that fairness would not work in the long run.

It was frustrating to face resistance every time I took a stand for "equal rights" because not only the prison staff but also those prisoners who had been here for a long time and who had gained certain privileges considered my actions to be driven by jealousy of their status; I was getting tired of trying to understand such thinking. Although my health was beginning to improve, my mind was in a confused state: I began to wonder whether being in jail was really not a waste of time. I saw the incredible roughness and cruel behavior of some prisoners as well as the guards, and inconceivably underhanded things done by educated prisoners.

Besides, the prison laws, which had not changed since the colonial era, were being misused for the advantage of those in power. Although I considered my time in jail as firsthand experience with an assortment of characters, which would make for great material, was it worth it, really? What final goal was I hoping to reach by standing firm for the right to freedom of expression while I had to give up all other freedoms? Was my goal, just as our goal for democracy, about being released before eighteen more years had passed? Could I not do more? Was there nothing else I could do to be free from these four walls, to be free from the bitterness and pain, and to be free from the despicable behavior of the humans I saw around me?

In the political arena, in late November Ma Suu pulled the NLD representatives from the national convention, saying that it was not in line with democratic principles. It looked as if the political situation was getting tense again.

~

In the outside world, negotiations began to end the war in Yugoslavia, and the prime minister of Israel, Yitzhak Rabin, was assassinated. The UN brought Radovan Karadzic of Bosnia to its war crimes tribunal. The world was trying to solve violent conflicts with peaceful means and had forgotten our fight for democracy. Although we were still hoping with all our hearts, the chance of having a dialogue was slim.

~

I was getting depressed with these thoughts when I received terrible news; I remember clearly it was the end of November. The authorities had been tipped off and the cells of my male colleagues were thoroughly searched, and their guards were even digging up the cement floors. Ma Chuu and I were in a panic when we heard that, because we had some books in our possession. We thought we should not waste any time as the inspection could come to our women's side at any time; we needed to remove all traces as quietly and quickly as possible. Luckily, most of the books were printed on cheap newsprint, so if soaked in water they almost dissolved and turned into pulp. Our cellblock's back wall was against the fence that separated us from the men's side, where there was an empty plot used as a garbage dump, so we rolled the damp pulp into balls and threw them over the fence into it. We could not ask any cleaners to help so we used our walking time to get rid of the literary evidence. Since one of the prisoners in our block often checked on us when we were walking by looking in a hand-held mirror, we dared not ask anyone in our block either. By the time the inspection team reached our cellblock Ma Chuu had only a few pages torn out of an English-to-Burmese dictionary and I had nothing at all.

I became extremely worried because my parents told me that Myo Myint Nyein and some others were being punished with a ban on family visits and that they had been sent to live in the cells where guard dogs used to be kept[4] after many sessions of interrogation. They had been caught with a lot of contraband such as handwritten pamphlets and copies of weekly journals and magazines, including *Time* and *Newsweek*. Many prisoners were involved, ranging in age from U Win Tin and the NLD MPs of the 1990 elections (in their late 50s; U Win Tin was slightly older) to student activists. We heard that they would all be charged, including those who had only about a month left to serve on their sentences; that to me was tragic. I also worried that if they reopened old cases it would get messy and that I might be incriminated for sending the shirt with their messages to the UN human rights conference. The end of 1995 was filled with news of terrifying events and I began to reflect even more deeply on my situation.

Every time I heard about my med-school classmates, they were studying for master's degrees, going abroad for fellowships or work, or working in public hospitals here and being transferred from place to place; their lives were springing forward. And what of my friends in the literary community? They continued to write; there were many new magazines and I noticed many talented new writers. I began to think of my dream that by the time I reached forty I would have a hospital and a mobile clinic—both of which would provide free health care—a nonprofit printing press, and an orphanage which, in my dream, would be nothing like ordinary orphanages. I had drawn plans for all three of these in detail on my wooden bed with the sharp end of a safety pin. Although I was confined to a twelve-by-twelve-foot cell for twenty-three hours and fifteen minutes a day, my health was at least good enough to keep me from dying. My speech and attitude would surely not help to shorten my sentence. If I did not daydream about each day being my last in prison, I would have to face that I would remain in prison for the next eighteen years. Even with some time off,

---

4. The German Shepherd dogs died or ran away during the 1988 prison riot. Putting humans where dogs used to be kept is a very offensive punishment.

for sure I would not be free in the twentieth century and very likely not even after ten years into the twenty-first century, when I would be nearly fifty.

Meanwhile, nothing was happening in my life. As a believer in self-reliance and a faithful supporter of freedom, all I could do was eat the food my parents brought me, suffer from ill health, and sit there watching time go by, every day, twenty-four hours a day. How could I still believe my time in jail was not in vain? Was it because of those birthday parties and support ceremonies held for me by others? So what was my contribution toward making sure it would not all be in vain, that I could survive for twenty years in a small cell? What was I doing— I, who wanted to create change on my own? Was I just sitting here, waiting for the day of my freedom? Ever a pragmatist, I said to myself, *Ma Thida, think carefully before you answer* and then proceeded to ask myself some hard questions, all of which filled me with dismay.

Chapter 13

Looking for Answers

Look at that—I, who so loved self-reliance and who wanted to stand on my own two feet all the time, was simply waiting to be released. If I had no wish to stay where I was, then what was my goal? Was my goal to sit and wait for the day of freedom? Whichever way I thought about this the answer was just that. This could not be happening! Then what else could I do? Nothing! That answer came out easily since I had taken the path of "not getting freed anytime soon" by answering the questions from Military Intelligence months ago with my eagerness to protect my rights to express myself freely. Some prisoners thought that if they were "interviewed" then it was closer to their freedom. They could give pleasing answers and sign any oath in exchange for their release, and then wait hopefully for the day. When that did not happen, I saw how crushed they were, regretting the promises they had given. One clear answer was that my freedom did not depend upon me so I had no responsibility to try for it. In that case what should I do? Should I, as usual, pray to the Buddha, count my beads and fast while I waited? That created more questions.

In fact, I have been trying to keep the Five Precepts since I was young. I have never attempted to do anything for personal gain nor have I sought an easy way out. I have always tried my best to ease the pain and anxiety of my patients with empathy and kindness. I know I would not be regarded as a model by many but I have lived my life with my own set of principles. Who was the culprit for me being jailed, in ill health, and unable to have any contact with people of my own profession?

Then I got my answer: it was my karma,[1] the result of what I had done to others in the past. I am a believer in its law of cause and effect. Therefore I did not want to go for the easy answer of pointing to the Military Intelligence, as I knew they were also the victims of this military dictatorship. What about the culprit behind my suffering? Was it the doctor who would not cooperate and would not do anything for me unless she was bribed? No. She was a victim of corruption as well. What about me? I have never seen myself as a victim. From a political point of view, the culprit of my incarceration was the military dictatorship and its system. But why did I suffer illness more than the others?

I got goosebumps with terror from the thought of having to repay all my bad deeds from previous lives. Buddhists say we cannot avoid prison if that is in our karma. I compared myself with Ma Hmwe; she had often said she would leave me out if she were ever detained or interrogated, but she was never arrested. There were many others who were involved in this struggle, but not everyone was jailed. The depth of involvement may have varied but some narrowly escaped—some even to other countries. Therefore, it was logical that my incarceration had everything to do with my karma.

I began to see my past sins as the original cause and my political involvement as the current cause. Then when would I finish repaying my past sins? By military law, I had been sentenced to twenty years for political activities. What about the sentencing from my karma? How long was it going to last? Oh, Lord Buddha! I came to realize I would have to repay my bad deeds even in the next lives, maybe by being jailed, detained, and handcuffed if I could not complete the payback in this life. Even if I became a celestial being,[2] would I escape all past misdeeds? All that I had learned from books came back to my mind, and it told me I could well be kept in bondage as a celestial being. What I did in this life would determine how I suffered—or not—in subsequent

---

1. Karma means action, good or bad. Thus what happens to one is not random but depends upon one's own past actions, committed in this or previous lives.
2. Celestials in their six heavenly realms are also creatures that remain in Samsara (the cycle of rebirth) as heaven is not Nirvana.

lives. Even if I gained a better existence by means of Thamahta meditation,[3] I would still be not free of the cycle of rebirths, so I could end up in purgatory. If I lived without being aware of what I was doing . . . A million light bulbs seemed to switch on in my head.

As a Buddhist I had the right to choose my fate. If I could not pay for all past misdeeds in this life I would have to pay again and again in my next lives, maybe also by confinement. If I lived without Vipassana and if I were doing misdeeds without being aware I was doing so, I might be reincarnated as an animal: if a bird, I might be caged; if a fish, I might have to live in a bowl. If it got any worse I might end up being an ant or mouse in Insein. Or perhaps I could be reborn a human— maybe not be a political prisoner in jail but a lowlife criminal. Or even a drug dealer. My tears fell in terror of that thought; I had seen how criminals were treated in jail. What about me? When did they ever treat me politely?

I tried to calculate it like a mathematics puzzle: twenty years in prison, a political prisoner, the precious gift of being a human, not uneducated or mentally handicapped, not bodily disabled, a self-reliant person and yearning for freedom—what could such a person do? There was only one answer. I could be free due to a political change or some unforeseeable event, or it could also happen that I would not be free until I had done my time. But the only sure thing was that I would be free in twenty years' time if—a big if—I did not have more years added to my sentence like had happened to U Win Tin. I could not do anything to change this answer. Bending to my jailer's whim and signing to promise that I would never do such-and-such could not guarantee my freedom; at any rate I had no wish to just go along with whatever they told me. So my freedom was completely at the mercy of my jailers. I had no ability to change these circumstances.

I tried to assess the circumstances again. I was a human being, not uneducated or mentally handicapped, not bodily disabled, a self-reliant person, and confined to a cell. I had once thought of becoming a nun

---

3. A form of meditation to gain supernatural powers.

to escape from this samsara, and I knew Vipassana, the method of insightful awareness, which would lead to such an escape. Would this set me free? Yes, this method guarantees this kind of freedom from all sufferings, sufferings from the day I was conceived and into old age, until death. To take this path I needed no mercy or permission from anyone else; there was no need to bribe, no need to promise anything to anyone. It was completely on me. If I wanted to practice Vipassana to escape from this samsara all I needed was my own body and mind. The freedom that I would gain from this practice would be nothing like the freedom of being released from prison, because the whole country was like a prison anyway. This freedom would liberate me from samsara—a freedom with no strings attached. Who could give me this freedom? No one. Not the military government, not the Military Intelligence, not the judges. None of them. The only one who could was me. I finally found something that I could control and that would set me free for real.

My thoughts wandered to atonement and the four nether worlds, which are purgatory with its eight levels, the animal realm, the Pyaitta[4] realm, and the Athurakei[5] realm. I did not know what it would be like to be reincarnated as a Pyaitta or Athurakei but I did know how animals live. I was afraid to become an animal for the one reason that they had no control over their fate—even a dog in a wealthy home, living in luxury. All I wanted was the chance to create my own fate, to think for myself. I had never taken sleeping tablets because I feared that it might make me fuzzy-headed; I did not even like to sleep off pain. A brain that is not alert can make wrong decisions, and although ignorance can be excused, knowing what is right or wrong but making a mistake anyhow for any reason was unacceptable. So to become an animal was my biggest fear.

I shuddered at the thought that I might have died while resisting the unfairness of the wardens and doctors, because in that period I

---

4. The realm of beings who can never have what they desire.
5. The realm of invisible beings who have fun all night and suffer all day.

was angry and bitter and so I would not have been reincarnated into a good life. With such a disposition, even if I could remember Vipassana during the very last minutes of my life it would not be effective since chances are I would be out of practice. According to sayings, if I died in that scenario I would be tied down with the very last thought in my mind, which would most likely be anger, and that meant there was a possibility that I could come back as an animal in this jail again. Lord Buddha! More tears fell from my eyes at this indescribable fear.

I had never been particularly afraid of anything, but now complete terror overwhelmed me. I feared the four nether worlds and the atonement I needed to do for my past misdeeds. As long as I was susceptible to these four nether worlds, nothing could guarantee that I could become a creature in control of my own fate. What was certain is that in prison not all my rights were gone. As long as I was alive I could practice Vipassana to seek real freedom. I realized that I needed to pull myself out of this despair and let go of this fear of being in prison for the next eighteen years.

Chapter 14

The Steps

It was nearly the end of 1995 when I decided to practice Vipassana. My health was improving and another x-ray showed I was healed of tuberculosis. My period stopped altogether but I did not mind. I also knew I would not be able to practice Vipassana here the way it was done in retreat centers, as unlike at the retreat, it would not be convenient to fast while observing the Eight Precepts. I could be stricken with tuberculosis again if I became malnourished, or it might be misunderstood as a hunger strike. So I decided to keep Ajivahtamaka Sila, which is similar to the Eight Precepts. The Eight Precepts are the basic five plus abstaining from eating solid food after noon until dawn of the following day, from wearing cosmetics, perfume or flowers or enjoying performances such as movies, dance, or music, and from sleeping on a comfortable bed. Someone observing the Ajivahtamaka precepts must abstain from saying frivolous things, gossiping, slandering, and being harsh in speech, and practice purity in thought, word, and deed. I realized it would be much easier to keep these precepts in a place like this, although I might still hear music. Therefore, I chose to keep the Ajivahtamaka precepts, as all of them are also important for meditation. I would not be able to concentrate like in a silent retreat and so it would be important to reach an understanding with other prisoners and the guards.

First, I notified everyone and explained that I had no idea how long it was going last. Nonetheless, I promised everyone that I would be involved whenever we faced problems and that by meditating I did not intend to cause trouble for anyone. I could not be choosy about where and how I meditated; I had to turn my cell into a retreat. Perhaps there are places unfit for humans to dwell but there is no place unfit for practicing dharma and meditation. Besides, there is a saying: where there have been good deeds done throughout past lives, that place can always be suited to overcoming all obstacles in the path of freedom from samsara.

One communist prisoner sneered, "Well, so Insein Prison is to be turned into a retreat!" Some warned me to be careful, as they had heard that some people went crazy after meditating. Actually, the ones who warned me about this believed that no political activist should be religious because it could weaken activists to the point that they would give up the fight. Their principle was "When in Rome, live as Romans do," and therefore they would just obey the rules and commit bribery but be recognized outside as those who had sacrificed for the sake of others. Although they took different stands according to if they were in or out of jail, they were largely respected as strong activists.

Although I had read many books about the merits of meditation, I had only practiced Vipassana when I was very young, so it was difficult at first to set my routine. At a meditation center you have to stick to its routine; for example, you might get up at 3:00 a.m., wash up, meditate in a seated position, eat breakfast, pray, keep the Eight Precepts, meditate while walking, eat lunch before noon, listen to the afternoon sermon, meditate in a seated position, then meditate while walking, bathe, meditate in a seated position, then meditate while walking, after which you discuss with the teacher-monk your experiences of the day and which state you have reached, and then again meditate in a seated position before going to bed. The whole day you have people meditating around you who even by their presence encourage you not to falter. In prison, there was no one but me. There was no presiding monk with whom I could discuss things and none to examine which state I had reached. Besides, there were few people considerate enough not to be noisy when I was meditating, although the others in our block were fairly obliging. I could not have asked for more since this was not a true retreat, after all, but one I had to create on my own.

I had never thought that fear of falling into the four nether worlds would give me such resolve. From day one, I neither cheated nor slacked off. After some reflection, I then realized that I would not be this diligent if I was hoping to attain Nirvana; it was my fear of the nether regions that was the driving force. In the repressive political environment after 1988, participation dwindled from fear of the regime's brutality. Nonetheless, the main reason many people got involved was in fact their desperation to escape economic hardship rather than any devotion to the principles of democracy. Similarly, my own fear was pushing me to seek freedom from purgatory rather than any desire to attain Nirvana, the end of the cycle of rebirth.

Many who meditate are concerned about falling ill, so I submitted the welfare of my health into the care of the Buddha.[1] I also spent considerable time sending out feelings of *metta* (loving-kindnes) to make myself feel gentleness, so that I would become gentle through the power of *metta*. I also decided not to follow a strict routine. First, I was in prison and had no control of my own time. Second, according to a revered mediation teacher, since our bodies are not permanent[2] we should never force ourselves to control them. In prison, we could be ordered into the lineup position at any time. If our cell doors were opened for bath time, we had to go out for it. Besides, I had to practice until I could both feel and see that there was no control over myself, there was no "I," and there was no one making me do this. Therefore, it was only natural not to overdo it to the point of exhaustion.

With all that mental preparation, it went rather well from the beginning, although as I tried to focus on the tip of my nostril where air touched on its way in and out with my breathing, my mind some-times wandered away so wildly that within seconds I would have to refocus. While pulling back my focus I also needed to be aware at the same time that *my mind was wandering, I got angry, I am pulling it back.* When I could concentrate I was able to be completely mindful for long stretches of time, but at first when my concentration was disturbed even the tiniest bit my thoughts would fly away.

---

1. A Buddhist ritual of prayer.
2. One of the main principles of Buddhism is that nothing is permanent.

The experience went something like this:

> *Breathe in, breathe out, breathe in, breathe out, breathe in,*
>   *breathe out*
> *oh, footsteps!*
> *who could that be? must be that nasty guard*
> *breathe in, breathe out*
> *which cell is she going to*
> *breathe in, breathe out, breathe in, breathe out*
> *why didn't I hear the key in the lock?*
> *breathe in, breathe out*
> *who's she talking to?*
> *breathe in, breathe out, breathe in, breathe out*
> *please, please, I hope it's not a problem for anyone*
> *breathe in, breathe out, breathe in*
> *oh . . . whatever, I am doing what I have to do—stop thinking*
> *breathe in*
> *oh, my mind slipped away again*
> *I am thinking, thinking, thinking, thinking*
> *breathe in, breathe out*

I noticed my mind wandering all over due to my lack of *viriya* (strong endeavor). I began to realize my mind had to be wide awake to be able to concentrate better. It was no longer enough to just concentrate with *breathe in, breathe out* so I tried not only to do that but also to direct my attention to my stomach rising up when I breathed in and going down when I breathed out. I tried every possible way so that my concentration and mindfulness stayed undivided from the beginning of my breathing in to my stomach expanding to my stomach falling upon breathing out. When I was able to do this, my thoughts stayed stable more often.

As time passed, I began to feel itchiness, aches, and pains but kept on practicing while being mindful of all these sensations, as I was taught. During the seated meditation, I was mindful of altering my position while thinking *itchy, itchy, wanting to scratching it, yes, scratched it* without my concentration wandering elsewhere. During walking meditation, I was aware of *lifting my foot, stepping forward, putting my foot down* at the beginning, but later I became aware in more detail of even the "want" and "know" states of mind, such as *wanting to lift foot, lifting foot, stepping forward, putting foot down, knowing it.* From there, I progressed in awareness:

> *wanting to lift foot*
> *lifting*
> *wanting to step forward*
> *stepping forward*
> *wanting to put foot down*
> *putting foot down*
> *foot touches floor*

I tried to move slowly to fully sense that "want," and finally it became a natural step in my meditation. Similarly, when I bathed:

> *wanting to pick up the bowl*
> *picking it up*
> *wanting to scoop up the water*
> *scooping it up*
> *wanting to pour water on me*
> *pouring it*
> *it's cold*

When I ate:

> *wanting to reach out*
> *reaching out*
> *wanting to scoop up rice with my hand*
> *scooping it up*
> *wanting to lift my hand*
> *lifting it*
> *wanting to bend my elbow*

bending it
wanting to put the rice in my mouth
putting it there
wanting to chew it
chewing it
it's spicy
knowing it

In reality, my mindfulness and concentration were more than I can explain in writing, but I became good at being mindful in every little detail. I was able to constantly be mindful of *ariyapoat,* the position of the body, such as standing, sitting, or lying. At this point, although I did not learn anything else from this practice, I felt more at peace than when my mind was flying all over. My movements, concentration, and mindful awareness were all in sync, in a calming rhythm. However, my wandering mind was still present although it no longer strayed too long or too often.

Then the next problem was the sense of hearing. At that point in my meditation, there was nothing to disturb me in what I saw, as most of the time all I could see were the walls around me. The senses of smell and of taste were also nothing special—especially the latter as I had nothing too delicious. The sense of touch never changed, as all I had was a wooden bedstead on which I slept or sat to meditate. The problem was what I heard: I could not block my ears, and people being kept in cells become heavily reliant on hearing and thus very good at it. My sense of hearing was therefore acute whether the sound was near or far. In fact, we were all very adept at analyzing sounds to learn what was going on.

The women's side of prison was almost always noisy, like a blazing hell, but if it became quiet, we knew prison officials had appeared for a surprise check. If the noise level then went up slowly or there was a short silence before louder sounds, we in the cells knew that meals had arrived or an announcement of some kind was to be made; there was no need to see, we knew for sure. Likewise, we knew the footsteps of each guard in our block and of the other prisoners as well. Just by hearing the key turning in a lock, we knew which cell it was. So, my habit of relying on what I was hearing caused me more effort in my practice than any other sense.

Mindfulness practice became easier and more pronounced during the night, when it was silent. I could even clearly know and visualize the entire process of air flow during breathing: my wish to breathe in, the air that I breathed in, the air touching my nostrils, the air entering my nose and causing my stomach to expand, my wish to breathe out after that, the air going out and causing my stomach to subside, the air flowing out of my nose, and finally the air touching my nostrils on its way out. It was great.

During the day it became something like this:

Want to breathe in
breathing
touching
knowing
hearing somebody swearing
knowing exactly which guard was swearing
disliking it
I don't want to hear it
wanting to breathe in
breathing in
air entering
knowing it . . .

Sometimes I heard someone singing, and then it became *hearing someone singing, liking it, I still want to listen to it* and I would then have to try harder to drag my mind back to my practice. It was worse if I knew who was singing. Moreover, when I was in a calm and peaceful state of mind, it was frightening to even hear the next cell's door opening and shutting, seeming to be as loud as thunder. I could not ask them to open and close the door quietly when I was meditating, and I began to feel annoyed for having the sense of hearing.

I first blamed *thanya,* comprehension or perception—in this case regarding sound; it was because of this perception that I could not just hear a sound but would end up thinking of all that it meant. Because of this perception, it took me a lot of effort to not analyze its meaning but only focus on my practice. It was worse if I heard something from outside, such as fire-engine sirens, the toot of a train whistle, or a song played over speakers from a nearby village:

> *hearing*
> *hearing fire engines*
> *getting worried*
> *don't want to hear it*
> *hearing still*
> *hearing a train whistle*
> *feeling longing*
> *longing for Mom*
> *wanting to go home*
> *becoming unhappy*
> *wanting to breathe in*
> *breathing*
> *air entering nose*
> *knowing it*
> *hearing*
> *hearing singing*
> *it's Twante Thein Tan's song*
> *is that coming from a feast?*
> *liking it*
> *thinking*
> *thinking*
> *hearing it*
> *hearing*

I had to follow my mind and bring it back from all the places it wandered, so I incorrectly thought that I only needed to be mindful of just the "hearing" without the perceptions that followed.

I tried to be mindful of the steps of awareness as closely as possible and in as much detail as I could, and then my reasoning changed. While I was taking a bucket bath, in the early stages I could only be mindful of

> *wanting to lift the bowl*
> *lifting it*
> *wanting to scoop the water*
> *scooping it*
> *wanting to pour on myself*
> *pouring it*
> *it's cold*

But later I could focus in more detail:

> *wanting to lift the bowl*
> *lifting it*
> *it's cold*
> *knowing it*
> *liking it*
> *wanting to lift the bowl again*
> *lifting it*
> *wanting to scoop the water*
> *dipping the bowl into water*
> *it's cold*
> *liking it*
> *scooping it*
> *wanting to lift*
> *lifting it*
> *wanting to pour it on myself*
> *pouring it*
> *it's cold*
> *liking it*
> *wanting to do this again*
> *reaching out my hand . . .*

Then I understood that the awareness of "wanting" was coming easier and in more detail. I recognized it even when I wanted to drink water and was sitting next to the water pot. I began to know and be aware of every step of the process of drinking:

> *thirsty*
> *wanting to drink*
> *wanting to reach for it*
> *wanting to reach out*
> *reaching out*
> *wanting to touch the cup*
> *touching it*
> *knowing I'm touching it*
> *wanting to lift the lid of pot*
> *touching it*
> *lifting it*
> *knowing it*
> *wanting to remove the lid*
> *taking it off*
> *wanting to scoop the water*
> *scooping it*
> *it's cold*
> *liking it*
> *wanting to lift the cup to my lips*
> *lifting it*
> *wanting to bend my arm*
> *bending it*
> *drinking the water*
> *it's cold*
> *liking it*
> *wanting to drink again*

I got to where I knew a lot more and was able to be mindful of smaller details and steps of whatever I was doing. Then I recognized that the culprit was not *thanya,* which allows us to recognize the feeling and whether we like it or not; the real culprit was *ahyon*—our own consciousness—which allows us to know our perceptions; Then comes *vinyan*, the awareness of knowing our feelings. In my case, the awareness of hearing was first, then came the recognition that it was a song or something else; the next step of my feeling about it was knowing whether it pleased me or not, and close on its heels came the thought of whether I wanted to keep hearing it or not. The sense of hearing happened when my ears caught the sound waves, which led to awareness followed by a string of other types of awareness—what kind of sound, what or who made it, what I felt about it, and so on—and as simple as that I saw *khanda nga par,* the five aggregates embodying a being: (1) physical and material form, (2) feeling and sensory reception (i.e., either good or bad or neutral feeling), (3) cognition or perception, (4) the phenomena of stimulation and change, and (5) conscious awareness of two physical and mental existences.[3]

The ear and sound are physical origins of the sense of hearing. This sense leads to the instant appearance of other aggregates of cognition, feeling, and reception as well as the phenomena of change. That is the nature of all physical and sensory existences. What about the culprit at the origin of problems? The culprit is the act of knowing, or consciousness. From this consciousness what follows are greed, anger, and delusion. My feelings of wanting to hear more or not, wanting it to happen or not, led to suffering and only now did I realize the true culprit. Not knowing this had caused my wish to know more. I was striving to know, and from this knowing, sufferings came.

Once I realized that suffering was the result of knowing, I understood more clearly how the cycle of samsara turns. Because of knowing, physical and mental states change.[4] When other people or situations affect physical and mental states, they change, causing sensations that lead to feelings of wanting something or feelings of not wanting it. If these feelings do not dissipate the person will strive either to get it or

---

3. (1) Rupa Khanda, (2) Veyda Khanda, (3) Thanya Khanda, (4) Sinkhara Khanda, and (5) Vinyana Khanda.
4. Impermanence.

to avoid it and thus will either attain it or avoid it. This is life and in life there is always wealth, health, and longevity that people want to have and old age, ill health, and death that people want to avoid.

However, we never analyze it to this extent, so we do not see samsara for what it is and we keep striving to be in it rather than to become free of it. For example, we hear something and do not stop there but continue on to liking it or disliking it. We want to hear more if we like it and we pay more attention, and then our physical and mental beings become preoccupied with it. Our wish to hear it is desire *(ta-nha)* rising within us, and if it increases it becomes obsession, so that if we do not hear it we become restless and try harder to hear it more and so do indeed continue to hear it. The consequences of first hearing a sound would be a cycle of liking, wanting, desiring, striving, obtaining, fearing for its loss, and so on. In the same way, we are caught in samsara without seeing that suffering is the final result. We keep on wishing to be alive because we do not realize the suffering that life brings according to the law of impermanence.

Our will to live keeps us alive. Once we are alive we own mental senses and physical bodies, and through these we feel, we suffer, we desire, we strive to have those we desire, we possess them, we lose them, we suffer, we live, we die, we are reborn, we live, we die . . . With this knowledge I was in awe of the Buddha's dharma, seeing that his Way is absolutely right.

I kept on with my meditation. When I began to understand physical and mental existences it became easier to concentrate. When I was younger I used to think that the instruction to see the existences of material form and mental sense was about trying to see them as separate entities. I now knew I had misinterpreted it; I was supposed to see that nothing exists apart from these two, so I should not have been thinking of "I" (i.e., the self). It was about asking us to practice till we understand the characteristics of material form and mental sense. In fact, many disturbances happen in our physical body when we are deep in meditation, such as pain, aches, itchiness, and numbness here and there in our bodies. Sometimes it can feel as if the head is about to explode or as if one leg has vanished.

The most common sensation is the feeling that something is moving under the skin around the nose or mouth. Sometimes, we can even see ourselves in out-of-body experiences. At times, we might feel as if the whole body has disappeared, and we can only sense our minds. However, if we realize that to know the characteristics of the material form and mental sense is the truth of the Buddha's dharma, then we will not be easily derailed by such magical and extraordinary experiences.

I kept concentrating and reasoning on the nature of physical and mental beings. Once perception or consciousness of knowing our sensations has gone, all aggregates of mental existence are gone too.

While concentrating on hearing, if the mind veers to itchiness then our ability to hear or know what we hear has already left our consciousness. Once we lose this, all other experiences and sensory feelings—*thanya,* knowing what kind of sound; *vedana,* feelings about this sound as either bad or good; and *sinhkara,* deciding whether to continue to listen or not—disappear as well. Once we know it is itchiness, other types of knowing and desire—knowing where that itchiness is (which is *thanya*), the feeling of knowing it is undesirable (which is *vedana*), and wanting to scratch to take that itchiness away or change the situation (that is, *sinkhara*)—rise up. This urge to take itchiness away causes the conscious mind to send out a message to the physical body to do something about it. The body must move or do something because of our wish to do so. Our knowing, or consciousness, and desire control every bit of our physical movement; it is the mind which causes the body to do something. Likewise when something happens to the body the mind becomes aware of it.

The steps are: we sense through the mind and it names the event, such as an itch; at the same time we know where and how the itch is; and we also know that the itch gives us a bad feeling. Then comes the desire to change that event, such as to stop the itch. Then it continues toward asking the physical body to do something about it, which spurs the physical body to lift the hand, move it to the spot in question, and scratch. Then again when this change—relief from the itch—takes place, the mind knows of it and we feel it, and the body changes (i.e., the hand stops scratching and drops back into its previous position). Here

I saw a mutual correlation and harmony between the mind and the physical body, and I continued to meditate by being aware of seeing it, recognizing it, and understanding it.

After being able to practice more efficiently and becoming more aware of my physical body, it became distasteful to me. In a small cell, it took not even ten steps to reach the toilet basin. However, let's see the whole process of mindfulness practice, starting from where I sat on my bed:

wanting to go to the toilet
wanting to get up
wanting to rise to feet
rising
wanting to straighten legs
straightening
wanting to be on feet
being on feet
wanting to stretch body
stretching now
wanting to stand upright
standing now
wanting to move feet forward
wanting to lift feet
lifting
wanting to take a step
stepping
wanting to put feet down on the floor
putting down
foot touching the floor
knowing foot is touching the floor
the urge to relieve becoming more pronounced
wanting to go
wanting to lift foot
lifting
wanting to take a step

stepping
wanting to put foot down
putting down
touching the floor
knowing it is touching the floor

That was the process of mindfulness practice when I wanted to go to the toilet. Then I would go through being aware of the steps of cleaning up to finally getting back on my bed to do more meditation.

So here was the suffering of going through all the steps just to relieve myself; if I had to write every detail of the whole process it would fill ten pages. There are numerous steps to be mindful of in just one action like this and it is not something one could choose not to do, like feeling hunger and choosing not to eat. The disgusting aspect of a decaying body is made more apparent. Where was "I"? Where was my "self"? There is absolutely no "I" or "self" who can make that "wanting to do something" go away. We will have to take every step that our minds ask of us, no matter how many—a billion steps and endless moments of conscious awareness.

Anissa (impermanence), *dukkha* (suffering), *anatta* (absence of self). I no longer saw myself as in "this is my body, this is my hand, my leg" but saw my body as something that moved only when my mind told it to do something, and on its own could only decay. Apart from that physical body and the mind that saw what was happening to it, I found nothing else. Apart from the unending cycle of *body changes, mind notices it, names it, has feelings about it, has desire to do something about it, asks body to do something, body obeys,* I found nothing else. In this cycle there was no longer any "self"—even my mind appeared only when there was something to notice. As soon as it noticed something, that moment of "noticing" was immediately followed by naming of it and that was immediately followed by "feeling" something, and as soon as that appeared it was immediately followed by the "desire" to do something about it. As soon as I became aware of what my mind had noticed, that changed to the next step, which I would again become aware of and which would lead to the next step. It was as if the things my mind knew were like balloons that kept appearing, one after the other, and my awareness the pin that kept bursting each one; one step disappeared as soon as the next was taken, in nanoseconds.

When I first began to meditate, I thought that I was able to be aware of something while it was happening. In fact, it was nothing like that. As soon as I became consciously aware of what was happening, that event disappeared and there was only one thing left: awareness. So what came into my mind and my awareness of it were two different things that existed sequentially and not simultaneously. I understood clearly that it was like dropping what I was holding to take up something else. As soon as I became aware of hearing a sound, the perception of hearing it had disappeared already. My awareness that I knew of it was also gone already when another perception of hearing appeared again. The steps appeared and disappeared so fast that it was like a magic show. Sound waves entered my ear, I heard, I became aware of the hearing sense, recognized the sound, felt something about it, wanted to hear more, the sense of hearing became awareness of hearing (and so the sense of hearing and its attachments disappeared), the next note of the sound entered my ear, I heard, I became aware of the hearing sense, and so on.

This cycle of sense and awareness ended only when the origin of the sense (the sound) stopped, the tool of the sense (the ear) stopped working, or another new and distinct sense appeared. I could not stop such things from appearing or disappearing. In this rapid flow of cause and effect I could not find myself, and since there is no "self," the nonexistent "I" had no control over the flow of my steps.

Chapter 15

Interludes

A problem with our rice came up just as I was trying to go deeper into my mindfulness. One day, the lunchtime hospital fare arrived very late, around two o'clock, and the rice was undercooked. Ma Chuu and Ma Don asked the guards to return it and get properly cooked rice. The guard responded that rice for the prisoners in the group hall was worse than this but they did not complain, so why should we? Ma Chuu and Ma Don became angry—they were not griping about the quality but simply saying that it was inedible. With the insights I had gained so far, I would not have minded eating it because in a meditative state, the annoyance I would feel about the taste would be dissipated by my awareness of that feeling. Nevertheless, I did not want to risk my health, which had not yet fully recovered. Besides, the way the guard had responded to this request was not acceptable. As I was thinking about what to say, an elderly prisoner in my block asked me to stop meditating and intervene. She was worried that the problem might get more complicated if Ma Chuu and Ma Don responded with anger.

While holding on to my conscious awareness, but not too deeply, I told the guard to inform the relevant authorities that as we could not eat this rice we would only accept a replacement if one of the doctors brought it to us. At the beginning of my meditation, the guards had thought I was just trying to show off or that I was a bit crazy, but after they had seen me meditating while I sat, walked, or even lay down and witnessed that I was sleeping only three or four hours night, they began to understand that I was really meditating, so they no longer dared say anything disparaging about me. And so they did not say anything when I asked them to just report the matter to higher authorities.

Soon after that the doctor arrived. We did not have to say or do more than show him the rice, and he immediately saw it was inedible. He promised that another batch of rice would be sent in half an hour. Within thirty minutes, we received hot steamed rice that was even better in quality than the rice we normally got. I told the guards that it was always better to just report any problem regarding our food to the higher authorities rather than responding themselves. From that time on, they realized that when I asked for the doctor it was often not about my health but to solve problems in our block. Though our food was sent from the hospital kitchen, I did not deal with the guards there but with the doctor, so the problem was solved without any need for argument, and I could go back to my routine of meditation. Other prisoners in my block who had thought that I would walk away from worldly affairs—politics, human rights, and other issues—and that I would accept injustice silently could only thank me.

I had never intended to forsake helping others and to remain silent on injustice, even while meditating nearly twenty hours a day. In fact, it was my love for truth and justice that caused me to meditate in order to find them within myself. I was already determined to seek and defend truth and justice because I believed there was no difference whether we were looking from religious or secular perspectives.

Therefore, practicing Vipassana did not mean abandoning politics, human rights, or the rights of prisoners. In the same way, defending and protecting these rights did not necessarily mean any lessening of *sila, samadhi,* and *paññya*—morals, integrity, and wisdom. Most problems I saw in prison were the result of the guards' lack of goodwill, lack of education, mismanagement, fear of repercussion, and lack of control over their own fate. Instead of solving even minor problems easily without any loss for guard or prisoner, they had the idea that they should bully prisoners; the prisoners tended to think all guards were unjust, and they focused more on what they felt rather than on solving the issue at hand. Therefore, there were only winners or losers for each incident, causing grudges and resentment. Besides, there were some prisoners who wanted to maintain their privileges and were not reluctant to distort the truth, and so more problems were created.

Therefore, I continued to meditate to be liberated from believing in "I," "me," and "self" because I saw everyone else being caught up in this "I," "me," and "self" whether it was a prisoner "I" enjoying her privileges or a guard "I" abusing what little authority she had.

Because of my weeks of dedicated practice, the ability to be mindfully aware of impermanence came back quickly despite the interruption of the rice problem. I began to more fully understand the process of being mindful, to see the truth of impermanence in how fast and far our minds traveled and changed. The happening and disappearing take place so fast, in the same way that strobe lights can seem to be a single ray, flashing so fast that we cannot see the interruption. I saw that in reality it is just the event of things that is impermanent—happening or existing and disappearing or vanishing, the cause of suffering. The nature of all physical and mental existences is that they will cease to exist one day.

Around this time, Ma Chuu became friendly with a guard who kept our doors open for longer periods, once in the morning and once in the evening, and with the help of some cleaners she grew some vegetables in the yard. As I no longer spent my evenings talking with her about our "tonics" she seemed to be compensating for it with other interests. Besides, this gave her fresh vegetables, and as for me, since the day I embarked on meditation I had needed no "tonic" to pass the time. After our doors were opened, I was able to do more walking meditation and I saw Ma Chuu's plants. Some were thriving but some looked sickly, and in them I saw the truth of impermanence where earlier I would have only seen food.

When small leaves from the rain tree fell around my feet while I was walking, I could fully comprehend the process of death and rebirth, of sentient beings as well as non-sentient beings. I could truly appreciate and believe in the truth of suffering being impermanent. I began to feel annoyed with my physical body as I started to see the sufferings that humans must go through. I was always the one trying to control my own fate, but when I realized that there was no "I," no "me," no "mine," I began to accept that there was nothing I could do to alter these things. When I looked at myself, I recognized my body as a being filled with suffering, a being that could do nothing without its conscious mind ordering it to act—smile, cry, sit, stand, breathe. Without this conscious mind, the body would decay in no time.

When Ma Chuu asked whether it would be a good idea to plant gladiolas, all I could say was, "Everything is impermanent. It will just die."

"Then we'll grow more," she persisted.

"That's right, but the problem is that it grows again and again. If there is existence there will be an end to it, and it goes on reexisting and dying, again and again. That's why we must create a situation where there is no reexisting," I tried to explain this to Ma Chuu while trying to remind myself as well.

In fact, I was disturbed by the thought that things decayed or died because they existed. The event of existing could not be stopped, and since it could not be stopped, deterioration and dying could not be stopped either; I found this terrifying.

At that stage, it became easier to concentrate; I noticed immediately when my mind wandered off and was able to pull it back to the instant of awareness. Aches and other disturbances in my body would disappear suddenly like a balloon popped with a needle, and then I would feel as if my whole body were floating like a puff of cotton wool within a ray of light. I also felt that in my mindful awareness I was in that light for a long time. I could fully sense *pharana piti,* the pervasive delight that was spreading inside me, making me very calm and easily able to continue my mindfulness practice. Although the happening and disappearing were taking place rapidly, my awareness kept in step with each; my mind was clear and my *viriya* (effort) was strong. I did not get tired or weak even as I was meditating long hours at a stretch. My concentration was so strong that my awareness had no need to deliberately go through each step of the process, but I could become fully aware with just a light grasp of the process of concentration. It gave me so much happiness that I wanted to share this with Ma Chuu and the others and wished that they would also meditate.

While I felt I was floating in light, my mind did not wander anywhere but remained in awareness, so I was filled with delight at how true the

155

Buddha's dharma was. I felt serene, without any care, and I felt as if I were soaking in a cool stream. Yet I was also able to understand that this light and delight were not real dharma. They were only feelings that I needed to be aware of, and once I became aware, they ceased. My awareness became faster after this. Being conscious of the happening—which led to the ceasing of it—was so fast that I could almost see each step of the process dropping like ripe fruit to be replaced by the next one.

I could see clearly this fast process of happening and ceasing. I was even able to be aware of more steps of ceasing than ever before, such as in the process of the air touching the tip of my nostril on its way into my lungs when I inhaled and the air coming out when I exhaled. My awareness was working so quickly that I did not feel individual steps, such as "wanting" and so on, but groups like "happen, know, disappear" all at once, so that my awareness was in a continuous flow.

Eventually the disappearing part became more obvious than the happening part, and I felt fearful again, for there is nothing as frightening as seeing the act of disappearing and happening within a tiny space of time. I could not stop it from happening. I could not keep from being aware of it. Absolutely no one could stop this, and there was no "I" to stop it. "I" did not have any control. I felt miserable and anxious that there was no one I could turn to for help. I saw I could not escape from the events of ending, disappearing, and dying, and I began to sense the truth of the phrase "nowhere to run." So long as there was body and mind, there was no escaping the events of ending, disappearing, or dying. Whether I was in a prison cell, a retreat, a forest, or heaven or hell, there was nothing I could do to escape from the phenomena of appearing, disappearing, and then appearing again in a renewed cycle.

No escape whatsoever. It was terrifying, and there was nothing good I could hope for out of it. At that point, there was nothing in my awareness except "existing, disappearing, emerging, and ceasing." I began to get tired of knowing that there was nothing but the event of appearing and disappearing in this world. Please stop! No more existence! No more happening! And no more ceasing! I had wanted to know the truth and thus I had sought for it but now was suffering from knowing it. I did not wish to know it any longer.

However, I knew I could not just sit there, suffering. There had to be a way out of it. What should I do next? I tried stopping meditating; it did not work, as conscious awareness came on its own. There was nothing I could do but continue in my meditation, and I became even more aware of each minute step. But then the awareness became somewhat loose, so I changed my posture to different positions so that it might become compact again. I meditated in such unusual poses, like lying on my back with one leg over my raised knee or half-lying, half-sitting, that anyone peeping into my cell would have thought I was doing yoga.

Still, things did not improve. I tried harder to gather my awareness and with this determination things soon improved; the process became easier and smoother, without any disturbing feelings of fear or insecurity, and there was no boredom; I could see dry leaves or green leaves and simply note things as they were. My pace during walking meditation was neither fast nor slow; in sitting meditation I could sit for hours without any discomfort and only knew the passage of time through the sound of the gong every fifteen minutes. During that period my awareness was tranquil. In this way I went on to search for the end of physical and mental existence.

There was no presiding monk to help me on my meditation journey, so I wrote down a synopsis of everything I had gone through and smuggled it out with Ma Chuu's help to my parents, whom I asked to forward it to the abbot of Chan Myay Yeik Thar Monastery,[1] where as a youngster I had attended meditation sessions. (After my release I went to the *Sayadaw* to pay obeisance and told him about this book that I was planning to write. He advised me not to include the later part of my meditation process and so I will not write anything about what followed the period of tranquility mentioned above.)

---

1. One of the most revered monasteries in Myanmar, and one of the first to open a meditation center for laypeople.

One thing I can confidently say is that after this endeavor I became a true Buddhist. I came to believe in the Buddha and his dharma unconditionally. I became able to understand true freedom and found a serenity that exists without any need for me to feel it. I also understood impermanence (*anissa*), suffering (*dukkha*), and nonself (*anatta*). I had seen the root cause of suffering. I no longer wished to have new life. I no longer had any desire for high status or fame.

Around that period I was thinking that even if someone had strived to the utmost to be successful or famous in this life, without an effort to prepare for the endless cycle of samsara, it could not be said that this person had found true security. Whenever I heard of how someone was successful or wealthy and had achieved a high level of success in education or career, I no longer felt admiration or jealousy. I no longer needed such achievements to feel fulfilled, for to be wrapped in awareness was such a calm, joyful, and peaceful experience in itself, complete and fulfilled.

Previously my mind would fly to the past or future, running between feelings of ambition, anger, and delusional thoughts, getting exhausted. Even if I were sitting as still as a rock, these desires and emotions roiling in my head were enough to make me feel as if I were on fire. Now, just being aware of these disturbances made them disappear, and they did not return. Even if I had to run around physically my mind was clear, filled with tranquility. The past did not disturb me; the future no longer created anxiety. If any of those disturbances should emerge, in an instant my awareness would do away with it. There was nothing as tranquil as just objectively looking on as things and thoughts appeared and disappeared; there was no longing for anything, no attachments to tie me up. To walk steadily on this path of freedom from samsara became my life goal.

As for what I would become in the future, let it be as my morality, integrity, and wisdom[2] dictated.

---

2. *Sila, samadhi, paññya.*

Chapter 16

Existing in Vipassana

My parents were delighted to know how much joy I was getting from meditation, and they believed that I would be released soon because of this good merit. As for me, I could not expect anything as I had been out of touch with world news; most of what I heard during visits was about internal affairs, and I only knew that the political situation was getting tense. Although Ma Chuu and I talked some, we did not completely resume our regular evening chats or taking "tonics." I was a bit uncertain about going back to that routine, as I was finding such joy in the tranquility of meditation. On the other hand, I wanted to live in harmony with others. There were changes in relationships among prisoners and other developments, such as new guards being appointed. I decided not to increase my meditation time but to set a timetable for regular practice.

In March, twenty-four political prisoners, including U Win Tin and Myo Myint Nyein, were given an additional sentence of twelve years to their original seven years for distributing in the prison bulletins about the diamond jubilee of Rangoon Arts and Science University and other things they had written, for sending open letters to the UN, for having several international and national magazines, and for even possessing shortwave radios. I was saddened by this news—especially for Myo Myint Nyein and Sein Hlaing, who had been about to complete their first sentence. Although it was not unusual to sentence them without bringing them to court, I felt it was unfair to sentence them with two different charges. I was grateful to Myo Myint Nyein for not giving me up to the authorities regarding the shirt that we had sent to the UN human rights conference. I had been able to help him and his family when he was first arrested, but now I could do nothing for them.

In the same month, some NLD members, including Ma Suu, attempted to take the train to Mandalay to attend the hearing of the comedian troupe the Moustache Brothers—consisting of Pa Pa Lay and his brothers—who had been arrested for making jokes about the military regime at the Independence Day celebrations held in Ma Suu's compound on January 4. However, the carriage she was in was uncoupled and left behind. It was disappointing and surprising that the matter had been handled so childishly. On April 1, the government loaned money to civil servants that was ten times their normal monthly salary and ordered them to repay in two years. The prison guards did not know whether to be happy or sad; at the end of the day, they were left in the same dire straits because the prices of basic commodities immediately soared.

During that time, we had someone in our block who was diabetic. The prison's chief doctor allowed her to have bread and green vegetables three days a week, and she shared this bounty, so the rest of us were also eating better. She was from a well-to-do family, and as there was someone from home coming with a parcel of fresh produce for her every other day she was receiving an abundant and regular amount. It was a season of feasting for all of us as there were stir-fried vegetables as well as fresh vegetables. Since we had no right to read or write in prison, the time we spent preparing food was precious to us. It was rare to have freshly-cooked food; we were used to food that could be kept a long time, such as fried dried fish and fried dried shrimp. The new diet of vegetables was excellent for our health.

Our warden was transferred elsewhere and a new one took her place, so the guards did not dare to keep our doors open. Led by Ma Chuu, the prisoners in our block tried to negotiate with the new warden, but it did not work. Those prisoners who were already enjoying privileges through years of bribery took the warden's side and suggested we should not push the matter further. Yet these privileged women went on sharing their food with us; were they bribing us as well, to keep silent? That thought bothered us a lot.

I vividly remember that Buddhist sermons were first given in Insein Prison on April 5, 1996. At first, famous abbots were invited; they preached in the group prison hall and the sermons were broadcast to other buildings. The inmates of the buildings where the abbot preached in person had the opportunity to pay obeisance and offer food or other gifts. Most prisoners were happy with this arrangement and it was very helpful for me too. Since the cell doors were kept locked I could no longer do much walking meditation, but I was able to keep to my routine. I was glad to listen to the sermons and I strongly urged Ma Chuu to take up meditation—and she did for short periods but said she could not do more as it was nothing like a proper meditation center. However, she was willing to keep a regular routine.

We then thought we should begin on that very day—April 5, 1996— to fast and observe the Eight Precepts three days a week:[1] Friday, on which the Buddha was born, Monday, on which the Buddha took to the forest to seek enlightenment, and Wednesday, on which the Buddha attained enlightenment.

By this time, I no longer needed to take tuberculosis medication; my period had stopped, so healthwise I was in good shape. I was eager to fast on the three appointed days each week since by then I had reduced the time I spent in meditation. Besides, I was beginning to dislike having to depend on others for fresh food and I saw this need as *tanha*—craving. I was afraid that this was not just having *tanha* but also being immoral. I wanted to challenge my craving for food, which I knew was obtained by means of corruption, even when it was needed for a legitimate reason. Moreover, I could soon become used to doing without fresh food and I would become indifferent to its absence. Cravings for this food, and its preparation, were not worth the short time of its consumption; there was too much wasted time and too much craving involved.

---

1. This practice of fasting three times a week lasted up to six months after I was released from Insein.

Ma Chuu and I informed all the others that we were going to fast three days a week. We had to do this; otherwise, they might think we were on a hunger strike when we missed a meal. We also said we would be avoiding good food during our fast.

From analyzing myself I began to understand the mundane world, which pushed me to challenge myself further. Ma Chuu kept to fasting thrice weekly, but out of friendship she accepted a good dish once in a while. I, however, was determined to keep on abstaining. Those who had used to think scornfully that I would become weaker or unbalanced through religious belief were surprised to see how committed I was. I could never have a clear conscience if I had to depend on those who oppressed others for the sake of having better conditions. As a political prisoner and a Buddhist, I could not allow myself to survive by gaining privileges while urging others to accept prison life without question.

I explained to my fellow inmates in the block that this was a challenge to myself to see if I could survive without craving the rare fresh food and live contentedly within the boundaries of morality, integrity, and wisdom. I must admit that I also wanted to prove my meditation had not turned me into a weak person who could easily be persuaded to accept gifts, however valuable they may be. I wanted them to know that I gained contentment by removing craving as much as possible through my beliefs in Buddhism and my own discipline, not out of necessity due to poverty or paucity. I wanted them to know that gentleness gained from meditation was not weakness but rather the strong and confident contentment of living in tranquility. I had never been a slave to cravings even before I was sent to jail, and so this place was the best to rid myself of it even more.

I spoke coolly and objectively and as they knew I would do my utmost to keep my word, soon they were referring to me with a crude idiom[2] meaning that I might look weak but was not one to mess with.

---

2. "Cat litter may look soft, but it stinks."

In fact, I was not sacrificing too much since I still ate the food my parents brought me and only refused that offered by others. There were many worse off than me as most prisoners had only prison fare and small amounts of food their families brought, if they even had that. Besides, as I ate with mindfulness there was not much difference whether my food was good or bad; the sensation of taste stays on our tongues for only an instant, and after we swallow the taste disappears. Awareness of having tasty food in my mouth was just momentary bliss, and awareness of tasting bad food was also as brief; I was able to see things as they were from this practice of accepting reality. I no longer thought about the past and I no longer dreamed about the future; it was very comfortable and peaceful to live like that.

Ma Chuu and I did not resume our evening chats while we were fasting; the few times we did, we talked mainly about Buddhism. Nothing out of the ordinary happened during that time. In early June, we heard that the authorities had banned public gatherings in front of Ma Suu's residence. In that same period, we also heard about a comment from the Singaporean prime minister, Lee Kuan Yew, that Myanmar would become like Bosnia if Ma Suu gained power and thus it was better for the military regime to continue ruling over us. Many people were angered by his remark, but we did not hear any response from Ma Suu. Within a year, the political situation had turned worse. The military government announced 1996 as "Visit Myanmar Year," while Ma Suu campaigned for boycotts on tourism. With that tension going on, hope of an amnesty dissipated among the prisoners. Ma Chuu was also having difficulties with smuggling in new "tonics." Consequently we were cut off from the outside world.

In early June, my parents said they heard that an organization of writers and authors called PEN had given me an award. My parents did not know the whole story, and I had no knowledge about that kind of award.

"Dharma is the one thing I should be getting, not an award. Don't give much attention to it. I have to be grateful, however, that they haven't forgotten me. Please say thank you for me if anyone asks," I told my parents. My father had also responded to someone who brought the news by saying "I can't be happy about it; I will be happy only when my daughter is released."

Later I learned that it was the Barbara Goldsmith Freedom to Write Award from PEN America in New York, and that the award was given on April 25. My only understanding was that I was given an award for my endeavors to write and express freely. Many people thought that the way the authorities decided on my prison term would be affected positively by this recognition. My parents thought otherwise: the international attention on me would upset the authorities and they might keep me in jail longer just for that. As for me, I did not know what to think of it. It was possible that I could be released as others thought, or not, as my parents believed. However, I was no longer too concerned about freedom from jail now that I was trying to seek freedom from samsara, which no other freedom could match. Besides, I knew that I had no control over when I would be released and could not guess what sort of impact the international attention would have on it.

Media and organizations around the world called for Ma Thida's release. *Left:* An Amnesty International newsletter recounts Ma Thida's twenty-ninth birthday celebrations at the Fourth World Women's Convention at Beijing in 1995. *Right:* The Lancet, a leading medical journal, spreads awareness of Ma Thida's imprisonment.

Time passed as usual, with days of fasting and meditating. Previously I had marked the time left in prison in fourteen-day periods, marking when I could next see my parents, but when I could dwell exactly in the present with mindful awareness I learned how to live in the moment, so my yearning for the future grew faint. On August 15, I was summoned to be interrogated. This time it was a major from the MI. He asked if I had heard anything special from my parents; I said no, my parents had said nothing to me. After a pause, he asked me if I had not heard of winning an award. At the time I did not know the name of the award, so I said it could be for one of my novels and that my parents would not know either. As usual he asked me about my condition in general and also about my meditation.

Finally, he asked, "What is your opinion on the government?"

He gave me a weak smile when I answered, "According to dharma, everything is impermanent (*anissa*) and I only see things as such." He then asked what I thought of Ma Suu. "She is doing what she has to do and facing hardships (*dukkha*) knowingly," was my answer.

As usual I was asked, "What is your political goal?"

He looked at me perplexedly when I said, "I'd like to do what a good citizen should do for her country and I wish to have the right to do so. I have no other goal apart from that."

This time I did not answer as before about what I wanted to be, but what I wanted to do; my answer had changed. After a while, he left after saying, "It's no use discussing anything with you," and I said to myself that my time in prison was not going to end anytime soon. It was not even our day to fast but I had no regrets because I had not said anything with an eye toward shortening my sentence. The others in the block laughed when I told them of the interrogation. They said, "So you failed the test again!" Yet I passed the test I had set for myself.

～

Ma Chuu was able to get some new "tonics," and I learned from them that a lot had happened during July. In Russia, Yeltsin was re-elected president. The International Criminal Tribunal in The Hague had issued a warrant for former Serbian president Milan Milutinovic. There were lots of wonderful things happening in the world of science: the first clone was produced, a sheep named Dolly. At the end of August, South Korea's president, Chun Doo Hwan, was sentenced to death for treason.

~

In domestic political news, at the end of October there were reports of a small riot breaking out after a fight between students and townspeople at a Yangon highway bus station, but I did not know whether to believe them. The minister of railways, U Win Sein, had publicly said at one meeting of the Union Solidarity and Development Association[3] that Daw Aung San Suu Kyi should be killed. I was appalled at his hatred for her without any history of personal connections or grudges. Even more horrifying was that Ma Suu's car and other vehicles in her convoy were attacked by a group of thugs on her way from her residence to U Kyi Maung's residence in Chin Chaung Avenue. I felt disturbed and worried that these people in authority really wanted to kill her.

It reminded me of the five kinds of enemy in Buddhism: water, fire, king or ruler, thief, and those who have no love for you. The authorities regarded Ma Suu as an enemy because they did not love her. For her and the people of Myanmar, the authorities were the rulers so they were the enemy.

In Burmese culture we have the ten virtues of rulers:
1. *Danan*—charity
2. *Silan*—good morals
3. *Parissagan*—benefaction or patronage
4. *Issavan*—fairness and honesty
5. *Maddavan*—gentleness in speech and deed
6. *Tapan*—modest upholding of moral precepts

---

3. Formed in 1992 by the military regime, it became the political party Union Solidarity and Development Party in March 2010.

7. *Akodhan*—benevolence or lack of anger
8. *Avihisan*—avoidance of cruelty
9. *Khanti*—patience
10. *Aviyodanam*—avoidance of conflict with the people

What kind of ruler did we have? The ten kingly virtues are guarantees that subjects will be taken care of and protected, yet here subjects were considered enemies of the state. The people in turn considered the rulers to be enemies because they were not ruling according to the ten virtues.

Around then, something happened to raise our suspicions. Behind our cellblock was a fence, and beyond that some vegetable patches, an empty plot, and the men's death row. The fence was made of galvanized iron sheets and we could see through the holes and gaps in it. That empty plot was where Ma Chuu and I had thrown the water-soaked pages from our magazines. Now from there we could hear sounds and voices of men at work, and by the clang of iron fetters we knew the laborers were prisoners. We tried to look when there was no one around and we even used a mirror to see more; it seemed that about thirty prisoners were constructing something in the empty plot.

The building was not big. It faced death row, so we could only see the back. The construction work would carry on the whole day, and it looked like they were in a hurry. When the guards were not around we called out to the prisoners and asked what they were doing. They said they had no clue what it was for but that they were building a small bungalow with a living room, one bedroom, a bath, and a toilet. After considering the political situation, we worried that it could only be for Daw Aung San Suu Kyi. Their attitude toward the person to be incarcerated there was obvious as it was facing death row.[4] It was strange how they were hurrying to finish it, as if it was needed urgently. They also seemed to be furnishing it—one prisoner told us that they had put in a dressing table and also that the toilet was the Western type,

---

4. Symbolizing bad luck, inauspiciousness.

obviously meant for someone of high status. From our guards, we heard that their colleagues from the head office would be posted on duty there.

I could not find any peace when I sensed what was going to happen. The guards were not happy to hear that only those from the head office were to be on duty there; in fact, most of them were sympathetic toward Ma Suu, not that they dared show it, for obvious reasons. I never heard anything bad about her from them in the likes of what we saw in the state media. They did not adore her but did have a lot of interest. We did not know if the outside world knew about this and if so, how far the news had spread. All of us in the cellblock agonized over the thought of Ma Suu being at such risk, but no one was brought to that little house, up to the day I was released. And I never did find out what it was all about.

~

During those days, there were changes of governments on the world stage. In November, President Bill Clinton of the US was elected to a second term. In Pakistan, Prime Minister Benazir Bhutto was ousted on allegations of corruption.

~

In early December, we heard that a huge student demonstration took place at Hledan,[5] and sure enough two students arrived in our cell-block on December 6. One was an NLD member who had participated in the demonstration, and another had handed out water bottles to the demonstrators. They arrived with only the clothes they were wearing, so we all rallied to help them. Not long after, another group of students was brought to the front cellblock. There were also many men arrested, and they had all been manhandled. The road in front

---

5. A busy, crowded area next to the Rangoon Arts and Science University campus.

of Ma Suu's residence had been blocked by the police and her gate kept closed so that she could not leave even at the very beginning of the demonstrations, cutting off any chance of communication between her and the public.

The new arrivals had to bear the unexpectedly cold winter with not enough clothes or blankets. As this was their period of detention while still in trial, they were not allowed any prison visits by their families, and we were also unable to give anything to them as their cells were frequently being searched. We sneaked food to them and made sure that they left no trace of it. They were locked in a larger cell and even the wooden flap over the screened opening was kept down to prevent easy communication between us. We wanted to know more about what was happening outside and we told them to get a twig while bathing, and at night to prop up the wooden flap. That way we could hear each other better.

Judging from what they said, the situation was not good. The demonstrations had been brutally crushed even before they had gained momentum. The authorities used fire hoses and tear gas to disperse the crowd, and the police beat them up. I heard many new names from the NLD member, and I was encouraged to know that a new generation had joined the movement. However, it was obvious that they had no knowledge whatsoever about some of us NLD members from the earlier times, we who were now scattered in prisons all over the country. I started to wonder—was there going to be a huge gap of ignorance between the generations within the movement?

～

In the same month, Kofi Annan became the secretary-general of the UN. There was also a labor strike in South Korea, but the news was apparently censored out of all the print media, so we knew nothing about it at that time.

～

Ma Chuu and I were being careful about getting "tonics." We could not let the new arrivals know about this as they were not yet accustomed to being in prison and might be careless about what they said. We had to be careful of the long-term prisoners too because we did not know how deep they were in their dealings with the staff.

As a result, we read more religious books, in particular those written by the abbot of Mogok Monastery. After reading them I was better able to analyze my practice, and I began to gain an even deeper faith in the Buddha's dharma of self-seeking and self-understanding. I felt embarrassed at myself for years ago having sought logical explanations in books without undertaking actual practice. Now that I was practicing meditation regularly, the truth was no longer ambiguous; grasping the dharma needed a practical approach and could not be fully understood just by thought. In fact, the Buddha's dharma lies beyond seeking a logical solution through reasoning, and with correct practice, the understanding of it appears instantaneously and directly. The books I was reading now confirmed my findings. I thought to myself that the dharma could withstand any challenge and test. I also became aware that the practice must be done according to the path set out by the Buddha; other methods of meditation would not work. That was the reason, I told Ma Chuu, that the Buddha said if you take this path you can obtain Nirvana. There are other useful types of meditation, but to reach Nirvana, to be free of the cycle of rebirths, the only way was to follow the method of Vipassana.

At the end of December, after returning from her family visit, Ma Chuu told me I had won another award. I thought it had to be the same one that they had been talking about before. However, when my parents came they also told me about it.

"You got another award; it's called the Reebok Human Rights Award. Your friend Myaing[6] received the award on your behalf. It was in America. We don't know the whole story exactly. We heard it on the radio," my father explained.

6. Myaing was a childhood friend; we had not seen each other since September 1988.

I later learned that I was among five recipients around the world given this award. The award was given to young people who defended human rights, and the award money would be given to nongovernmental organizations nominated by the winners. I could do nothing but be grateful to the world, which had not forgotten me. How did they know about me and how did they come to choose me? I did not know what to think. There was a saying that prison walls have ears, but now I understood that the world's eyes and ears were able to penetrate them. The world was trying to keep Myanmar in the international spotlight so that no one would forget it. I believed this award was for everyone who participated in our cause. My parents were happy and sad at the same time; the best prize for them would be my freedom.

Nonetheless, I told myself that their suffering (*dukkha*) of having to come and see me and my younger brother would be somewhat eased as he was about to be released. For me, the best award that I could receive

Musician Michael Stipe of the band REM and Guatemalan activist and Reebok Human Rights Award winner Jesus Tecu Osorio participate in a candlelight vigil on December 10, 1996, for Ma Thida organized by the Reebok Human Rights Awards committee.

was from my parents, for they climbed into crowded buses, carrying heavy bundles large and small, in order to see me. Not only that, but my mother was filling in for me at the classes for poor children held in a monastery where I used to teach free of charge. My father was volunteering by auditing the accounts of the monastery of the abbot of Shwe Taung Kone. I always told my parents that I was most proud of being a citizen of Myanmar, being a devout Buddhist, and being their daughter. I was just happy and grateful to receive the other awards or prizes.

Just like that, 1996 was over, and 1997 opened with another new arrival to our block; Lay Lay Mun was only eighteen years old, a first-year student from Dagon University. She was imprisoned with nothing more than the clothes she was wearing, and that year it was very cold so we all felt sorry for her. She was put in the bigger cell where Daw Ohn Mya and Daw Nyunt used to live before they were transferred to the cell next to mine. Lay Lay Mon was stronger than the two earlier arrivals. When we were planning to send some food and things to her, she said, "It's their responsibility. If they leave me like this, then this is how I will live. You don't have to give me anything." We also told her to get a twig to prop up the wooden flap, and talked to her in the evenings.

At that time, Ma Chuu and I were trying to memorize two more sutras; we had already memorized eleven. During those days, my daily tasks consisted of reading secretly until late, getting up at 5:00 a.m. for the lineup, having my meals, cleaning, bathing, washing, giving food and miscellaneous items to new arrivals during our walking time, memorizing sutras, and meditating during the afternoon from noon to two o'clock. After the evening lineup I regularly prayed to the Buddha, talked with others and read "tonics" when we could get any—if not I would resume meditating. Hence, I was busy and barely had enough time for all the things I wanted to do. Unlike the period when I was meditating full-time and did not notice the day's passing, now I had to take care to fill my time with other things.

After my younger brother was released he came to visit me once and never came again, but through my parents he often sent food he had cooked. Soon after that, he left for Singapore to join my other brother. Around that time, I learned that the relationship between Ma Suu and the authorities became more difficult. I also heard that more female students had been arrested and put in the other cellblock.

In early February, three more students were put in our block— Nilar Thein, Ye Ye Tun, and Thin Thin Aye. Ye Ye Tun and Nilar Thein knew me already, but my memory was a bit hazy. They lived around Sule Pagoda Road and 33rd Street and knew me well from my work with student activists. Before I was arrested, some students held a reconsecration of the abbot of Nyaungdon, who was a political prisoner released in the general amnesty of 1992, and I had assisted them; we talked a bit about that time. I had to smile when Ye Ye Tun said that the MI interrogators had told her to study Buddhism as another "-ism." They were using what I had said to them, and passing it on to the new generation of activists! Maybe these guys were fast learners.

They were spending more time chatting with me, but regarding Ma Chuu they did not think of her as an active participant in the '88 uprising but as someone who got caught up in the chaos of the period. Around that time, the women's doctor-in-charge was granted a transfer according to her request. There were several turnovers in both wardens and guards around that time, and as a result some arrangements also changed. The new inmates were not yet sentenced, but we could not persuade any of the new guards to keep their doors open.

Then one of the new ones said to me, "A prisoner in this block told me not to get friendly with you because you don't have a good relationship with the guards. She said you have a bad record with the intelligence and that you won't be released even if there is an amnesty because your sentence is twenty years, and that we would be blacklisted if we became friends. Besides, it was you who got the doctor transferred." I was amazed at that and could only say, "Well, I didn't know I had so much power that I, a prisoner, could have an officer transferred. She asked to be transferred. It's okay if you don't want to be friends with me as long as you are happy. I can only tell you if I will be released or not when I am actually released."

In the middle of all that, I received news that an American academic organization had honored me. As usual, I was not sure how or for what.

I only found out later that it was an honorary award from the American Association for the Advancement of Science. In our cellblock, not everyone knew about it as I did not want to tell anyone since I was not sure of anything about it.

After that, the situation in our cellblock got complicated. Everyone believed that the students, like those before them, would be transferred to other buildings after they had been sentenced, but they were kept on here. At that point, there was a small problem between Ma Chuu and me. I was trying to persuade her to give up smoking, and Ma Chuu was refusing adamantly, even using rough words against me. In the eyes of the others it was a falling-out between us, but in reality she was suffering from blood clots in her toes as a result of smoking. Although she reduced the number of cigarettes each day, she was still suffering from it and was just lashing out at me from fear. I simply wanted her to get better, and I kept trying patiently in a thousand ways to make her quit.

In March 1997, Ma Chuu got into trouble as she smuggled in a container of steamed rice in her parcel after a family visit. She lost her temper with a guard when it was confiscated, as she was feeling stressed and edgy while trying to quit smoking. In prison, rice from outside was not allowed; good or bad, we had to eat the prison rice given to us. Since Ma Chuu had been in prison for a long time, once in a while she wanted to have home-cooked rice and curry. Consequently, she was punished with a ban of one week on family visits, bathing, and exercise periods. I tried to convince her to stay calm and to talk to the prison authorities. However, the matter was already out of our hands and I could only try to help reduce the hardship caused by her punishment.

I persuaded the cleaners of our block to refill Ma Chuu's pots with water while they were doing other things in her cell so that she could bathe in her cell, and the guards were also agreeable to helping her. Other prisoners in our block also did what they could to help her, apart from the long-timers who were not pleased that she could bathe; they felt she should follow the rules. Actually, everyone in our building was already eating hospital fare, including rice, which was somewhat better than that for the general population, so the smuggled rice was considered a needless offence and got blown out of proportion. For one plate of white rice, Ma Chuu's rights to receive family visits, bathe, and walk were denied for a whole week—plus a red mark was put on her record for bad behavior. In this way, some prison guards who could not even sign their own names thought they could do anything they wanted with educated prisoners.

One guard even quoted a famous actor, saying, "If you want to be like me, wait ten years, okay?" In other words, prisoners would have to wait until they were freed to be like the guards, and until that time no prisoners could be their equal. Others got infuriated by this remark; in the old days, I would have been angry too but now I said to the guard, "I feel sorry for you that you think it's a great life to have a little power in this locked up place, and how little sense your parents had that they brought you up to think like this. Even if you wait ten years, your life is not going to get better, so you should wait for the next life and pray you'll be reborn to educated parents who do not teach you stupid ideas." They could only comment with disdain that they were surprised I would speak like that, even as a prisoner, and that I was too proud. I was satisfied that I had told the guard off calmly and coolly.

In mid-March we heard about some violence between Buddhists and Muslims, and everyone believed it was the work of the military regime to take the people's attention away from real problems. Ma Chuu and I were not able to get hold of new "tonics" during that time, so we missed some world news, like the massacres that were happening in Algeria. In early April, the daughter of General Tin Oo, the SLORC's secretary-2 was killed by a letter bomb delivered to his residence. Soon after, we had new arrivals—Ma Cho and Ma Khin Mar Ye, who had participated in a demonstration; Chaw Chaw, who was implicated in the explosion case; and Daw Tint Tint Han, who had given financial support to student demonstrators and whose son was in exile. So the two bigger cells were filled with more people and it became a bit crowded in our block.

We were facing another problem: not having enough water. Summer that year was scorching hot, but our six-by-three-foot brick water tank was not filled regularly. We had to take turns for our bucket baths, and some of the newer inmates used up a lot of water without any consideration for others; they said it was up to the guards to arrange something. The problem was that the guards knew nothing beyond asking water carriers to fill the tank, not even where to get more water to make sure the tank was kept filled for all of us. Fortunately, the warden on duty at that time was quite nice and would make sure the tank was kept filled, but the water level in the source was getting low. In the hall for the general population there were about five hundred prisoners, so no one had enough water to bathe or wash. There was another women's section for the sentenced, on the other side of the main gates; they were facing the same problem, and besides, prisoners from one side could not go to the other unless officially transferred.

The young inmates working as water carriers had to work until closing time, and on unlucky days they had no chance to bathe if the water ran out. We felt bad to see them covered with sweat just for us to have our chances to bathe while they could not. In the end, even the nice warden became fed up with this problem.

Finally, the chief warden announced a new rule to ration the water. Each prisoner was allowed only eighteen scoops for bathing. Everyone was upset and in an uproar. The heat was unbearable, and I began to feel sick. I was already being careful because I suffered from allergic reactions when I sweated too much, but then I started to feel nauseated. I tried to control this with meditation. In any case I felt I must intervene about being allowed only eighteen scoops of water, so I requested to see the doctor. Since I had been well for quite some time the prison doctor suspected that my request could not be for illness so he brought along the new head of the prison hospital as well as the new women's chief warden. I informed them that I had no problem having to bathe with a limited amount of water, as I knew it was the same for everyone, but that it would be fairer to allot the amount of water according to the approximate body surface of individuals.

Before I could finish talking, the new women's chief warden interrupted to say, "Talk for yourself in the prison, not for others." However, the new head of the prison hospital politely stopped her and allowed me to speak freely. I was grateful to him for this. Soon after they went back, two glazed Martaban jars about as high as our thighs were brought over; both of them were kept filled to give everyone a chance to bathe. It was definitely better than having to make do with eighteen scoops of water. Then I heard that some prisoners were saying behind my back, "Don't touch her. She has all those MIs behind her, and that's why she gets whatever she asks for."

After this incident, although we had no more problems about bathing with one pot of water, we still did not have enough, as washing our hair and clothes used up a lot of water, especially since many of us had long hair. So Ma Chuu and I soaked our clothes with soap and we wet our hair and applied shampoo inside our cells before we were let out for our turn. This way, it was easier all around. No matter how creative I was in dealing with the lack of water, in the evenings my body started to react to the intense heat and inadequate water: my blood pressure went down and red rashes appeared all over my body and I was almost fainting with nausea. I was in control of my mind with meditation but had no control over my body, which was sweating from the heat. I could no longer pretend that I was fine and asked to have my blood pressure checked; it was seventy over fifty. The nurses gave me an intravenous glucose drip and I got better but was sick again the next day. They wanted to say I had low blood pressure because I was fasting, but my blood pressure was low even when I was not fasting. The only way to solve this problem was to be allowed to bathe twice a day. My cell was on the west and it was getting the intense heat of the afternoon sun. So I talked to the guard on duty and the nurse and received their permission to take another bucket bath in the evening. After that bath my allergic reaction got better, my blood pressure improved, and I felt better. So through the guard and the nurse, I officially requested to bathe two times a day.

The authorities said no one had ever been allowed to bathe two times a day. Actually, many more significant things had been allowed by various "understandings" or bribery throughout the history of the prison. I could never obtain this right by any "understanding" and I would not bribe, either. So I asked them to hear me out and I finally obtained permission. Even though it was obvious that I had health and skin problems, some inmates in my block thought I received this privilege because I had pull with the MIs; I felt I had to respond to their allegations so I said, "If I really had the backing of the Military Intelligence, I wouldn't be asking for baths. I'd ask for my freedom." In reality, my requests were granted because of the demands from the international community regarding my health. So although the MIs were not that sympathetic toward me, they had to allow me certain things, as they knew I could not be faking my ill health. The summer of 1997 was not at all a good time for me.

The political situation outside turned very tense again. Álvaro de Soto was assigned by the secretary-general of the United Nations to be the special envoy for Myanmar, and he was able to meet with Daw Aung San Suu Kyi. Many of her rights were being restricted by the military regime as she was not allowed to see foreign reporters, and the seventh anniversary celebration of the founding of her party, the National League for Democracy, was not permitted.

In prison, the next problem we faced was about the lineup. As I mentioned earlier, I never sat in the required position but in a meditative pose with eyes closed and palms upward on my lap instead of arms folded across my chest. One visiting minister asked me, "Are you doing *tayar*?"[7] I promptly answered, "Yes, I am always doing what is *tayar* (justice)." The minister was somewhat confused by my response and said, "Stay healthy. Ask for anything you want to eat," before turning away abruptly. Another time, I sat in my position as usual when we were asked to line up for the chief warden. He asked me, "What happened to your arm?" I had forgotten I was supposed to sit with arms folded, as I never did so, and replied, "Huh, what? No, nothing happened," as if I wanted him not to worry. He sounded bewildered as he said, "Oh, so nothing's wrong?" before he left. It happened several times when the chief warden came for surprise checks. I did not know about the other cells, but an inmate who overheard the chief warden talking to the guard on duty told me that he had said, "How old is she? Isn't she only about thirty? She can really meditate a lot!"

---

7. In Burmese, *tayar* can mean either "meditation" or "justice."

However, one day prisoners from one cell were out walking during their exercise period while those who had their cell doors open the whole day through "understandings" were warming themselves in the morning sunlight. So it looked like there were many of us out in the compound. I was officially outside too, to receive medication sent by my family, and I was checking each item against the list. Without warning, the gate to our compound was flung open, and a loud voice called, "Line up! Line up!" The new chief warden entered with male and female officers following him. I glanced at them but kept on doing what I was doing. Daw Ohmar Oo, a warden who never liked me, said, "Ma Thida, why are you still writing when you heard us telling you to line up? What are you writing?" All their faces turned dark with anger when I answered, "I'm sitting here checking the list of my medication as I was asked." In their eyes, I, the prisoner had dared to talk back to the officer. The new chief warden, U Lu Hla, who was already known for being tough, did not say anything, but our warden was later summoned to his office and harshly reprimanded.

The matter did not stop there. The guard on duty came to tell us, "Everyone must sign a statement saying you'll be seated in the standard lineup position when senior officers come into the building. We'll call you out one cell at a time to do it." Everyone in the block held an emergency meeting about this, which meant we stood close to our doors and talked. Unsurprisingly, the "when in Rome" crowd were willing to sign. Ma Chuu and I were not that happy, since this was not a new rule; it was as old as the prison, so we decided that we would think it over, depending on what they had written in the statement. The students had different opinions; some did not want to sit in this submissive position while others said they were going to sign because they did not want any more trouble. Nilar Thein, who never accepted any orders readily, said she refused to sign. The only thing I could do was advise her to see how it was worded.

Their cell was called first. The statement said that we knew we had to sit in the standard lineup position whenever senior officers entered the building with or without anyone calling out the order to do so. All in their cell signed except Nilar Thein, as did those in the other cells too. Then it was my turn. The blank space next to my name was large, so I wrote, "During previous surprise checks or visits by senior officers, prisoners were often out of their cells for various reasons and not sitting in the lineup position, yet they were never asked to do so. Only now are we being asked to sign that we know about this rule. Thus, I state that I know this rule was not always followed," and signed it. (In Burmese, I wrote this entire statement in only one complete sentence.) I noticed that the warden could hardly contain her amusement as she read each word while I was writing. Although everyone thought Nilar Thein and I would be in trouble, nothing happened to me. They later summoned Nilar Thein and persuaded her to sign it. I remember that from then on, Nilar Thein's name was on their blacklist.

After that episode, during a routine check U Lu Hla paused in front of my cell and said "Do you have everything? Have you got enough clothes? Let me know if you don't get everything you should be getting." He then left without waiting for my answer. It made me smile. Maybe he had heard from the staff of how I often taunted them: "Any law in the prison is like a rubber band! It stretches wide for those who get along well with the staff and remains tight for those who do not bend to their will. The rules here are always stretching like a rubber band."

I noticed that they were very careful when it came to dealing with me, though Daw Ohmar Oo, the warden who disliked me, was somewhat clumsy in showing her ill will. She came into the cellblock occasionally to check if our cells were clean. Actually, Ma Chuu and I were cleaning not only our cells but, if the guards allowed, scrubbing the whole block once a month with soapy water without anyone telling us to do it. However, I would not clear away the spider webs in my cell. She had nothing else to find fault with, so one day she peeped in and said, "There are so many spider webs in your cell—why haven't you cleared them away?"

I said, "I can't live in my own home and so I don't want to destroy others' homes." She was speechless and left without saying anything and never came near my cell again.

Chapter 17

Existing in Illness

Then I got ill. My period returned and the cramps were unbearably painful. I was frightened as it was flowing very heavily and the color was not normal. I had ignored its abnormal disappearance for a long time, and meanwhile it had been growing worse. I thought I should not delay any further and reported it immediately. This time, both medical officers and the prison authorities arranged things quickly. Perhaps they did not want any more death in custody—a respected writer and activist, U Tin Shwe, had recently passed away in prison, in early May of 1997. The day that they came to check on me, the order for the lineup was shrill and my block went completely silent. Everyone in the cells had to be seated in the lineup position, and I also sat down as usual.

Footsteps stopped right in front of my cell. I heard the key turn in the lock, the door opened, and someone said, "Are you meditating?"

There were many officers including the doctor and the new chief warden.

"How are you feeling? Are you still having your period?" The doctor asked as I walked out of my cell.

I answered, "It used to be heavy but now it's just spotting. But I have cramps the whole day."

The new chief warden then sneered, "You look fine, though. You are speaking in a strong voice, aren't you?"

I responded to his taunt by saying, "That's right, adrenaline is spreading through my whole body now, and thanks to that I can face anything."

Then I started discussing my treatment with the doctor. The rest of them did not say anything more and left after a while. I later heard that the authorities had been instructed to do all they could to get me treated properly. The next day, a prisoner who was volunteering at the office told me that they were complaining about me. Apparently one of them had said, "She is not only a writer but a doctor as well so there's no point in arguing with her."

I was taken to Insein General Hospital, where Dr. U Win Sein from the gynecology department, a very kind and professional doctor, examined me. He looked worried, and upon hearing the history of my ailments he ordered an ultrasound. He believed that my ignoring this problem since 1995 had not been a good idea. I admitted that I had not asked for any treatment after no longer needing to take the tuberculosis medication and that my period had petered out painlessly. I did not tell him the real reason was that I'd had no wish to go through the whole unending procedure of getting proper treatment in the prison.

After some days, I had an ultrasound taken at Insein General Hospital. Dr. U Win Sein came along with the radiologist to explain the result. The looks on their faces were not at all good. Even the chief warden and the Military Intelligence men guarding me peered at the report curiously.

The doctors said with sadness on their faces, "Daughter,[1] how could you tolerate this much pain? I'm sure it's unbearably painful! You have 'rectovaginal septum infiltration' and it's all stuck there." I had an unusual membrane growth on the wall of my uterus, which had by now spread in a thick layer over its outer surface as well as around the large intestine. I now knew why I was having pain as if a strong hand was clutching and pulling at something inside the most inner part behind my womb. This condition was not easy to cure, and that was why they looked so crestfallen. Meanwhile I was busy trying to collect my thoughts.

It is not known what causes endometriosis; many women suffer from it, and no matter how much pain they have, it is still very difficult to find answers. There is no cure or treatment for it yet. It is not cancer

---

1. Friendly, informal and affectionate term often used between strangers to show sympathy in the same way of other types of address such as mother, aunt, uncle, son, brother, sister, and so on.

but can grow like cancer cells and can spread to other organs, like the intestines, where it can cause internal bleeding. It is rare to have a condition like mine, with the growth massed thickly between the large intestine and the uterus. It would typically be detected earlier because of pain, but I had not felt it while I was meditating. The main problem was that it could not be removed with normal surgery as there was a high risk of perforating the wall of the large intestine. If that happened, parts of it would have to be cut away, and the excretion of waste matter could no longer be done normally but would have to happen through a pipe inserted into my abdomen. There was no guarantee that even after this kind of surgery the disease could be completely cured. Dr. U Win Sein explained everything in detail to the authorities, and I was grateful to him for that.

At that point even the authorities became alarmed at my condition. That day, they sent me back to my cell while they held a meeting with the MIs. Within a short time, nurses came to check my blood pressure and pulse. From that time on, a nurse came to check every week. The pain grew worse each day and was like no other pain I had suffered before. The position of my uterus was not normal and so it had become closer to the large intestine. Going to the toilet became extremely painful. The pain started after lunch—around eleven in the morning—and by eight at night I would be so exhausted with pain that I would fall asleep. The pain I was having now was several times worse than the pain I had in 1995. If I had not disciplined myself with meditation I might have just passed out or died. However, I was not worried about either of those possibilities because I kept myself aware, so my mind was alert though my body was exhausted.

It still gives me goosebumps to think of the pain I went through. As I was fasting I would prepare lunch around ten o'clock. Previously I made efforts to make my food look appetizing, but I no longer did this and just ate with mindfulness instead. Knowing that the pain came around eleven in the morning, it was in my best interest to eat while I could. I did not have to do anything in prison, so fasting was easy as I seldom felt hungry since I was not moving around much. However, the pain was so intense that sometimes it caused me to throw up without warning, and I would feel worse afterward. Finally, it became difficult even to meditate.

Suffering is not "I." "I" am not suffering. There is no "I." Keeping my mind on this helped me control my pain, yet it was so severe it almost completely immobilized me. Attempting to be aware of the pain, being aware of it, and being aware of it disappearing did not stop me from suffering it constantly. I could barely breathe when it came on in full force, and I would feel as if I were gasping for my last breath. I could not even sit up anymore. I folded a blanket to press against my abdomen as I leaned forward but it did not work. Then I curled up on my side in a fetal position but that did not help either. Walking meditation was already out of the question. I had a rubber hot-water bottle that my parents had sent me, but although it and the vacuum flask were a mere five steps away from my bed I could not even crawl that distance. The slightest movement made me exhausted.

While I was determinedly trying to be mindful, a guard who passed my cell looked in and saw me lying back with just the whites of my eyes showing and ran for the nurse. By then, I was no longer aware of my surroundings although I was still wrestling with the pain and the practice of mindfulness. The nurse immediately gave me a combined injection of the strong painkillers Ponstan (mefanemic acid) and Voltaren (diclofenac) but it did not help. I could hear the voices of Ma Chuu and the others but I was not aware of what they were saying. Thinking that if I could focus on awareness of hearing my pain might become less intense, I tried to listen to their voices, but that did not work either. Almost every day, my pain increased and finally became very pronounced until I fell asleep out of exhaustion. The next morning, I was fine as if nothing had happened, so I would catch up on the things I needed to do, such as washing clothes while bathing, washing dishes, preparing meals, and other chores, until pain arrived almost on the dot at 11:30. It was not just one day or one week. Knowing that surgery would be difficult, Dr. U Win Sein continued to treat me with hormone replacement. Since I could no longer take medicines orally he would inject them. Every fortnight I was jabbed with two Depo-Provera (progesterone) injections, which is commonly known as the three-month contraceptive. Nevertheless the pain remained. I was, however, allowed to get regular treatment at Insein General Hospital.

In the middle of this, there came another annnoyance: lists of rules for both guards and prisoners were handed out and we were told to memorize them. I cannot remember them now, but I know the rules for prisoners were not consistent. I told the guards not even to think about testing me as I could not memorize such a messily written list. The long-term prisoners who "lived like Romans" did exactly as they were told. Ma Chuu and the three young new prisoners refused to memorize it. The guards only tested the new group, who simply refused to say anything, and as punishment their rights to bathe and exercise were stopped. The guards did not bother to ask anyone else. As usual, Ma Chuu and I made sure they could take bucket baths in their room with the help of the water carriers. After that, the new group understood that we were not really the bad guys. After their punishment period was over, we persuaded the guards to keep all the cell doors open during the day.

Because of the side effects of my hormone replacement therapy, acne was breaking out all over my face. I wanted to use their mirror in the guards' room in order to rub on skin ointment; Ma Chuu managed to persuade the guards to allow this, and on the very day that we had asked for our doors to be opened, I went to the guards' room. The mirror was in a corner next to the entrance, so I could not be easily seen as I stood looking into it, applying ointment to my face. I heard one of the long-term prisoners run up to the guard and say, "Don't do that! Don't open their doors. It'll get complicated for us if they get friendly. Go! Go and tell the warden to keep all the doors closed, and come shut ours too, immediately, so that they can't point at us. Come! Shut our doors at once!" I was flabbergasted. I could not believe I was hearing this. It seemed there was nothing else we could do.

Not long after that, some of the new arrivals were transferred to the other women's section. Just before Dr. Lei Lei Win left, Daw Kyi Kyi was admitted to the guarded ward[2] at Rangoon General Hospital, as

---

2. A dark hall in the basement of the hospital with a few small windows, within which is a cluster of iron-barred cells with beds packed into each.

her diabetes was out of control. Her family could visit her more often there and provide proper food for her condition. However, before that she had to undergo tests at the hospital, and once after her checkup she had come back with very high blood pressure, which sent everyone into a panic. It seemed that while she was being registered, she had proudly announced that she was a communist. The nurse on duty had replied, "Now, now, don't you be too proud to be a communist—don't you know the Soviet Union is falling apart?" Daw Kyi Kyi probably knew that already, but she exploded with rage to be told like this and her blood pressure shot up. In July, she was admitted to the guarded ward at the hospital, where she remained for a long time.

After several Depo injections, my pain eased a bit. For several months, every day from eleven in the morning to eight or nine at night the pain had persisted despite one injection after another. It was only through meditation, with which I was able to be mindful of the Buddha's dharma, that I was able to cope with it; otherwise I might have crumbled completely. It was the Three Gems—the Buddha, dharma, and sangha—that I kept in my mind, and this gave me the strength to withstand the pain. Thus it was not surprising for me to be indifferent to what I was eating or even to whether I had an appetite or not.

~

It was late 1997. The British relinquished ownership of Hong Kong to China, which announced it would rule "one country with two political systems." In Cambodia, Hun Sen came into power. The SLORC leader Senior General Saw Maung passed away, and I heard that very few people attended his funeral.[3] K. R. Narayanan was the first "untouchable," or Dalit, to become president of India. In Britain, Lady Diana was mourned after being killed in a car crash in Paris. In mid-August, some high schools in Myanmar that had been closed down the previous year due to student demonstrations were reopened. On

---

3. It is a matter of prestige for the deceased and family to have many attendees at the funeral.

November 15, the State Law and Order Restoration Council changed its name to the State Peace and Development Council (SPDC) but there was no change in the regime's top leadership, which consisted of Senior General Than Shwe, General Maung Aye, and General Khin Nyunt.

$\sim$

One night around nine o'clock, not long after I had fallen asleep, I heard Ma Chuu knocking on my wall. I asked her what it was and Ma Chuu replied, "They are coming to transfer me to another prison. Don't worry about me. I'm packing up—have to go now. I know you are not on the list, but I don't know who else is going."

I felt sad and distressed but realized I had no control over the matter. So I just stood near the door and told Ma Chuu to keep on trying to quit smoking and to keep on meditating, along with whatever other words of encouragement I could think of. Although we were not usually allowed to talk that late, it was highly unlikely that we would see each other again soon, so the guards left us alone. We remembered that it was not long ago that we had said to each other, "Even if one of us is freed first, the other will follow within a year." We had understood and cared for each other all these years, and it was heartbreaking to be parted so unexpectedly. I did not have a chance to give her anything as a token of our friendship; we said goodbye and I stood there watching her back as she, loaded with her belongings, disappeared into the darkness of the night.

Altogether about one hundred men and women were transferred to other prisons that night along with Ma Chuu, including Daw Ohn Mya, Lay Lay Mon, Thin Thin Aye, Nilar Thein, Ye Ye Tun, and a number of other political prisoners from our cellblock as well as some prisoners from the women's section on the other side. Actually, those transferred were, like me, women who refused to accept the status quo of life in Insein Prison. Our cellblock was left with mostly long-term prisoners who did not mind kowtowing to the demands of the authorities. That I was left behind could have been because of my illness, or it could well have been a deliberate move to isolate me socially. Later I learned that Myo Myint Nyein and Sein Hlaing were also among those who were transferred.

For several days, I felt so desolate without Ma Chuu that I had to turn my attention toward meditation without bothering to talk to anybody. It did not go easily as I felt too disturbed by all that had happened the past months. How complicated was this world we lived in! In spite of the situation, I never considered myself a victim. The only thing that could cause me trouble was my own mind—a belief I made sure to hold on to firmly at all times. This was about analyzing the process of impermanence, suffering, and nonself, so I had to see troubles and distress as mere challenges to the strength of my belief, and I had to find within myself ways to face them.

The cleaners who had been jailed for prostitution sometimes told me touching stories from their lives. I paid particular attention to one woman, Shan Ma, as she was a gifted storyteller. Her husband was a soldier, and when he died in battle the commander of his troop arranged for her to marry another soldier.[4] As the pay of her husband was not enough, she stole bullets to sell to the rebels, and then she would trek deep into the jungle in order to reach them, carrying the bullets in bamboo tubes normally used to store rice. She ended up having an affair with one of the rebel leaders, and she was soon stealing, trading, carrying, and smuggling anything, including weapons and heroin, to and from the army and rebels. Carrying heroin for the rebels meant she had to go into town, and sometimes it brought her to Yangon, the biggest city in the country. She hid packets of heroin in public toilets, which were so dark and dirty nobody dared go in them, and arranged for people to collect the drugs.

Shan Ma was never caught for this, and even if she had been she could have avoided arrest by offering to sleep with the police, which always worked. According to her, she had been arrested for smuggling weapons but had managed to get her charge reduced to the lesser one

---

4. A normal practice in the Myanmar military.

of prostitution after sleeping with a police officer. I did not know how many "night birds"[5] like Shan Ma were out there, married to a soldier but having an affair with a rebel leader and sleeping with the police. Other cleaners said they would tell their husbands they were working night shifts while instead working as prostitutes, sometimes in the back seat of expensive cars with tinted windows, parked on the grassy edge of Royal Lake. I found it very sad but also understood that I could do nothing to change their lives; I could eventually no longer bear to hear their stories, so I stopped asking.

On December 11, 1997, the SPDC issued order 1/97, which reduced long-term sentences like the death penalty and sentences over ten years down to ten years. I calculated the time that Ma Chuu had already spent in jail and knew she would be released very soon. I was happy for her; as for me, although my total sentence was twenty years, none of my individual sentences was over ten years, so the order was not applicable to my case. At that time, I missed Ma Chuu very much, as well as the "tonics" she would smuggle in, so I had to pass the time by meditating. In the last week of December, I heard that the SPDC had notified some of the NLD leaders that dialogue between them was not going to happen, and I also learned that one of the NLD leaders, U Kyi Maung, had resigned from the party.

Just before the end of 1997, Dr. Daw May Win Myint, the MP for Mayangone Township elected in 1990, was arrested and sent to our block; we called her Aunty May. She was placed in the cell where Ma Chuu used to be, and she was a good companion. Although she often spoke without thinking twice, she was a genuinely goodhearted woman. I got to hear about the NLD and Ma Suu from her, and there were many stories of internal conflict that worried me. Aunty May was friendly to everyone but she did not bend to the compliant attitude of the "when in Rome" prisoners. She was also a medical doctor, so it was comforting to have someone to discuss my health with, although I felt sorry for her plight. I briefed her about things that had happened

---

5. Common term for prostitutes.

in this block but mainly we talked about the NLD and the political situation. Neither of us lost hope of seeing dialogue take place, despite knowing the SPDC would not tolerate any consideration for Ma Suu. Moreover, we both hoped to see U Win Tin freed, as we had worked with him closely and knew him to be politically astute.

During my imprisonment I saw U Win Tin only two times, both from a distance. The first time was when I was on my way to the prison hospital to have a chest x-ray, and I saw him standing on verandah of its upper story; I waved at him and he saw me. The second time was when he was on his way to his family visit while I was going to mine, and he waved at me. He was hooded so at first I could not make out who it was, but then he pulled his hood up and gave me a thumbs up. Once when two male inspectors came to search my cell, I was surprised when instead of searching my cell, they told me U Win Tin said hello and for me to keep well. Another time, Daw Ohn Mya in my block came back from her internal family visit to see her husband U Zaw Htoo, also a political prisoner, and gave me two coffee mix packets sent to me through her husband from U Win Tin, on which he had written the initials "W. T." At that time, I thought about how gentle he was and if he was released soon how great it would be for him to mediate between Ma Suu and the military regime. I had full faith in him and if anyone had ever asked me, I would have said that if only one prisoner could be freed, I would want it to be U Win Tin rather than myself. Nevertheless, 1997 came to an end and not one of us was released.

The passing of years changed nothing in prison. Calendars were not allowed, so we tried to keep track of religiously important dates by a small verse—"Odd days, twenty-nine, for Tagu, even days for Kasone"[6] —to calculate the days and months. With this verse, we could work out the full-moon holy days. News in early 1998 was not good. On February 18, the famous and respected writer Mya Than Tint passed away suddenly at his home in Sanchaung. U Thein Tin, organizer

---

6. This lyric is about how many days are in the months of the Myanmar lunar calendar. Tag and *Kasone* are the first and second months; some months have twenty-nine days and others have thirty days.

of the NLD in Yangon Division, passed away in Insein Prison but we did not know the cause of his death. My health did not improve much although I was getting regular treatment, so the nurse came to check my blood pressure and pulse every day. I felt sad but also wanted to laugh, knowing they only showed me they cared whenever someone died in prison; it looked as if they were worried I too might die.

There were new arrivals in our block, and many of them were elderly. There was Ma Khin Swe Yin, owner of a photocopier shop, accused of typing out and printing pamphlets pleading for Buddhist monks to help ease the political situation; a Karen woman; and the two older sisters and two younger twin sisters of Ko Thein, who had been charged with planting bombs in Yangon under the direction of the armed student group on the border, the All Burma Students' Democratic Front. The twins were separately placed in two different blocks.

The crimes of those four sisters were giving money to Ko Thein when he asked and helping him to get a national ID card; plus the twins were accused of sending novels to him with the help of the Karen woman while he was at the border camp, and so all five siblings were in jail. The two older sisters, the Karen lady, and Dr. May Win Myint all had high blood pressure, so I said I would not have mine checked unless theirs was too. The warden refused, and admitted that they were giving me this care only on the orders of the Military Intelligence. I pushed further, saying the nurse need not do it, as I could. As usual, their response was to tell me not to speak on behalf of others. Finally they agreed to check the blood pressure of two others every time they came for me. I was regarded as a troublemaker once again, but at least it was satisfying to see these women getting some help.

In early March my parents told me that Ma Chuu had been freed, and they brought me food and gifts from her. She had comforted my parents by saying that for sure I would be released within this year. I was delighted that she was freed and sent a message to her not to resume smoking. I became friendlier with Aunty May and another inmate, Khin Swe Yin, who was single. Particularly, I had a lot to talk about with the latter; she too had her own timetable of religious practice, health care, and cleaning routines, so we got along well. In the same month, I heard that cracks had appeared in the relationship between Ma Suu and Ma Thanegi but did not know much else other than that Ma Thanegi had opposed Ma Suu's calls for economic sanctions. I recalled the campaign trips we had been on together; at that time I had been in my early twenties and had sometimes behaved like a child toward Ma Suu, but I remembered Ma Thanegi was willing to do anything for her. She would not even allow anyone to share her tasks, so I was perplexed to hear something like this. Later I found out that it was not a personal attack but that Ma Thanegi had written an article in which she urged Ma Suu to rethink her pro-sanctions strategy. I heard many other critical remarks concerning Ma Suu, but she always remained in my heart.

Senior General Than Shwe said in a speech on March 27, Revolutionary Day (or Armed Forces Day, as the military had renamed it to the chagrin of many), that he held no grudges against the registered political parties. This news was the talk of the prison and many again thought there would be amnesty; yet nothing happened. In April, a British and Australian citizen, James Mawsley, was arrested for distributing antigovernment pamphlets. Since there were no more "tonics" I knew nothing about the political situation and learned the news only when my parents came. In May, President Suharto of Indonesia was forced to resign. In the same month, I heard of the death of Aung Kyaw Moe, who had served his prison term but was not released. He went on a hunger strike and was tortured to death. I was crushed to learn of this and disconsolate thinking about all the political prisoners languishing in prison.

The Depo-Provera injections were easing my pain, but the latest ultrasound result was not good; it seemed there were even more complications. What was certain was that although the medications I was taking were not making any headway, my endurance was growing stronger so the pain was more endurable. In fact, I had suffered intense pain every day for nearly two months, so I felt numb toward it, and my meditation had led me to separate "me" and "pain" so that I no longer viewed it as a problem. Since I had started practicing Vipassana

I had not touched my prayer beads and had tried only to focus on strengthening my awareness.[7]

By this time, Dr. U Win Sein from Insein General Hospital had been transferred to Mandalay and my treatment was taken over by a female doctor. However, she did not have much interest in me and only suggested I continue with Depo-Provera injections. She too had been transferred by the time of my next appointment. So I requested to see a gynecologist from the Central Women's Hospital, because if things got worse I could end up with my large intestine being cut away and a colostomy opening in my abdominal skin. As usual, I had to give some time for the bureaucratic red tape to unravel. After several discussions with the authorities and being seen firsthand in agonizing pain, I was finally permitted to consult the gynecologist at the Central Women's Hospital. In the midst of it, some guards and prisoners gossiped that I was pretending to be in pain because I wanted to go out. If only they knew how painful it was for me to go to a place dressed as a convict where I used to wear a doctor's coat with a stethoscope draped over my neck! After I told them how I felt, the gossip stopped.

At the Central Women's Hospital, the gynecologist Dr. U Soe Aung attended to me and prescribed Danazol, which was more effective than Depo. The problem was that it was not available in Myanmar, so my parents had to ask my younger brother in Singapore to send it. I found out after I was released that organizations such as the Physicians for Human Rights from Boston helped to get this medicine. It was very expensive, but my brother was able to get it and send it quickly. The side effects of this medicine, which blocks female hormones, include changes in voice, hair growth on the face, uncontrollable weight gain, and loss of bone density. Dr. U Soe Aung instructed me to eat less and to do regular exercise, and he was relieved when I told him I was fasting three days a week. However, I would have to exercise more regularly. My body weight had gone up due to the Depo injections but as the drug increases liquid in cells, I was in truth bloated.

---

7. In Myanmar use of prayer beads is common, especially when people are sick or in trouble. Even though I was feeling pain I focused on meditation, not beads.

In June 1998, all the schools that had been closed since 1996 were reopened. On June 23, I heard that the NLD had demanded the authorities form a parliament no later than August 21. Political tensions grew but at least a proper demand and timeline had been set, so I was feeling happy, but the situation deteriorated even further. On July 7, Daw Aung San Suu Kyi was blocked on her way to visit Daw Hla Hla Moe, who was an elected MP of Minhla Township in Pegu Division. All the rumors of Ma Suu being sent to that new building in Insein flew around again. At the end of July, Ma Suu tried to go by car to Pathein to visit imprisoned MPs, and again her convoy was blocked near Htantabin Village. She refused to turn back and sat in her car for five days until she was forcibly removed. Also, many elected MPs of the NLD were detained and arrested. Even the guards were telling us about these events. In the prison around this time, we were often ordered to line up in what were probably attempts to keep us under control.

On the anniversary of 8.8.88, I heard that the home minister had invited the NLD Central Executive Committee members for a meeting but it was rejected because it excluded Daw Aung San Suu Kyi and U Tin Oo. The political situation was growing worse. In the prison, a wealthy and pretty young woman who was implicated in a case against a division commander and who had been sentenced to forty-four years was bribing practically all the guards as well as many prisoners by handing out dozens of packets of imported snacks, and for this grand gesture she was able to strut among her pack of followers. Then I heard that eighteen foreign nationals had been arrested for handing out anti-SPDC pamphlets in downtown Yangon but were later deported.

The date of the NLD's ultimatum to convene a parliament arrived, but the SPDC had not responded. The NLD then announced that it would form a parliament on its own with the other ethnic MPs. This was like the climax of a traditional drama, and many NLD members were arrested all over the country or detained and interrogated for days. Meanwhile, my health was improving with the new medication, but Dr. U Soe Aung wanted me to consult a more senior obstetrician and gynecologist, Dr. Daw Hla Hla Myaing. He was conflicted over whether I should continue taking this medication, since there was not much change apparent in the latest ultrasounds. We both feared the side effects of this medication, as there were risks of damage to the bone marrow, bone density, and arteries. The seriousness of the disease could not be calculated because of my ability to endure pain. For an intrauterine ultrasound, an ultrasound transducer probe could not be used, as in my unmarried state my vagina was not wide enough. He therefore suggested Dr. Daw Hla Hla Myaing in order to get a better diagnosis, but it was not easy to get permission to be taken out of prison to see yet another specialist, especially during times of political tension, regardless of how helpful or necessary the doctors were.

Around the end of August, some students held demonstrations in Hledan Township. Although the name of the ruling junta had changed from restoring law and order to bringing peace and development, all voices of dissent were being put down as brutally as ever. At the same time, a woman was put into Aunty May's cell. She was the mistress of a former army major. She had bribed to get into a cell because she wanted to avoid having to sleep with all the others on the floor as would happen if she were put into the large buildings. The guards treated her indulgently as she was very wealthy and could throw money around. She wanted to dominate everyone else too, but none of the political prisoners gave in to her. Aunty May tried her best to get along with her but found it difficult as she was of a too vastly different type, so Aunty May tried to move to another cell. At the same time, a young woman sentenced to death for a brutal murder was placed in Daw Nyunt's cell. In the end, Aunty May had to move in with Daw Nyunt and the young murderer. However, they left me alone in my cell, though I was also worried that either one of these two young women would be placed with me. Ma Don was all alone but no one was placed in her cell since her mother might return any day from the hospital.

Aunty May had high blood pressure and stiffness in her arms; both conditions grew worse, and she was finding it difficult to clean herself. As she had once worked at a hospital for the handicapped she knew she needed to exercise with machines, but for this she would have to go to a hospital outside for regularly physiotherapy treatment. Ma Don's door had not been left open after her mother (the one who had secured the privilege of the open door) was sent to the guarded ward at Rangoon General Hospital, but she was not released as Ma Don hoped. In addition, Ma Don's husband, Moe Win, also serving his sentence, was suffering from a serious case of ulcers and he possibly needed surgery. Ma Don thus became ill with anxiety for her family. For Ma Don and her mother, that year was in fact the last to be served in their sentences, but nothing was certain as the political situation was very tense. We heard that some political prisoners who had already served their full terms were kept on under Act 10 (A), which allowed imprisonment for up to five years without charge.

The mistress of the military major sometimes had hysterics when things did not go her way, and she would sing, shout, complain, or swear loudly. It was disturbing for the devout inmates who were meditating or counting their prayer beads. Meanwhile the one under death sentence would inform on us for any little thing so that she might have an easier life in jail. Consequently our cellblock was in perpetual turmoil and unease.

On September 16, the NLD established a group called the Committee Representing the People's Parliament with elected ethnic MPs and other individuals to work toward a genuine parliament. In response to this, the Union Solidarity and Development Association, backed by the military regime, organized public protests against Ma Suu, the NLD, and the new committee. The political prisoners did not know what to think of all this confusing news. We all hoped to be freed after a national reconciliation process or else a clear win of one side or the other, but in the current situation this hope was fading fast. The SPDC responded that they would accept nothing but their own national convention, and they began arresting a lot more people from the NLD and ethnic parties, including members of the youth and women's wings, saying they were only inviting those involved in the planned new parliament "to discuss various opinions at the government guesthouse." The arrested committee members and supporters ended up in the so-called government guesthouse such as the Ye Mon military camp, used for interrogations.

Luckily, obstetrician and gynecologist Dr. Daw Hla Hla Myaing was allowed to monitor my condition at the Central Women's Hospital. She was more succinct than any other doctors I had seen. The MIs who tried to come into the examination room were told to stay out. "Don't follow us in. Your patient here is not someone who would run away. So wait out there, do you hear me?" I was delighted at the thought that I had someone like her on my side. She later decided to give me two different treatments. First, she wrote a permission slip for my parents to be able to once a week bring me food and vegetables with lots of fiber. As I mentioned earlier it was very rare to have fresh vegetables in prison. Second, she recommended that I be tested with laparoscopy,[8] which would show my condition exactly. Depending on the finding, Dr. Daw Hla Hla Myaing would decide whether I should continue with the current medication or not. In her physical examination she had felt masses of tissue in the area. She gave instructions for me to have blood tests and a chest x-ray, as the laparoscopy would have to be done under general anesthetic. The day for my laparoscopy arrived. It was the morning of October 11, 1998, and I took along all the things I might need. I left my other belongings with Aunty May because I knew I would be put back in my cell right after surgery. Then a group of MIs came as I was being registered at the hospital, and they told Dr. Daw Hla Hla Myaing that they would be taking me back as soon as the general anesthetic wore off. Laparoscopy surgery during those days was done not as a test but as a whole surgical procedure; thus, Dr. Daw Hla Hla Myaing explained to them that the patient could not be discharged right after the anesthetic wore off but must remain under her care. The MIs said there was no guarded ward at this hospital to accommodate a prisoner and thus there was no guarantee of security. They warned her that unless they could take me back to prison right after the surgery they would not allow it.

Dr. Daw Hla Hla Myaing was very upset and said to me, "Daughter, I can't agree to something so irresponsible. I'm afraid I can't do this

---

8. Laparoscopy is a surgical procedure that uses a thin, lighted tube put through a cut in the belly to look at the organs inside.

for you. Besides, you've taken about three hundred tablets of this medicine by now, so it'll be better for you to stop now. Without knowing what your condition really is, it is no good to keep taking it. I'll make another appointment for you and we will see the next time about what to do. You have to understand why I decided not to have the surgery."

There was nothing I could do, either; it could get very complicated if I were to be taken back before the anesthetic wore off, while I might not be aware of what was happening.

I reassured her, "*Ma Ma,*[9] my uterus has been giving me so much trouble and all I want now is to take it out. But I do understand you and I understand everyone. I don't want to say anything more."

I did not wish to put the doctor in a difficult position; she had been very sympathetic towards me. The MIs were in the same spot as well; they did not dare take any responsibility in the current political tension, and I sincerely understood their predicament. I only blamed my own physical being that had been causing me so much trouble, so all I wanted was to get rid of my uterus.

I said to the MIs, "That's fine. I understand it's not the doctor's responsibility, if, through not being allowed to get a proper treatment, something goes wrong with me after the operation. Take me back right now."

The young intelligence man looked upset at my words. Dr. Daw Hla Hla Myaing gave me a look to reassure me that she understood. Soon after that, I was back in my cell. Others in the cellblock were unhappy upon hearing my story. "You are now very well known and talked about by the media outside and I think your case is handled directly by the higher-ups. It looks like they want to make no mistake in this complicated situation. Let it be, and let's see what happens at your next appointment. We'll see what happens after you stop taking the medicine," said Aunty May. After that incident, the prison authorities instructed the medical staff to be more careful of my health and also to try to understand in detail about my illness.

---

9. Customary polite and term by which a junior physician addresses a senior one.

Chapter 18

Conflicts

At the end of November, I heard that some NLD members had resigned from the party. In reality, the SPDC had tried every trick they could, with innumerable harassments, to cause a mass resignation. I also heard that the government-backed National Unity Party, as well as some pro-regime ethnic parties, voiced their opposition to the NLD's call for convening parliament. I noticed that the political situation was growing more complicated. Unexpectedly, on November 6, I was told that an appointment for a medical consultation had been made for November 12; on that day, even Dr. Daw Hla Hla Myaing was surprised to see me again. I explained that I had not made any request to see her earlier than the previously set date. My condition had improved a lot by that time due to my having stopped the medication and to the fresh vegetables I was eating regularly. I was no longer too constipated and my period had stopped again so I was not in so much pain now. All I knew was that the MIs asked her to check on my current health condition, and after that I was brought back to prison.

On November 15, I heard that the Ayeyarwaddy Division commander, Major General Myint Aung, had passed away. He was the main cause of the troubles and danger we had faced during our Ayeyarwaddy campaign trips, and he had held many bitter grudges against Ma Suu. He lost his position as commander when the SLORC became SPDC, and he died without any status. Ma Suu, whom he hated so much, was still wearing flowers in her hair and was still campaigning for dialogue. It was his karma from which we could learn something.

Around that time, Aunty May was sent to the guarded ward at Rangoon General Hospital to get regular physiotherapy treatment for her arm, which was getting worse. Ma Don's stomach pains grew worse and she was even sent to stay at the small clinic inside the other women's section, but she could not stay there for long as it was too filthy. By now, their family was getting exhausted, since Ma Don's mother, Daw Kyi Kyi, had not been freed as expected; she was still at Rangoon General Hospital, separated from her daughter. Ma Don put in a request to be sent to the hospital for her stomachache so that she could take care of her mother at the same time. For the rest of us in the cellblock, it was business as usual. Then, a Karen student who was a Christian missionary was put in our block after being arrested on her way to the border and accused of assisting the students in exile. Her name was Naw Wah Gay, a remarkably frank, honest young woman who was very interested in education, so we quickly became friends. Our cellblock was kept filled with new arrivals, even if many had left.

While I was waiting for my next medical appointment as well as watching for changes in my condition after stopping the medication, I got better. My mother came to deliver the fruit and vegetable parcel every Tuesday. I shared them with the inmates in the cell of Ma Khin Swe Yin and Ma Khin Mar Ye every other week but shared with Naw Wah Gay every day since she was all alone. My mother often brought vegetables that were difficult to obtain, so everyone got into the habit of eagerly waiting for what she would send in each week.

One Tuesday in early December I received her parcel as usual, but four mangoes on the list were missing. I handed the parcel back to the trustee prisoner who brought it to me and asked her to report that I would accept the parcel only if it came back with every item on the list. Within a few minutes, she came back and said to me, "Those mangoes were not confiscated, they were just not allowed."

(Not long before, nine paracetamol tablets had been missing from the medicines sent in by my parents. This was a normal practice. Often, prisoners would ask their families to bring cheroots so that they could give them to cleaners and water carriers as tips, as they were used like money in prison. The guards would ask the prisoners to contribute ten cheroots to the collective fund to give them out to the cleaners and others, but Ma Chuu and I preferred to keep all of them with us and tip people directly. Yet they thought they could get away with taking the paracetamol tablets. The staff said they would replace the missing tablets, but I told them I wanted my own pills back. I asked who was responsible and refused any replacements. That had caused quite a stir, and after making some inquiries they said that they had been used at the prison hospital. I did not take their replacements but told them that they could always ask me if they ever needed medication and I would not hesitate to donate some if there was such a need. They had been very careful about my parcels since then. Thus I already expected the answer of my mangoes being "not allowed.")

I told her to go back and ask why, as I had permission from the doctor to eat any fruit, including mangoes. The trustee went away, scratching her head. After a while she returned with a young guard who said that there was an outbreak of diarrhea in the men's side and since mangoes soften the stool, they had been banned.

I replied, "Exactly, I need to eat mangoes because I am very constipated—that is why I need them back. If I can't have them I won't accept the rest of the stuff." The guard went away again, sniffing in disapproval.

She returned soon and said, "No, they said you must take the rest of the items because all mangoes are banned. Please, Elder Sister, if you want mangoes I'll smuggle some in for you tomorrow. Please take the stuff—I'm getting really tired of going back and forth."

I told her, "No, I cannot accept this. Go back and ask them who made that decision, I want to know so I can ask that person directly." The young guard went away again, calling upon her mother to save her, followed by the snickering trustee who was still lugging my parcel.

She soon returned and said, "Sis, you won't get the mangoes back. This order came from the chief warden and they said the decision wouldn't change no matter who you asked. Please accept this now. This girl and I will die from exhaustion."

I sympathized with these two women but thought I needed to teach a lesson to the chief warden and his staff.

"All right, take those mangoes and this list and give all of it back to my mother and get her signed note that she has received the four mangoes. Only then will I accept the other stuff in the parcel."

Sighing heavily, she left. People in my block were saying that by the time I finished antagonizing the staff, the other vegetables in the bag would surely be rotten.

The two young women came back, and the guard, who was quite friendly and polite with me even in this situation, said, "Oh, Sister, just let me die! Your mother's gone already, she left once the parcels were taken in. What do I do now, huh? Do you want me to follow your mother to your house and ask for her signature that she has received these mangoes? Is that what you want?" She said this tauntingly, and I taunted her right back, "I might, if I were like in the old days. I would've set the whole sky ablaze with my temper. But now you can do this: go tell that officer who confiscated my mangoes to keep them until my next prison visit and she can return them, good or bad, to my parents right in front of my eyes. If she can promise me that, I will accept the other stuff." They again hurried back to the office.

The truth was that I could not accept the idea of the staff taking even one hardboiled egg from families who could only afford to send in ten for their loved ones in prison. They often took whatever they liked with the excuse that it was not permitted. I knew that the value of four mangoes was nothing, but I wanted the authorities and guards to know that they could not treat everything as theirs just because the stuff belonged to prisoners. It did not matter whether I could eat the mangoes or not. Soon after, the authorities sent word that they promised to return them to my mother and asked me to take the rest of the things.

I told the guard, "Okay, take note and tell the other guards here too that you can't just say something is not allowed and take away anything from what the families bring. The real owners are never the staff of the prison, understand?" She did not say anything but nodded.

I gave some cheroots to the young cleaner who had been carrying my parcels back and forth and remarked to her that she must be exhausted. The young woman said cheekily, "Yes, it's tiring but it's really fun. Ha ha ha . . . just kidding! I'm leaving now!" before she ran off, laughing. By this time, it was nearly noon and the vegetables were no longer fresh.

My parents could not stop laughing when they were handed four rotten mangoes on their next visit. They already knew the story as some guards at the parcel department had told them about it, saying, "We thought we might have to come to your home, your daughter is unbelievable."

My mother asked, "What do I do with them?" Both my parents laughed when I said, "Oh, Mom, throw them in the garbage bin! What more do you want with them?"

I gained an even higher rank in the troublemaker category after that episode. I could not help it. If we allowed this type of corruption because it was a trivial matter it would keep on happening and we would be accessories to the corrupt system. Even though I was causing trouble like this it had no impact on my morality, integrity, and wisdom.

In December, we learned that General Khin Nyunt had been sued by the NLD for injustice inflicted by his MIs on NLD members and the public. However, the international news was almost completely silent. At every visit we received only domestic news, so we had nothing to discuss about international situations. My family visits were even more closely monitored than before. A guard was assigned to listen and take note of everything we said, and a warden was also assigned to listen and make sure the guard had left nothing out. They now took my blood pressure every day and also had to give a weekly health report to the higher authorities. According to nurse's instructions, an officer from the MI came to collect my health record every morning at six. However, they did not know the irrelevance of their monitoring and caregiving to the disease I was suffering. At least I was happy to see that the other prisoners' blood pressure was taken and recorded.

Before the end of that year, Ma Don was admitted to the guarded ward at Rangoon General Hospital where her mother was. I was happy about it, thinking they might be released from the hospital without returning to prison. And so, 1998 came to a close.

Chapter 19

Death in the Family

Early 1999 in Insein was nothing out of the ordinary, and I had been given no chance to see the gynecologist since the mangoes saga. The next appointment with her was still some time away, and the authorities also seemed to fear I might tell this story to her. One day, a guard from the head office filled in for one of the guards who was on emergency leave. She went on with her tasks and then approached my cell, looking sad. She said abruptly, "I'm so sorry to hear about your younger brother. How old was he? How did he die?" I was confused and thought at first that she might have been mistaking me with someone else. Then I suddenly realized what it meant and demanded, "What do you mean? Who died? How do you know? Tell me!"

She was very alarmed at this. "I thought you already knew! Please don't tell anyone—I can get into trouble for this. The other day I met your mother and another lady at the gate and they asked me if you'd be allowed to attend his funeral. I just pointed to the staff on duty. I don't know what happened next. I am so sorry, I've upset you."

She seemed genuinely sorry. I felt pierced to the heart and began to panic . . . younger brother, younger brother, who could that be? Was it the one in Singapore or the one who was released only recently? Who could it be?

"Which one of my brothers was it?" I asked repeatedly. I was so shocked that I could not collect my thoughts.

"I don't know that either, I didn't dare talk to your mother and I didn't know how many younger brothers you have. I thought you knew and that you had been allowed to go to his funeral. I had better stop now or I'm going to get into real trouble letting you know. Please don't tell anyone and pretend that you know nothing when you have your visit next time." She quickly left and from that time avoided me completely.

My thoughts were in chaos. Kyaw, my brother in Singapore, was the only financial support of our parents as he was earning well and sending money to them. He also worked as a model and took good care of himself so I thought it might not be him. Yet it was a sudden death and I wondered if he could have had an accident in Singapore; I could not be sure of anything. Aung, the one at home, was the problem child, and my parents had suffered several times because of him. I had told my parents to take him to a doctor as I was told he had been coughing up blood, but despite that he rarely stayed home. After his release from jail, he even went to live in Singapore for a short time and then to Malaysia. However, he only found odd jobs, so he came home and was nothing but a burden to my parents. I had heard enough of his behavior during prison visits; I was not sure whether his drug addiction had been dealt with or not. I thought it was highly likely that it was him.

I could not imagine what my parents would be going through if it was the one in Singapore. And if it was the one in Yangon, they would have no children living with them. I was in despair at every turn of my thoughts. Tears rolled down my cheeks; I tried to reason that nothing was permanent, and slowly I regained control over my mind. I was not completely out of the emotional state but was able to control my tears. I kept on concentrating on awareness and being mindful. We all are mortal beings and thus we will have to meet and be parted. My younger brother died. My parents were suffering.

The cell door opened for my bath time. Before I went to bathe I ran up to Ma Khin Swe Yi's door and told her the news. I also asked her not to tell anyone else so as to keep this news away from the guards. I told Naw Wah Gay too. They both felt terrible and I was at last able to get a better grip on myself after having shared my sorrow with friends. I recalled a dream that I'd had not long ago, in which my parents and I, without my two brothers, were going somewhere in a luxury saloon car, the kind I had seen on the streets but had never been in before. I rarely dreamed and rarely remembered them if I did, so I thought it strange that I could remember this one.

My younger brother in Singapore, Kyaw, left in 1992, so he was not often on my mind, but I had been on internal visits with Aung while he was in Insein Prison. He had also come once after his release, and another time he had sent with my parents the watercress he fried himself, so he was in my mind more vividly. However, the question of which brother passed away remained unanswered. On the other hand, I was utterly amazed to know that people existed who would not inform a prisoner that a family member had died or give permission to attend the funeral.

I remembered that the writer Min Lu had been allowed to attend the funeral when his father, the famous writer and director U Tha Dhu, passed away in 1991. Although I never thought I would one day face a similar tragedy, something like this could happen to anyone. My parents were no longer young; at the time my father was seventy-one and my mother, sixty-four. Anything could happen at any time to them. My father had been consulting a cardiologist for his irregular heartbeat, so I was always worried for them but had never imagined either of my brothers dying. Now, it was obvious that age, sex, or gender made no difference in *anissa*, the dharma's truth of impermanence.

Then why would they not tell me and allow me to attend his final journey? I wanted to ask the chief warden right there, right then, to hear how he would answer. But I knew I should not. I should consider the guard who had blurted it out; she could lose her job for disclosing something they were keeping from me. So I could do nothing but wait for my next visit. I kept imagining how my parents were feeling right now. Even thinking about it exhausted me mentally and physically.

Although I knew and had no doubt that my neighbors and friends were looking after my parents, they had their own lives to attend to and would not be able to help with everything. How would they arrange a funeral if it was the brother in Singapore who had died? There were so many thoughts in my head. Some prisoners in my block found out and came to comfort me when they were let out for bathing or walking. I felt a little better, but I still felt upset about how things were being handled. Why would they not allow me to send him off for the last time? Why didn't they tell me about him? My questions and attempts to grasp

DEATH IN THE FAMILY

awareness went in circles. I reasoned that the grief and worry I was feeling were due to attachment—that it was because we humans were prone to desire life after life and did not accept the truth of *dukkha*, suffering. If we had not made up for all our misdeeds, our karma could always catch up to us in so many ways. Then my thoughts would go back to trying to understand why the authorities were not telling me anything.

At last I had to open up to Khin Swe Yin. "Ma Swe, the others are right. I think I will still be here even if everyone else is free."

She was startled and said, "Oh, why? What happened?"

I reasoned, "Well, if you think of it, I wasn't allowed to go to the hospital for security reasons. Now I am not told about the death of my brother and am not allowed to send him off for the last time. I think they don't want me to have any contact with the outside world, so I think I should just focus on my health and stay well. Better not to expect and hope for anything until the twenty years are over." She was speechless. I went on, "So, I won't chat with you tonight. I am worried that we might say something we shouldn't while others can hear us. But please don't worry about me—I'll be meditating anyway. And don't worry about me not being able to sleep either; meditation gives me good concentration and I can go to sleep if I want to." After saying good night to her I remained silent for that whole night.

Although I told her not to worry, Ma Swe was very concerned for me that night. I had seen affection, sadness, sympathy, and worry on her face as she listened to me. My own thoughts were all over the place, even as I was wrestling with them and trying to concentrate. Although I was grief-stricken, it not burning in my heart because I was meditating. It scared me when I thought, *What if there were no Buddha? What if I had never learned his dharma? What if I have not paid respect to the sangha? And what if I had not practiced Vipassana—in what state would I be, now?* I was able to get through the night only by contemplating the Three Gems.

Early the next morning while our doors were open during the distribution of rice porridge, Ma Swe greeted me, and it was obvious from her face that she had not slept the whole night. I felt very bad seeing her like this.

"Don't feel bad Ma Swe, we don't even know when we'll die and we don't know when we'll be released. We don't own our future and there is nothing to be attached to in our past as well. So it's important for us to stay in the present, all right? I'll try to live and survive for every single minute."

Ma Swe laughed until she cried. "You, you, I thought you must be so depressed because you were telling me yesterday that you won't be freed. Now are you saying you could be released soon? You are trying to console me! Your depression doesn't last for twenty-four hours, does it? I think no one and nothing can make you depressed at all. You are like a knock-about toy. You're so funny!" she said wholeheartedly, and only then did I realize how far I had crumbled the previous day.

Her words reminded me to be optimistic about life and survival no matter what I faced. I also wished to stay in the present, dwelling neither in the past nor in the future. Thus, I had survived and was ready to meet my parents, who I believed would be exhausted with grief but whom I also trusted to be insightful of the unexpected changes of life.

However, it was impossible to pretend not to know once I saw the faces of my parents; we all three burst out at once:

"*Hpay? May?*"[1]

"Oh, my dearest . . . "

"Who was it? Who? Aung or Kyaw?"

"It's Aung . . . Oh, my dear, did they not tell you?"

It was my youngest brother, whom we had considered a black sheep in the family.

I told my parents that I had not been given any information by the authorities. The warden on duty was nearby so I asked her for extra time. "I need more time to talk about this. Can you please give me an extra fifteen minutes?"

She said she would ask permission from the chief warden and sent one of the male guards to inquire.

---

1. Affectionate and touching versions of Mother and Father in Burmese.

"Why didn't they allow you to tell me? How did he die? When was it? When was the funeral?" I had so many questions.

On his twenty-eighth birthday, January 13, 1999, he had gotten up at about three in the morning to cook food with his own hands to offer to monks who had been invited to take breakfast at our house in the *soon kyway* ritual offering of food to celebrate his birthday. As he paid obeisance to the monks, he had promised that he would be good from now on. Then he went back to sleep and never woke up again. My parents had come to the prison to hand in a request that I be informed about this and allowed to attend the funeral, but although they accepted the letter my parents left, one of the guards had told them, "Aunty, don't expect her to be there. I don't think they will allow it as she is well known nationally and internationally."

They only realized the guard was right when I did not turn up on the day of the funeral. For whatever reason the prison authorities even refused to give us more time and asked me to put in a request before the next visit if I wanted extra time. I did not even know how I got back to my cell after I tried to console my parents and argued with the warden for more time. The only thing I remembered was that I told the guard who was taking notes, "I do not accept withholding news of the death of a family member and not allowing me to go to the funeral. Write down that I demand an explanation."

I told everyone in the block about my brother's death. I was so weary and I felt overwhelmed with their words of condolence. Everyone was worried that I would not even have the energy to unpack the parcels from home. As I had known about it beforehand, the news of his death was not a sudden shock that day, but I was still annoyed and dispirited for not getting the extra time to talk to my parents.

Although I had tried my best to overcome any challenges by practicing *sila, samadhi,* and *paññya,* for the first time I began to feel it was too much. That night, our block was not silent; there were too many questions about the way my young brother had passed away at such a young age. He did not wake up from his sleep! I remembered my mother saying that when the funeral tent was set up in front of the house, the neighbors thought it was my father who had died. I had thought that it was possible one of my parents might die of old age before I got out of jail, but I had not considered that death could come to anyone regardless of age according to the dharma of impermanence. An unexpected thing had happened, so could the expected happen, too? Of course it could.

Since I was under a twenty-year sentence I would not be freed in the twentieth century even if I received allowances for good behavior, and very likely the day I could be free would be a decade into the twenty-first century. By that time, my parents would be around eighty years old. If a twenty-eight-year-old had died just a few days ago, people of eighty could die at any time. I, their daughter, had succumbed to various illnesses by the age of thirty-three and could depart this life any time while trying to ease my pain or while crawling toward the vacuum flask. I had watched and been aware of the disappearing, ending, and impermanence of life and things. I had felt fear, ennui, and disgust about this process of emerging, existing, disappearing, and ending. That was why I tried to attain cessation of samsara and was still trying. Because of this endeavor I was able to endure this terrible loss. I felt satisfied with *sama sati,* my strength to contain right mindfulness, and *sama samadhi,* the strength to contain right concentration of the mind.

I would have to share this truth with my parents, and doing this would be what made it worthwhile to be a human. It is not enough to repay the debt we owe our parents by saying, "I'm not insulting others' parents, but I think my parents are the best." I was not interested in making huge amounts of money. They had supported me all the way in whatever I chose to do and had never complained. I decided that the best way to show my gratitude was to share the method of gaining what I had achieved. I was unable to accept even the thought of not being able to continue with my practice, for it meant that I would not be able to share it with them.

The time for my parents' prison visit came again and I got only ten minutes extra. My parents were allowed to come in five minutes before the others and could stay five minutes after the other families left. There were so many things to talk about, and time was never enough. Although my younger brother had not always fit in with the family, neighbors and friends loved him. My parents told me people were still coming to offer condolences—both his friends and mine. I was happy to know we had such friends.

However, I could see that both my parents were extremely tired. There were so many things for them to do, including a *soon kyway* ritual food offering to monks on the one-month death anniversary and other obligations. My parents had asked my brother in Singapore—who was shocked that his brother had died—not to come back as it would not make a difference. Besides, he could not come back, as he had just gotten a new job and could not get leave. I had no time to share my experiences of meditation with my parents, and I was not sure when I would be able to. There had to be a way, I thought.

I asked a guard on duty to please tell people from the MI that I would like to see them. This time I did not have to wait for long; in about three days, a major from MI came and said they had not been able to arrange for me to go to the funeral because the prison authorities failed to inform them on time. That was nothing new; as always, the prison authorities would say the MI was responsible and the MI would blame the prison people; finding the beginning or end of an egg would be much easier than figuring out who was responsible. Between these two bodies no one could ever pinpoint the real culprit. I was not prepared to discuss any of this as I had no time and simply told him the reason I had asked to meet him.

I informed him that in response to my request the prison authorities only gave me ten minutes more to talk to my parents. He said he would try to arrange for fifteen minutes extra.

"Fifteen minutes is not enough for what I want to say to them."

"So, what do you want us to do?" He looked at me with puzzlement on his face.

"I would like to write, and I would like the MI to arrange it for me. Please just give me paper and ball-point pen and put me at a desk. I will write everything in one go, and you can check every word when I am done. After that I want the MI to send it to my parents," I said bluntly.

"What are you going to write about?" he asked.

"About two types of awareness in Vipassana meditation."

"What?" He was now thoroughly confused.

First I tried to explain the whole logic of finding the truth about *anissa.*

"The reverend abbot of Mogoke said that there should and could be a clear explanation for those who are trying to meditate so that they know both the awareness of the physical and mental beings and the awareness of cause and effect. Only after understanding these two clearly would it be easier to go on to the next level of awareness, which is the wisdom of knowing *anissa, dukkha,* and *anatta.* Then people can go on to attaining higher levels of Vipassana. It is only possible for me to show my gratitude to my parents by sharing this knowledge with them. This kind of true dharma is not attainable just by gaining merit through donating money. I must write it down for them, as there would never be enough time during their visit. As you see, even my twenty-eight-year-old brother can die—either my parents or I could die anytime soon. If one of us dies without my telling this, how badly would I regret it? After that I can be at peace knowing I have shown my gratitude to them before any one of us can die before I am free. Otherwise I wouldn't be able to repay my debt of gratitude to the best parents ever," I tried to explain as clearly as possible.

He became interested and asked, "Can't you explain to me, too, about these two kinds of awareness?"

"Of course I can. It's like this. Many think that we would be able to let go of the "I" or ego in us only when we can separate the physical and mental existences. That doesn't mean our mental being literally getting out of our body and looking back on our physical being. It's about knowing and being able to distinguish the nature of physical and mental existences."

I thought it was good for people like him to hear about the Buddha's teachings because they were in a pitiful state, caught in this quagmire of a bad system in which no one was allowed to have individual thoughts and ideas. They were also prisoners of power and privilege and had been their whole lives. Every time I saw them I felt both pity and regret on their behalf that they did not even have the wisdom to know the difference between right and wrong, or even if they knew what was "wrong," they were unable to change it to "right." How could anyone like that be at peace in this samsara?

The major looked none too certain about my explanation but before he left he said, "I'll get back to you as soon as possible. I'll report about this to the higher authorities at once, and after that we might be able to arrange it so you can write it—it's very likely to happen."

This time it was not an interrogation, so he did not ask the usual question of "What is your political goal?" For me also, this was not a test so I had no need to worry about failing or passing it. Everyone in the block thought it was the usual interrogation session. They reassured me after I explained what had happened and said, "Good, good! Who knows? You might be freed."

For me though, my wish to write all these things down was more profound than my wish to be freed. The next day, Ma Khin Mar Ye said she'd had a dream last night and in that dream I won a *mahadoak* lottery[2] and had been allowed to carry the Buddha image. She said in her dream I was wearing a plain dark-brown waist garment worn only by yogi, people who meditate for months or years, and that I carried an emerald alms bowl[3] slung across my shoulders. She said this was a good omen and that I was really going to be freed.

---

2. *Mahadoak* is a lucky draw not for cash but for a chance to make merit by undertaking the expenses of a man entering monkhood.
3. An alms bowl made of green glass, only used in ceremonies.

Chapter 20

Freedom

On February 11, 1999, around eight in the morning, a guard came to my door and said, "Ma Thida, you have to go for an interrogation session, so put on your whites."

I thought it might be about my request to write to my parents. However, I was not particularly fond of the word "interrogation" as I did not want to face any test again. But I put on the uniform over my clothes and waited. I knew it could well be that they were going to allow me to write, so in my mind I was planning it out. It was time for taking bucket baths, and that day my turn was last. Because of recent transfers and changing cells I was in the room where Ma Chuu used to live. Ma Khin Swe Yin, Ma Khin Mar Ye, and the "aunties" advised me to talk carefully and comforted me by saying I might be freed. Everyone thought I would at least get the permission to write. It was Thursday, so I was not fasting. My turn to bathe came close to lunchtime, and as the interrogation could take several hours, I hurriedly ate my meal first. It was a bit uncomfortable as I wore the prison whites on top of other clothes. *Why call me to be interrogated during this particular period?* I wondered.

Then, it was time for me to bathe and to walk . . . what was I to do? Thinking that I could do my laundry later, I took a bucket bath. While pouring water over my body I tried to focus on the awareness of what I was doing because I would need to be calm during interrogation.

I heard the warden talking in the cellblock: "Ma Thida, come out. Hmm, you're not in the room . . . Oh, are you bathing? Didn't they tell you about the interrogation? Why didn't you wait and bathe later?"

She approached me while shooting questions from her mouth as if firing a machine gun.

"I was waiting the whole morning. It was my turn to bathe, so why couldn't I? I'm almost done."

She walked over to where I was.

"Finish up now, change quickly. We don't have time."

"Well, they didn't come when I was waiting. Nope, now they can wait for me." Surprisingly, she laughed when I said that.

"Oh, come on, change into dry clothes. Here's your *htamein*," she said, handing it to me.

"Hey, no, Sis, don't do that![1] I'll stop when I've used up all the water in the jar," I said.

"Don't worry, you can have another bath in the evening."

"Don't care, I'm going to use up my quota."

She was still shoving the *htamein* at me impatiently so I finished my bucket bath quickly, changed out of my wet *htamein*,[2] and walked back into my cell. She followed closely and said, "All right, pack up your belongings, but be quick!"

I got a bit scared at that, thinking they were going to transfer me to another prison.

"Oh! You said it was an interrogation, why would I need my belongings? Elder Sister, tell me the truth. Are you transferring me somewhere else? Tell me or I won't pack my things."

"You're going to the hospital. Quick, quick! Everyone's waiting for you."

She started to pack my stuff while urging me to be quick.

"Hang on, it's not the day of my appointment. Did someone arrange it? Am I going to have a laparoscopy now?"

---

1. Handling a woman's *htamein* by another woman not of the same family is considered inauspicious for her, and the owner would feel bad about it. Men, family or stranger, would not touch a women's *htamein*.

2. A woman bathes in public by pulling her *htamein* up to the armpits and tucking it around firmly before pouring water on herself. In changing into a dry one in public she first pulls it on to cover her body and allows the wet one to slide out from under her without showing anything more than her bare arms and shoulders.

She just nodded to every question I asked.

When I took out the white prison garb she said I could wear ordinary clothes. I was surprised to hear that because on my several visits to the hospital I had to wear the prison uniform. Looking into my questioning eyes she said, "Be quick. It looks like it's going to take forever the way you are packing your things. I'll have someone do it for you. You go ahead, just tell me what you want to take with you."

"I have to take everything since we are going to the hospital. I'll leave behind the fresh stuff like onions. I'll take all three of my plastic commodes, okay? I'll really need them in the hospital so please don't forget. Wait, I don't have a *htamein* good enough to wear."

I was beginning to get muddled. I then put on a white top and a Kachin-made *htamein* that my parents had sent in 1995 just after Ma Suu was released from house arrest, with the hope that we would all be freed too.

"Yes, yes, just go . . . you can comb your hair on the way," shoving a comb into my hands. At that time, I had thick, waist-length hair as I had not obtained permission to cut it for some time.

"Don't leave anything behind. If something goes missing, it's your responsibility," I warned her.

I hurried out of my cell and rapidly informed Naw Wah Gay, "They said I have to go to the hospital but they asked me to wear normal clothes, and I don't understand why. Please be alert for any news of me and inform my parents if you find out they transferred me to another prison."

I then walked quickly in the direction of the office, at the same time trying with some difficulty to comb my tangled hair. The warden followed on my heels. We went through the door of the women's section and then we were at the door leading to the room between the two huge metal gates. While stepping over the high lower edge, my *htamein* split apart at the hem.

"Oh no, Sis, I'm in trouble—I can't go like this and I don't have another to change into either."

In the large room between two prison gates, the personnel on duty were all men; a young officer from the MI saw me and said, "Hey, aren't you happy? You're about to be freed!"

"What did you say? I was told that I am going to the hospital!"

"Oh. We told them to tell you that you're being released."

"Ah, so she was lying to me."

I turned to the warden but she took my hand and pulled me into an empty room.[3]

"Just turn your *htamein* around here to hide that tear."

Looking straight into her eyes I asked, "Why did you lie?"

She did not give me an answer but said somewhat sternly, "You talked too much. Because of you mouthing off, you're being released only now. Otherwise, it could have been since last month."

"What did you just say? What have I said that I was kept in jail longer? Why wasn't I released last month? What happened? What makes you say this for sure? Tell me right now or else I'll file a complaint." My tone hardened increasingly as I kept questioning her, and then someone knocked on the door.

"Enough, enough! You're ready now, aren't you? Let's go." She opened the door and went out quickly.

She took me to where the chief warden was standing in front of his office door and I saw my pile of belongings along with the three commodes. He said to me, "All your belongings are here and nothing is left behind. Do you want to check?"

"I told them to bring everything because I was told I'd be going to the hospital. But if I'm going home I'll take just a couple of things, and please return the rest to the cellblock."

"Be assured, I'll have everything sent back without a single thing missing. All right, they are waiting for you, please go in." He gestured toward a room. What he said and how he said it were confirmation that he knew he could not mess with me.

Lights flashed as I entered just like when Senator Richardson was here. I had to walk carefully, as it would be very embarrassing if my *htamein* tore again, and this time I would not be able to turn it around. All the officials in the room had smiles plastered on their faces. I

---

3. It would be highly unseemly for a woman to loosen her waist garment and tuck it in again in public, especially in front of men.

remembered to concentrate, and my awareness returned, so I was able to look calm. They then read out from a paper that I was being released under Act 401 (1).

"Ma Thida, you know very well that we tried our best to help with your health problems while you were here, but you were not happy about it." These words were from the man who had once murmured behind my back that there was no point in arguing with me. Before he could finish I interrupted him by saying, "Your best was not my best. It was not that I was unhappy—all I did was point out what was best for me." They did not know what to say after that and kept silent.

"Anything you want to say about your time in prison?" asked the chief warden.

"Recently you had the guards memorize a list of rules, which I overheard as they were reading them out loud. One of the rules was to treat the prisoners well, as they are all citizens of our country, but I would like you to know that none of us were treated well. Now, can you tell me, where are my parents? Do they know I am going to be released?"

One MI said, "Yes, your parents are being informed at this very moment. Our plan is to take you to our office and meet up with your parents there, and we will hand you over to them. Is there anything you want us to tell them?"

"Yes. Can you ask my mother to bring me a *htamein* for me?"

"Sure, and what else do you want to say to us for the last time?"

"Well . . . I would like to say thank you for giving me the chance to meditate almost twenty hours a day. If I had not been in prison I wouldn't have had this much time and even might not have meditated at all. That's why I would like to thank all of you. I would also like to thank myself for making the decision to meditate." They looked stunned and uncomfortable to hear a prisoner thanking her jailers for keeping her in prison.

I walked out of the office while camera lights flashed all over the room, and I saw the last thick metal gates leading to the world outside. Some officers came with me so instead of the small door through which we needed to bend our heads to come in or go out, they opened the big doors. As I walked out my awareness was with me, sharp and strong, and so I left prison with dignity. My mind was incredibly clear and calm. Before I began meditation I had said to myself, "I'll walk out of here the way I walked in," but now I realized how wrong I was; there was no awareness within me when I walked into this place. Now, awareness was with me at every step I took away from that place. The difference was huge; no one knew exactly why, except me. There was some truth in a saying I had often heard before, that one comes out of prison a new person with a new mind. Every step I made out of this prison was proof of it.

There was a long luxury car waiting. The driver opened the door of the back seat for me and there was another man sitting there, smiling at me. As we drove off, the driver began to talk: "Ma Thida, I am Hla Thet Maung and this is Major General Tin Hlaing. You look as if there's nothing out of the ordinary! Don't you feel happy? Aren't you surprised that the major general himself has come to take you in his personal car—a Toyota Mark II, you know, the latest model. If people saw us us, they would think you're his younger sister! I must say you're the only one to be released in this way."

"I'm happy, but this is nothing strange or special. If there is entering there will be exiting as well. I knew on the day that I walked in here that I would walk out someday." They smiled upon hearing my calm response.

"How long were you in there?" Major General Tin Hlaing asked me as the car passed by the visiting room.

"Five years, six months, and six days" I answered him within a few seconds, and he exclaimed, "Lord Buddha, were you counting the days every day?" I did not bother to tell him that I had done the calculation right there in my head.

"Now you are free. What do you want to do? How can we help? Just ask."

"If so, I'd like to get a passport."

"What? Why? What happened? I don't think you can apply for it right now. Where are you thinking of going?"

He looked and sounded shocked. The car we were in was not even out of the prison compound and I was already talking of going overseas.

"I want to go for further studies; if I can't apply now, when can I?"

"You might have to wait about six months. You already have your license to practice, right?"

"I have to apply for an extension. I just need to continue doing the things I was doing before—nothing so special." He stared at me but did not say anything more.

I was brought to the MI office 7 on Taw Win Street in Dagon Township. They had sent someone to fetch my parents, but my father was downtown so it was taking them longer to track him down. One of the officers brought a *htamein* from my mother: it was plain dark brown. Just before I left my cell I had grabbed a green-colored handkerchief, and while I was changing I recalled the dream Ma Khin Mar Ye had about me wearing the dark brown of a yogi and holding a green alms bowl. While I waited for my parents to arrive, Major General Tin Hlaing gave the expected speech about how the leaders of the country have such great goodwill for the people. After his speech he asked me what I had to say.

"I thought I should ask you. I was supposed to be freed last month but was not, is that true? Why? Was it because of how I spoke?" He looked panicky and said, "Oh . . . Who said that? It's not true! What a mess . . . Even us, we only knew today." I told him that I found out from the warden.

"Impossible. It's nothing like that, for sure. How can they know something like this? They can't. That's not true." He became a bit upset. (Months later I bumped into a prisoner trustee who used to do chores in the office, and she told me that the warden was asked for an official explanation for saying so and was denied the chance to take the test for her promotion that year. I felt bad for her and thought she might still be calling me a troublemaker even though I was no longer there.)

It took quite some time for my parents to reach the MI office where we were. As soon as I saw them I knelt down on the floor and paid obeisance. In fact, that day, February 11, was their thirty-fourth wedding anniversary and my parents were filled with delight, as they had not been expecting this.

I said, "Okay, everyone's here so let's go home." An officer replied, "Wait, there's a religious celebration at the Shwedagon Pagoda. A new crown[4] is going to replace the old one. Our chief[5] ordered us to take you there, Ma Thida, before we take you home."

I felt that they were prolonging things just to annoy me but thought that as it was the Shwedagon I would be going there anyway, so I did not protest. We all had to climb back into this Mark II luxury car. My parents and I were in the back; I had waited more than half a decade to sit between my parents like this. It did not matter if it was Mark II or any other vehicle, but I thought of the dream I'd had and how I had remembered it though I usually couldn't recall dreams. At that time, awareness and concentration were flickering in and out of me. In the

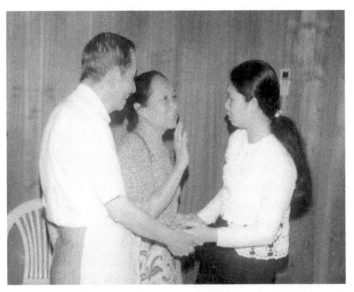

On February 11, 1999, the day of her release from Insein prison, Ma Thida met her parents at Military Intelligence office number 7 on Taw Win Roadin Yangon.

---

4. The pagodas spire is topped with a bejewelled crown called a *hti* in Burmese, meaning umbrella. It is sometimes replaced when damaged or too old. The new one would be adorned with additional jewels donated by the public so it would remain on the pagoda platform for several days before it was hoisted up.
5. General Khin Nyunt.

car they played a tape of a famous singer. The car was nearing the Shwedagon Pagoda when I noticed it was turning in another direction.

"Hey, you said we're going to the Shwedagon."

"Well, it's lunchtime already; let's eat first at Shwe Ba restaurant."

"But I'm not hungry, I want to pray at the Shwedagon and go straight home."

"You may not be hungry, but we are. Your house won't run away, you know. Relax! Let's eat first."

"Okay then. *May* and *Hpay*, please pay for lunch. I'll eat only if you agree."

My parents knew why I requested this and immediately agreed while the MIs insisted that it was their duty to pay for our meal. We entered the restaurant and we might have looked like a family because they were not in uniform. However, one man who was already in the restaurant and who looked like a businessman came up to say hello to the MIs and repeatedly called them by their ranks. The major general introduced me as a doctor and a writer. The man was not aware of anything and soon went back to his table. They knew that it was Thursday and I was not fasting so they ordered as many dishes as they liked. I did not eat more than usual. Afterward, my father prepared to pay the bill only to find out that the man who had greeted them had already paid for us. I felt relieved that at least it was not the MIs who had paid the bill.

"What powers you have! Your wish came true—someone else paid. It's getting quite scary, right? What did you really wish for?"

I did not reply but just smiled, thinking about how shallow they were.

Finally, we arrived at the Shwedagon Pagoda; they tested me right away by asking, "What do you think? Isn't it better and more beautiful? Doesn't it look more glorious?"

I could only say, "Whatever the appearance is—red or white or any color—it's all impermanent and that is the true dharma."

They then talked about the benefits of *dana*—donating—and I could no longer stand it. So I said, "Be careful, Uncle. No *dana* can get you out of hell or the other nether worlds. Even if you donate money in a pile as high as a tree you would only reap merit the size of its seed if you obtained your wealth by misdeeds. Morality is the most important factor and the very foundation of Buddhism."

The officer who had driven us murmured, "We are no longer enemies although we have yet to become friends." I said nothing to this.

People were looking because there were many cameramen following us, taking photos as I prayed. They must have been wondering why this woman who was not an actor or someone famous was having photos taken of her praying and pouring water.[6]

The major general bought a religious book for me. He asked, "Did you know in advance that you would be released? Such as in a dream or any omen?"

They had no understanding of Vipassana meditation, and I could only say, "The insight gained from Vipassana is nothing about omens or signs."[7]

After circling the spire, my parents and the authorities said goodbye; we would be taken home in a Land Rover by a captain. I later heard that the whole group of MIs, officers, and camera and video men went straight to the Office of Military Archives, where General Khin Nyunt was waiting, to show him taped documents of my release. Just as the Land Rover turned into my street, I thought, *This home I left behind is no longer the same; now there is no Aung Aung[8] and I did not even have the chance to say goodbye.*

The captain took more photos as I was going into the house. Some neighbors and friends who knew about my release were waiting for me.

Looking at the dim living room filled with spider webs, I walked straight to the altar room, saying, "I must clean this up." I greeted everyone when I came back after praying. Soon, more friends arrived. I was very happy to see Ma Hmwe but could not help crying when I saw Ma Chuu. We thought we would be freed within a year of each

---

6. Pouring water on the image at the compass point of one's day of birth is a normal practice of Buddhists at pagodas.

7. True believers of Vipassana meditation do not aim to uncover signs or omens, but in many cases they achieve it to some degree.

8. Repetition like this is a form of endearment in Burmese.

Ma Thida and her parents at the Shwedagon Pagoda upon her release from prison.

Ma Thida and her father pour water over the image corresponding to Ma Thida's day of birth.

other and it came true. That day, my concentration was definitely not with me.

In the evening, I called my brother in Singapore. More friends who had heard on the radio as well as by word-of-mouth arrived one after another. I told them of my experiences until very late. That night, lying in my own bed, I was wide awake; the mattress and pillow were too soft, and there were no mosquitoes! How were my friends in the cellblock? How would they be sleeping? By now, they would know about my release—what would they be thinking? How would they be feeling, missing one member of our regular evening chats? My thoughts and mindfulness were coming and going in turns all night, and I could not sleep until dawn.

The next day, I realized that although I had been freed from the four walls of Insein Prison I was still in a much larger prison.

Chapter 21

Aftermath

While we were eating breakfast, the captain who accompanied us home the day before appeared and said that the major wanted to see my parents and me. What they wanted was for me to sign a statement in my parents' presence that I had been warned by the MI not to continue participating in party politics. They knew me enough not to ask me to sign anything saying I would not participate in certain things.

The major asked, "What are you thinking of doing now?"

Everyone laughed when I told them truthfully, "I need to clean the house. It's really messy."

"I mean, what is your goal regarding politics?"

They nodded when I said, "I told you all this already. I want to go abroad for further studies. I must publish a novel that was all ready to be printed when I was arrested. I will go back to volunteering at the Muslim Free Hospital. Just like before. I'll do things I was doing before."

They seemed to think that I had not had enough time to think everything through and sent me home. Friends old and new and relatives were already waiting to see me, so I had no time to think about what the MI had wanted to know.

At that point my father's health was not good and he needed a thorough checkup. He was on medication for ectopic beats and atrial fibrillation[1] and was also suffering from transient ischemic attacks[2] so he sometimes lost consciousness for a few minutes. My parents were finally able to

---

1. Skipped heart beats and abnormal heart rhythm.
2. Mini strokes producing similar symptoms but usually lasting only a few minutes and causing no permanent damage.

let go of the strong fighting spirit they'd had to cling to before my freedom, and now the loss of this determinedly held inner strength meant that the toll from years of heartbreaking anxiety and the trauma of losing a son became too much to bear.

The financial survival of my brother in Singapore was at the time somewhat uncertain. I, the eldest child, had put my wishes first and had dragged my parents into my problems, so I felt I must repay this debt—although it never entered their heads that I should; if I remained safe, it was enough for them. For me though, it was the biggest promise to keep as I did not wish to stray from the path I had chosen and did not want to leave a bad personal record.

All my writer friends felt that I would be doing my fair share for the literary world just by continuing to write. All my friends from the hospital said I should not be too long away from the medical field. People from the international media seemed to want to lead me into new political arenas. Friends from my period in politics wanted me to use the present attention on my experiences to become politically active.

Knowing I was losing my concentration and mindfulness back in this distracting world, I longed to enter a retreat to get some peace, but there were too many things to do—especially spending time with my parents. I had no wish to be parted from them again anytime soon. I also had to go for a checkup and follow-up treatment for my illness, the diagnosis of which was based on a single ultrasound and had yet to be confirmed. With different things pulling at me, I began to feel like a fruit trying to grow inside a nest of thorns; it felt as if the twelve-by-twelve-foot cell had been much larger than this. Now I was tied down and surrounded by many attachments and expectations wherein I had no room to turn.

Right after I was freed, I visited the NLD headquarters at its new premises on Shwegondine Road, where Ma Suu had her office. She was in a meeting, so as I waited I thought about the time I had last seen her. It had to have been before July 19, 1989, when she was placed under house arrest, because when she was released from house arrest in 1995 I was already in prison. It had been almost ten years, or roughly 3,300 days. I had only been able to receive a message of love from her through Senator Richardson. When I thought of how I could only see her now after all that time I became overwhelmed with sadness. After their meeting, U Aung Shwe and the others left Ma Suu and I alone in the room. I did not know where and how to start as I had so many things to tell her. Finally, I could no longer control myself and tears rolled down my cheeks. Ma Suu too had tears in her eyes. The two of us were not crying audibly but our tears were falling. However, it lasted just a few moments, and then I asked Ma Suu to understand that right now I had too many things to attend to. She too asked me apologetically to understand her; she said she was just a human. I had to wait more than 3,300 days to be reunited with her: my Ma Suu, my sister.

For about a week after getting out of prison I could not sleep at night. Friends came the whole day long, and my parents and I would talk about family affairs late into the night. Once I was in my bed, I kept thinking about how my friends in the cellblock were doing. My concentration and practice of Vipassana was no longer constant or strong. By the time I rolled out of bed I would be seeing the first light of day. Meals were difficult too; the rice was too soft and slid down my throat before I remembered to chew. I would think of those in the cellblock and then I could no longer eat. When I bathed and I scooped water out of the cement tank at home, I imagined how they would be bathing and washing their clothes with what little water they had in the Martaban jar.

The day after I was released was Union Day, and the day after that was the birthday of our national hero, Bogyoke Aung San, as well as Children's Day. It was one month since my brother had passed away, so we held a *soon kyway* food offering ceremony for monks and invited friends as well. I was very happy to see many friends whom I had not seen for such a long time, and there were new faces among them; some were new NLD members, writers, and friends of relatives. All my old friends looked the same. The only ones I did not recognize were my nephews and nieces, whom I had last seen as toddlers or babies.

Later, I attended the one-year death anniversary of the writer Mya Than Tint and visited the famous cartoonist U Pe Thein, who had suffered a stroke. Ma Hmwe came and slept over one night to bring me up to date on the news of the past five and a half years.

When she saw I was able to discuss some issues already she exclaimed, "You know everything! Not about the news but about people and their attitudes. You seem to know everything." She remarked that I had changed a lot. I knew that, too; I still spoke up for things I believed in but in a different tone and manner. I still did not like behaving in a feminine way but I no longer complained about being a woman. Actually, I now found these things so boring that I no longer cared about resisting them or wanting them changed.

Later, I went to pay homage to a famous abbot, Thamanya Sayadaw, in Karen State and made a pilgrimage to Shwe Set Taw Pagoda in central Myanmar. I then tried to get permission for the publication of two books—a collection of my short stories and the novel *True Color of the Sunflower*. I could not yet volunteer at the hospital but I was never home. My parents told me that they noticed a man sitting everyday in the car repair shop opposite our house and watching us. I did not see him but it became a bit annoying for my parents after a whole week, so I rang the number that the MIs had given me and asked them to come see me.

A captain came over and I asked bluntly, "Did you assign someone to watch me? My parents said there's someone watching our house from across the road all day, every day."

He denied it so I cut the conversation short by saying, "Okay, I'll give you three days to deal with it. Please ask around all the intelligence units and the neighborhood authorities. I think they might have put someone on duty without your knowledge."

After three days, my parents said he was still watching us. As usual, I was busy with my own stuff and was never home so I had not noticed. The captain came back then and said, "I already asked around. No one was told to watch your house and no one is watching you. You might be mistaken."

He lost his composure when I said, "All right, I can't say for sure because I never saw him myself. I'll help you out, that's what I'll do. Tomorrow, I will cancel everything and stay home. I'll take photos of that man for you and I might even go over and ask him for his name and address. He could be someone pretending to be an intelligence officer, you know, so you should nab him."

He laughed nervously and took his leave, saying, "You don't have to do that." As I expected, the man was not there the next day and never returned.

Extending the validation of my license to practice medicine went without any hitch. I again wanted to enter a meditation retreat for some days before I resumed volunteering at the free hospital but could not as something happened that shook us all: Ma Suu's husband, Dr. Michael Aris, passed away in Oxford. I visited her to give my condolences, and she looked very calm, being a strong person who was always prepared to face any challenge in her life.

When I came home, there was no calm for me. I received a phone call from Hla Thet Maung, the officer who had driven us home the day I was released. I had not heard anything from him since then, but now he ranted at me angrily, "Why didn't you report it me? Didn't you know you have to report in advance to me if you are going to visit her like that? What now? Are you going to blame us? Do you think you can just go to that place?"

I thought to myself, *All right, we'll see about that.*

I said, "Wait a minute—are you sure that I've been released from prison?"

"Being released is one thing. Doing anything you like is another. You want to ask why you can't do anything you like, don't you? You want to blame us, don't you?" He continued to rave.

I said to him icily, "Uncle, please control yourself and talk nicely, will you? I haven't said anything out of line to you yet and you're saying whatever you think. If you use that tone of voice with me, I will talk in that same tone to you, too. Remember at the Shwedagon Pagoda, I didn't respond when you said we were no longer enemies although we had yet to become friends. I didn't say anything then because I wanted to wait and see. You should be aware that you're making me want to say no to that possibility. If you want me to talk respectfully to you, you should do the same for me."

"We didn't say you can't go. I'm just saying you should inform us before you do." He still had some rage in his tone of voice.

"Look, you never told me I have to tell you if I'm visiting anyone out of social and personal consideration, so I had no idea I had to do it. So I'm not the one responsible here. If anyone should take responsibility it's you, for not telling me earlier." My voice was cool.

"Hmm, well, I thought there was no need to tell you . . . everyone let out of jail knows they have to." His voice had lost its rage, but it still sounded impatient.

"How could I know? This is the first and only time I've been jail. I have no experience of being released apart from this. It's not reasonable for you to say everyone knows. How could I know? You didn't tell me! So I assumed I could go anywhere and meet anyone I wanted. That's how I understood it and that's what it means to be free. Now it looks like I haven't been released after all, from what you are telling me now."

"All right, all right. You didn't know before but now you do. So tell us if you are going to do something important like this, all right? I am telling you now, officially. You are free, that's true, but we also have a lot of problems, and if the higher authorities should find out something like that before we knew of it, it won't look good for us—we'd look stupid."

It was obvious they had problems among themselves.

"Well, that's your problem."

"That's true, but you would be helping us if you tell us in advance."

His tone became softer but I thought, *Nope, I cannot let you off that easily.*

"It's not natural that you are using that tone while asking for my help. Please change your tone and the way you talk. Please tell me officially and properly that although I have been freed from prison, you want my help to tell you if I am going to visit important places or meet important people. If you don't tell me officially about your needing my help, it will be very difficult for me to believe I'm a free person. Moreover, I'm not responsible for anything relating to my visit to her since I wasn't told about the need to tell you: it's your responsibility. Only if you tell me properly and officially will I agree to let you know in the future." I made my demands clearly, talking nonstop.

"Well . . . let's leave it, its fine. It's our mistake that we didn't tell you officially before, and I apologize for that. Now it's official, Ma Thida, so in the future, please tell us in advance, okay?" His tone had already softened but was still somewhat sarcastic. I did not wish to keep on winding him up.

"All right, Uncle, I agree to do that. In the future, if you don't want to be enemies before we can be friends, please talk to me nicely."

With that I hung up the phone. The conversation had been tiring!

That was the only time he called me; after that he assigned his subordinates to deal with me. He was probably worried that he might have to apologize if he called again. (I do not know whether he was sacked when General Khin Nyunt was dismissed and charged with corruption in 2004.) Then I decided to go to the *soon kyway* ceremony on the seventh day after Dr. Aris's death. I rang the MIs just before I left home. They told me to wait and said they were coming. Within five minutes, a captain turned up at my house who did not say much but said he would be coming back to see me in the evening.

While I was telling Ma Suu about the phone call she got angry and asked, "Why didn't you tell him off?" She smiled when I said, "I didn't tell him off, but I made him apologize."

I kept trying to get the Press Scrutiny Board to give permission for my books to be published. Although the personnel there tried to give me trouble like usual, it gave the green light after the MIs intervened. I was not happy that my manuscript of *True Color of the Sunflower* was heavily censored, but at least got it published. It took a decade from writing it until its publication. I was also able to publish a collection of short stories, titled *Acidic-Sweet Honey Swamp and other Stories*, that I had written during the early years of my career. Another published collection, titled *Core of the Spectrum: The Insight of Different Literary Persons* consisted of interviews with thirty-three short story writers and essayists whose work had been published in the literary magazine *Message*. I was able to publish these three books with no difficulty since the MI was involved. However, it was very difficult to get permission for my short stories written in and after 1986 because I had not informed the MI about them. Finally, after waiting months for it to be approved for publication, I received permission, but there were so many things cut out from it that nothing made sense, so I gave it up as a lost cause. Also, none of the short stories that I had written during imprisonment and had sent to magazines passed censorship. Some editors were even afraid I might submit my stories to their magazines. One writer was so terrified he even backed away in alarm when I was unexpectedly introduced to him. Some sneered, "Do you even know how to write any more?" I responded to their malice with just one question: "Why don't you go and ask the censorship board whether I can still write or not?" Thus my life as a writer recently freed from jail was indeed colorful.

I must admit I felt as if I could not write anymore at that point, because my mind was too steady and devoid of feelings. A short story writer must have feelings and emotions to write, but now as soon as my feelings or sentiments rose my awareness immediately jumped in to tackle them with the mindfulness of *happy, happy* or *sad, sad* until they disappeared, and I was left with the "knowing" and then the "ceasing" of those feelings. That effectively stopped me from following my emotions into the creativity of writing.

That made it rather difficult for me, although I was grateful to those friends who had encouraged me to get back into writing. Unlike when I was younger and wanted to write down whatever I was feeling, I now concentrated on awareness rather than allowing my feelings to grow. In the end I simply edited old short stories and submitted them.

While Vipassana practice was not helpful in my writing, it was extremely useful in my work as a surgeon. By this time I was already working again at the Muslim Free Hospital. Although I had been away from my work, the imaginary surgeries I had done in prison paid off. A doctor colleague also encouraged me to have confidence in myself and shared all the latest methods with me. Within a few months, my hands regained their dexterity. Both my colleague who had helped me, and the general anesthetist were amazed to see how quickly I improved, saying no one who did not see it would believe it. They said they could see a difference too because they had seen me operate both before and after my incarceration. Since my concentration had improved, I could operate more neatly and tidily without any fear or excitement obstructing my work. Some people asked me whether I could still treat patients and perform surgery, and I usually told them to ask my colleagues. However, my success was because I could concentrate well; hence it was not surprising that a surgeon with a steady mind and steady hands could do a good job.

My father needed another operation after his appendix was taken out in 2006 by another surgeon as his stitches had become infected, and my colleagues were surprised to see me do it. Usually, surgeons prefer not to operate on their own family members as the emotional stress can interfere with their concentration, but I simply concentrated on the area where I had to operate without thinking of anything besides the existence of only mental and physical beings; I also thought of my father as a patient like any other, so I was able to perform the surgery smoothly and successfully.

Although I was busy with work, I did keep up with social obligations, particularly in attending funerals. At that time, an NLD member who had testified as a government witness against me got seriously ill and had no one to care for him, so I went to help him out. He looked at me and thanked me with his eyes as I did not talk about the past but asked only of his health.

Someone I did not know came to see him while I was there and, pointing his finger rudely at me, asked, "How many dollars have you been given by now?" I was so disgusted I did not want to answer, but I explained that the award money came with a stipulation that I would donate it to an organization of my choice so I was planning to donate it to the Muslim Free Hospital to buy new equipment for the operating theater.

I met people who offered their help after my release, knowing I would be struggling to establish myself, but there were also those who said things like this and even some who forgot to ask if I was well while trying to borrow money from me. I wondered how the old me would have responded! I no longer got into quarrels with those kinds of people, but I could not help reacting somewhat angrily to the captain who came to my house one day without warning and without being invited.

I did not understand when he said, "Ma Thida, please hand over the roll of film."

I had no idea what he was talking about so I asked, "Captain, please tell me clearly—what is it that you are asking me to hand over? What roll of film?"

He said, "Oh, I mean the photos you took this morning when you went to the food offering ceremony for the death anniversary of Thakhin Kodaw Hmaing.[3] We heard that you also went to his tomb and took photos."

I had gone to the ceremony but left early to be at the hospital before the outpatient department opened at 8:30 a.m. I had not even had a camera with me. I tried not to react in anger, although I was quite cross. He looked confused when I said, "Oh, well, we seem to be thinking of the same thing, I was going to ask copies from those who took photos there as it would save me the cost of film and the printing, too. Maybe you took some? Can I have copies?"

"Um . . . we heard something different. It's okay if you didn't take any photos. We are not going to be miserly by asking you for copies. We just didn't notice." What he was saying was all over the place.

After that we had a good chat. He was a nicer person than normal from that organization and did not seem to resent my usual tactic of seeking the advantage over them. He was a middle school teacher before he enlisted in the army, so he was polite and not arrogant like the graduates of the Defense Services Academy.

Later he would often show up at my house but as neither foe nor friend. In February 2001, twenty-two SPDC officials, including General U Tin Oo, the SPDC general secretary-2, died in a helicopter crash. After that event, I told him, "Look what happened! It's an example of not being able to balance *kuso* and *akuso* (virtuous act and evil deed). If you do *kuso* you'll get the fruit of good deeds, if you do *akuso* you'll get the fruit of evil deeds.

---

3. A much-revered poet and national leader who passed away in July 1964 at the age of eighty-nine.

A little bit of *kuso* from good deeds will not replace the *akuso* of cruelty done to others. It'd be a different story if you were at the stage of *magga*[4] where no karma can touch you. Otherwise, you have to take the punishment of *akuso* the same way as you gain rewards of your *kuso*." This time, he did not say anything.

The thing that most people fear most is death, so they equate daring to die with courage. But the courage of "daring to live" can only be gained from a true comprehension of events such as *jati*, which is being conceived to be born as a human, *jaya* (old age or decay), *marana* (death), and samsara, the cycle of life. By my own experience I know that just "daring to die" is not real courage.

While in prison, they had played for us the taped sermons of the abbot of the mountain ranges,[5] a missionary monk who said that he lived with a goal of attaining Buddhahood in a future lifetime and that he had the courage to die and the courage to live. When I heard that, I realized the significance of daring to live. Although he had known very well of the suffering within the endless cycle of rebirth, he wanted to continue spreading the Buddha's Way of finding true freedom. I felt so much reverence for him for daring to live for the sake of his mission.

The neither-friend-nor-foe MI who visited me would often ask general questions according to what he was sent to do, but he readily accepted my answers. One day—six months after my release—I went to buy an application form at the passport office. The person at the counter selling application forms turned out to be the MI who had once interrogated me.

He asked if I recognized him and gave me a wry face when I replied, "How can I forget someone who helped to make me suffer?" He said shamelessly, "I heard you've published a novel, so give me a copy, will you?" All I could say was, "Buy it if you want to read it. Whatever

---

4. Path leading to renunciation of desire in order to attain Nirvana.
5. He walked throughout the Chin Hills and other remote regions to spread the teachings of the Buddha.

money I get from that book isn't one tenth of what you get here as 'tea money.'"[6]

I heard nothing more about that application, so I kept pestering the captain who came to my house about it. Finally, he seemed to have asked his superiors about it, because he came by one day and said, "It's too early for you to go abroad." I had already told him that I wished to go for further studies and wanted to do so while both of my parents were healthy enough so that I could leave them without having to worry too much. I explained that if I wanted to, I could just cross the border but that I had no desire to live abroad as an exile and that was the reason I was officially applying for a passport.

I did not know what to make of it when they said it was "too early" for me to have a passport. Finally, I got impatient as we talked about it, and said, "Tell your superiors I can't wait any longer and I will make my own arrangements to leave."

He stammered, "What!" and I continued, "Yes, I'll get out on a flying carpet. So please tell your superiors who go on to pagodas' tops to scatter money and puffed rice[7] not to worry if they bump into something. Tell them that it's only me on my flying carpet passing by them just to say goodbye. But tell them to be careful—they might fall down from the pagoda if I bump into them."

Upon hearing this, he sighed with relief but wore an expression of wanting to cry and laugh at the same time. I did not know if he talked to his superiors, but that was the last I saw him or heard from him. I received my passport only after General Khin Nyunt was ousted and his intelligence department completely demolished at the end of 2004.[8]

Thus I was finally able to travel outside of Myanmar but I still lived there by choice, in that prison bigger than Insein.

---

6. Bribes.

7. Scattering money and puffed rice is a gesture of celebration during an act of merit or a traditional wedding.

8. The department's work was taken over by the Bureau of Special Investigation, which had previously handled only criminal cases.

Chapter 22

Myanmar, the World, and Vipassana

I continued to live my dream of being a surgeon and a writer and when I wrote this memoir still hoped to fulfill the dreams of setting up a mobile clinic, a nonprofit press, and a family-style orphanage. The difference from before was that I no longer wished to take the lead in these projects but wanted to work with like-minded people or organizations in whatever way I could contribute. It wasn't a matter of giving up but of not putting my ego ahead of things that mattered to me. I continued with my volunteer work at the Muslim Free Hospital doing what I love, surgery, as well as working as an editor for a newsweekly.

In the early days after my release my health was not bad, but my period returned with the same pain. Although ultrasounds showed some improvement, it was still extremely painful; if it happened while I was in the middle of an operation, I could no longer continue. Two obstetricians and gynecologists from the Muslim Free Hospital, operated on me in November 2004 and removed my uterus, fallopian tube, and left ovary. The lab results after the operation came back with three different diseases—adenomyosis, leiomyoma of the uterus, and cervical polyp. I regretted that I had not followed through with a laparoscopy after my release.

Before the operation I had asked the anesthetist to give me spinal anesthesia as I wanted to be mindful during the procedure and he scrubbed around my spine with iodine and mentholated spirits, but somehow it did not work so they had to rush to give me a general anesthetic. I was given an antibiotic injection after I regained consciousness, but the combination of that with the iodine and mentholated spirits caused a serious allergic reaction, and the skin on my back peeled off in layers as if I were a snake. Patients who had had operations on their abdomens were usually asked to sleep on their stomachs to encourage scar-tissue growth, and since I had this problem it was convenient for me to sleep on my front, anyway. A day after the operation I was walking around, so people did not even realize I had already had my operation and asked me when it would be done. Some senior and experienced nurses remarked, "Doctor, you don't seem to feel any pain at all." As we were of different faiths it was quite difficult to explain Vipassana to them.

I stopped fasting three days a week in early 2000 as I sometimes needed to operate around noon, so fasting became inconvenient. Instead of meditating regular hours, I tried to be mindful at all times while I went about with my life—especially when I noticed rising emotions. When I was on long fights I would pass the time with meditation. When I watched movies my mindfulness kept me from getting into the story, so I turned to watching documentaries. Although I was of course still human and prone to having small desires, I was able to be aware of the bigger and more worldly ones.

I told the revered abbot of Shwetaung Gon about my meditation in prison and the conversations I had with the MI officer. He remarked, "Those who are heroic try to benefit both themselves and others. One cannot just help oneself but not others. I am very happy to hear that you were able to do good for yourself while being imprisoned for serving others. I am also happy that you answered that angry phone call calmly and wisely." I felt encouraged by this and wanted to do more to benefit both others and myself. Before, I was more interested in further studies in medicine but now I wished to learn more about how I could benefit others.

However much I enjoyed my voluntary work, it was not always smooth. Once a senior colleague had asked for money from a patient, who then reported it to the hospital board. The doctor accused me of being behind it and said he wanted to kill me. I replied, "Don't worry.

I'll die one day even if you don't kill me." That made him angrier, and he told me I was "a very scary woman." After that exchange he tried to have me fired and said, "If you think I cannot manage and if you don't want to work under my management, you can quit." At that time, I was volunteering at the hospital without being paid, so even someone like a medical superintendent would not have wanted to fire me. Later he apologized for accusing me without proof, and those who knew of this incident were amazed that I could still work with him.

At first it had troubled me a lot, but I was able to regain my peace of mind once I decided to just do my job and deal with him only in professional matters. My principle was that I could allow him to become neither an enemy nor a friend, and I simply carried on doing what I wanted to do—help and treat poor people. Every workplace had bad and good people, and it was not the working relationship that was important to me. I was not at the hospital to find friends. Even if I moved to another hospital I would still meet many types of people, if not this one.

I no longer judged anyone just through hearsay, and in fact, I no longer judged anybody except myself. Each individual has the right to decide how they live so I have no reason, no right, and no interest in judging anybody. I would always say, "Worry that you might harm somebody, not about others wanting to harm you, because that's their problem."

To this day I remain a true believer in the concept of karma and its effects. Thus I believe there is no way I or anyone can have any impact on someone else's life. Since everything is impermanent I cannot be hating or loving anyone forever; I am also aware that no one can sit there loving or hating me twenty-four hours a day. Thus, without anything superfluous attached to the knowledge, I can see others and myself as just being in the present.

In 2002, when I immersed myself in the literary world, I found Vipassana a great help. My writing style changed, and my stories became more based on true happenings than they had been, and I also concentrated on the presentation. Prior to my experience with meditation, my style could have been described as shrewd and obstinate, but afterward it became sharp and deeper but also polite and sensitive.

At the hospital, too, I became more tolerant and tried to be more understanding of difficult patients. The changes in me were so obvious that friends like Ma Hmwe would get frustrated to see me being patient with demanding people.

I became an editor of *Budding Teen* magazine, which gave aspiring young writers more space to have their work published. The magazine did not make much profit, and the others criticized me for being too lenient with young people. I wanted to give attention to everyone's wishes in the magazine while not favoring anybody, including myself.

My wish to give everyone a chance to voice his or her view is rooted in my deep understanding of impermanence (*anissa*), suffering (*dukkha*), and nonself (*anatta*). This understanding has given me so much strength that I am able to open my heart to everybody. It is almost like my heart is an empty space for everyone to enter, and I welcome them with open arms. If anyone sees something useful in my heart they can take it. If they wish to throw trash into my heart, I can accept that as well. Good or bad and happiness or sorrow, nothing is permanent and thus it makes no difference. In the end, the result is *dukkha*—suffering. Every living being shall end and shall die one day; thus there is nothing that we can control. We may not wish certain things to happen to us but they will, one way or the other. We will get things that we do not want and we may not get things that we wish to have. That is *anatta*.

From late 2002, the ability to work at the hospital in the morning and at the magazine in the evening from Monday to Saturday gave me enormous satisfaction. As a surgeon I had to think like a scientist, and as a writer and editor I was an artist. So every day I used both sides of my brain, which helped me focus my mind on the middle path.

I completed my diploma in health systems management in 2004 from the University of London. In February 2005, I was issued a passport to attend "London Night," the graduation ceremony, held in early March. That was my first overseas trip. Before leaving, I got in touch with old and new friends as well as organizations in Europe, North America, and Asia to arrange observation trips, which began in February and ended in December 2005, lasting about ten months. I was able to visit England, Belgium, the Netherlands, France, Spain, Italy, the Vatican, Thailand, Singapore, Malaysia, the United States, and Canada. About half of them were observation trips, and the others were for tourism. My last stop on the trip was to attend the International Writing Program at the University of Iowa in the United States. In 2006, my parents and I traveled to China, Hong Kong, Macao, Singapore, and Thailand. Later I went on another observation trip to Thailand and the Netherlands.

The year 2007 was my busiest for travel, with a total of eleven trips. However I was in Yangon during the famous Saffron Revolution. The overseas trips in 2007 were to Vietnam, Greece, Thailand, Norway, Sweden, Germany, Czech Republic, and Australia. In early 2008, Brown University got in touch with me while I was attending a course on Conflict Resolution at the University of York in England. At the end of April I went back to Myanmar and was there when Cyclone Nargis hit in May. I went with a group of medics and doctors from our hospital to Myaungmya, a delta town, to treat victims. In September 2008 I was awarded the International Writers Project Fellowship at Brown University. Amid all these activities I took part in a literary festival in Algeria. In early June 2009, before I completed my tenure as resident writer, I was awarded a fellowship by the Radcliffe Institute for Advanced Studies at Harvard University. So I went back to Yangon from July to September and then returned to the US. I attended two literary festivals in India, one in October 2009 and another in January 2010. I finalized this book while I was at Harvard University.

In those days I tried to keep a low profile, attending several international literary panels and seminars. I would ask the audience not to put my presentation in print or on the Internet, and some of them commented that this was unusual because as a writer I should promote myself. But at that time I was living in a country that could be compared to a prison. In spite of that and although I traveled abroad often, I only ever wished to live in Myanmar. Thus my security was more important to me than fame. The second reason for eschewing personal attention was that I only wished to raise awareness about Myanmar—the prison—and its citizens—the prisoners. Thus I was happy as long as these two objectives were met. Besides, international friends I talked with after giving my presentation at the Radcliffe Institute observed that I seemed more interested in working together to solve problems rather than in using confrontational methods. Many of them asked me about the key to not being bitter despite everything that I had gone through, and why I chose to live in Myanmar despite having opportunities abroad. My answer to both questions? My practice of Vipassana.

I believe that readers of this book see by now how true this is.

Ma Thida–Sanchaung
February 27, 2010
Allston, Massachusetts

EPILOGUE

The Burmese version of my memoir ended here. The original was written while I was at Harvard in 2010, without any expectations of it being published since censorship laws in my country were then still draconian. So I thought I should try to publish it first in English and I asked my friend Ma Myint Myint San from Sydney to translate it. I am very grateful to her for her kindness in accepting the project and for doing such an excellent job. At first I thought I should write the English version myself, but I became so busy that I realized I had neither the time nor the energy for the endeavor. In fact, going back mentally into prison life to write about it was not an easy task; however, it was very useful in getting rid of the remaining feelings I had about that experience.

After I came back from Harvard I went back to my editor's desk, but I could not spare enough time even for my daily volunteer work at the charity clinic, which I loved. The demands of writing became stronger, as writing affects a larger number of people compared to what one surgeon can achieve, so I could only volunteer once a week as a medical doctor and the rest of my time I spent as an editor and writer.

I continued to travel abroad after my return from USA in 2010. Since I could never keep silent on situations in Myanmar, I asked the kind people who had invited me to not publicize my contributions to their conferences. What I feared was not another term in prison but to be put on the publication blacklist and silenced in my own country.

When the election was held on November 7, 2010, the well-funded Union Solidarity and Development Party—which used to be the long-standing Union Solidarity and Development Association of the military regime, won most of the seats since there were few opposing parties. The National League for Democracy, the opposition party led by Daw Aung San Suu Kyi (who was released from house arrest in November 2010, two weeks after the elections), decided not to take part because of doubts that the elections would be free and fair. So the political situation was uncertain and I did not dare to have my words on record. Then my documentary fiction *The Roadmap,* about the 1988 uprising and its aftermath, written in English while I was at Brown University, was published by Silkworm Books of Chiang Mai in late 2011 under the pseudonym Suragamika, meaning "brave traveler" in Sanskrit.

After my return, I focused mainly on my work with *Budding Teen* magazine. It was welcomed by parents and young people who finally found a publication seriously addressing their issues as well as by emerging young writers who were able to practice and to test the limits of their freedom of expression. However, it came to a stop due to financial problems. Many young writers from this magazine became well-known during its existence of over a decade, and many are now established writers. Both our senior editor, Myo Myint Nyein, who also spent twelve years in prison as a political prisoner, and I will always be equally proud of this publication.

Another effective support for new writers was *Shwe Amyutay* magazine, where we were also editors at the same time as we were doing *Budding Teen,* and we have continued this work. It has been a prestigious literary magazine since its debut in 1990 and since 2006 has held the annual Shwe Literary Awards, which exceed all other awards in terms of prize money, media attention, and credibility of the judges and the magazine itself. Although both Myo Myint Nyein and I were detained soon after *Shwe Amyutay* came out, the editor-in-chief, Win Nyein, the eldest brother of Myo Myint Nyein, was a steady and capable hand at its helm. In addition to the awards, *Shwe Amyutay* has a regular section under my charge that supports new writers. Every year aspiring writers from all over the country send hundreds of manuscripts which I read and choose to comment on—an average of fifty a month. About thirty short stories by new writers are published each year, and some of the authors are by now famous award-winning literary figures. By the time I was invited in 2008 to be an International Writers Project fellow at Brown University, and after that a fellow of the Radcliffe Institute for Advanced Studies at Harvard, I had read and commented on nearly seven hundred short-story manuscripts before I left for the USA.

In April 2012, there was a by-election in Myanmar and all but one seat were won by NLD candidates. Since there was some relaxation in press censorship, Myo Myint Nyein and I started a weekly news journal called the *Myanmar Independent*. I also started to think about publishing my prison memoir in Burmese. The first step was for the publishing house to submit the manuscript to the Press Scrutiny Board. However, one publisher declined to do so as he thought he would get into trouble even by taking the first step. Then Myay Hmone Lwin, a young writer who had become known through *Budding Teen* magazine, offered to do it. His publishing house, Ngadoe Sarpay, submitted my manuscript, but we received no reply. Only when pre-censorship was abolished in August 2012 were we free to publish it under the title *Sanchaung—Insein—Harvard*, and it came out in November 2014. The title referred to three places that have had a great deal of significance to me: Sanchaung Township in Yangon, where I grew up; Insein Prison; and Harvard University, where I was able to write this book in safety.

In April 2013, the *Myanmar Independent* was discontinued by the publisher, and later our team of editors started a new weekly called *Pae Tin Tharn,* (Echoing Voice); that also closed down in April 2015 for various reasons, in spite of its success.

Now, the situation of press freedom is slightly improved compared to three years ago. Some of my old and new friends, such as Vicky Bowman and the Indian-British writer Salil Tripathi, encouraged me to start a chapter of PEN International in Myanmar. In fact, it was already my dream. Therefore I gathered some writers who were interested in PEN International, and on behalf of all of us, Nay Phone Latt, who also spent years in prison and won the Barbara Goldsmith Freedom to Write Award, went to Iceland to submit our application for PEN Myanmar at the 79th International Congress of PEN International.

We were accepted and began an awareness campaign. On November 27, 2013, which was our National Day for that year, PEN Myanmar held its very first conference and I was elected president out of nine board members (now extended to eleven board members). Since then, PEN Myanmar has been active in defending and promoting freedom of expression, encouraging a vital literary culture, and trying to be a bridge for literature and school curricula.

At this time I am thinking of starting some new writing and publishing projects. I have received a lot of feedback on my prison memoir since its first publication, and by now the Burmese version has been reprinted ten times.

Through this memoir I have gained better access to a wider audience, including leading religious and political figures and those from the grassroots, especially young people. Many have encouraged me to publish in English but I was always busy with traveling within or outside of Myanmar for literary talks and conferences. Friends kept pushing me about it, so I worked on this project during whatever time I could spare each day. I was also lucky to have a friend (who doesn't want to be named) voluntarily help edit a previous version of the translation in late 2014. It took me a long time since I have not had the time to sit at my desk since the end of 2012.

Now, my prison memoir in English is finally complete. I hope readers will continue to keep an eye on our country's situation in the near and distant future since you have learned about some aspects of our past through this book. What we, the people of Myanmar, want is for everyone to continue following the progress or decline of the human rights situation in our country.

Thanks to all of you,

Ma Thida-Sanchaung
June 21, 2015
Yangon, Myanmar

ACKNOWLEDGMENTS

I would like to say thank you to U Win Tin for his kind foreword to this book, to Radcliffe Institute of Advanced Studies at Harvard for giving me a place to write this account in safety, to the American writer and Harvard professor Jane Unrue for initiating the process, to Lena Bay, a Harvard student who was my research assistant, to my original Myanmar publisher Ngardo Sarpay (Our Literature) for being committed to this book in the beginning and to my readers and friends who sent so many messages of support.

I am grateful to myself for choosing Vipassana, and my thanks go to my jailers—generals of the military junta—who gave me enough time (by sending me in prison for so long) to make my determination and practice of Vipassana possible and to those guards and prisoners of Insein Prison who assisted me to comprehend and see the truth of life. May you see the truth of *anissa, dukkha,* and *anatta,* and with this comprehension may no one be able to make others suffer.